Dear Bandi
Thank you for your interest to
read my book & your support
for my writing -
Best regards,
Kunnudi

WHO
STOLE
MOTHER'S
SOUL?

A Fictional Memoir

R.E. SILIENTE

FriesenPress

One Printers Way
Altona, MB R0G 0B0
Canada

www.friesenpress.com

Copyright © 2022 by R.E Siliente
First Edition — 2022

"Disclaimer: This book is a Fictionalized memoir, which is a new term for an old genre; they are different from standard memoirs because of the inclusion of fictional writing techniques - names or places are changed to protect those involved - and since the narratives of the events are based on one person's perception. The author wishes to confirm that other than the words Mother, Father, brother, grandmother, and grandfather, all names that appear in the text are fictitious. If any name would be identifiable to a reader, that would be considered as a pure coincidence."

ISBN
978-1-03-913207-8 (Hardcover)
978-1-03-913206-1 (Paperback)
978-1-03-913208-5 (eBook)

1. BIOGRAPHY & AUTOBIOGRAPHY, PERSONAL MEMOIRS

Distributed to the trade by The Ingram Book Company

TABLE OF CONTENTS

For Father

Acknowledgements

With love and gratitude I acknowledge my family in Ottawa and in Sri Lanka, for making this book possible by living their lives, and intertwining those with mine.

I gratefully acknowledge my friends Sharon Hamilton, J.R. Keenan, Donald Bertrand, Julie Lawson, Clive Morris, Rick Taylor, Lynette Wilson and Janna Klostermann for their dedication of time and efforts to improve my writing.

Last but not least, I gratefully acknowledge all the educators who crossed my path during my formative years, for their support for me to learn English, and their encouraging words that nudged me to write what I know.

"Biology is the least of what makes someone a mother"

—Oprah Winfrey

"I can be changed by what happened to me.
But I refuse to be reduced by it"

—Maya Angelou

"Success is not final, failure is not fatal:
it is the courage to continue that counts"

—Winston Churchill

$\mathscr{P}$ROLOGUE

It was January 2017 in Ottawa, Canada. I was standing by the bay window of our family room overlooking the crescent, where I had been living for over eighteen years.

Without a doubt, the winter has taken charge of the land.

The ground was frozen, and a thick layer of snow mixed with sleet and ice blanketed it, stretching to the horizon in a pale and indefinite colour; a poor contrast to the clear blue sky above. The world stood still without chirping birds or human interventions.

I shivered at the sight; it warned me loud and clear: stay warm, stay indoors.

Upon me was the thirty-seventh winter after migrating to Canada. Now I call this land my home, which is 10,000 miles from where I was born and raised; warm and sunny Sri Lanka.

The distance between the two countries is great. Although continents and oceans separate them, the threads connecting my heart to the land of my origin are naturally very strong, like the attachment of the petals of a tropical flower to its central bud; unwavering and stubborn.

The childhood struggles, the awkward behaviour during my teenage years, and the decisions I made as an adult are fresh in my mind. All associated memories had followed me to Canada like a hunger that would pursue a starving homeless nomad.

Life in Canada has been challenging since I landed, but all in all, adventurous and fruitful. Yet, it all changed in December 2016 because of a life-altering event: Mother's unexpected death.

Since then, my life has been engulfed by an internal struggle.

Two weeks prior to that, Mother had celebrated her ninety-third birthday at the senior's residence where she had lived for nearly five years. The facility manager, the caregivers, and a few of her resident friends had attended the party.

In the photos the manager shared later, I witnessed Mother had dressed in a long party dress, cut a chocolate cake, eaten a piece placed on a small delicately decorated tea plate, and drunk some milk tea in an elegant teacup. How fitting were those images of a lady who always wanted to present herself to the world as a sophisticated woman, and who had not been bashful to describe her heritage as 'royalty'.

Ironically, that chocolate birthday cake turned out to be her last meal.

Soon after the party she was rushed to the hospital, as she had experienced difficulty with swallowing food. There, she had been immediately placed on an intravenous saline solution.

After hearing of her admission to the hospital, I kept calling her cellular phone, hoping to speak with her. There was no answer; it was eerie to listen to the continuous ringing of her phone. My gut feeling was that she may never answer it again with her shaky but sweet voice.

With teary eyes, I still wonder what Mother's reason was to leave her cellular phone at the residence. Was that intentional because she did not wish to say goodbye to me? I would never know.

Gradually, her organs began to fail. On the eighth day, her heart stopped beating. When she closed her eyes for the last time, I was 10,000 miles away from her bedside.

Since scheduling a flight to visit her in Sri Lanka at a moment's notice was not feasible, I never had the opportunity to say goodbye to her. Apparently, no one else was there either, not even her beloved son, who had been entrusted with her well-being after Father's passing.

Soon after her death, I realized that the loss of Mother had led me to find myself as much as to lose it. The internal struggle has been unimaginable. Accepting the facts of life has been painful. This revelation has resurfaced all repressed memories that I had categorized as forgettable into the realm of being haunting. It made me understand how my life has been inextricably linked to that of Mother. It made me realize that unknowingly, I had held her close to my heart.

In *ABC of Impossibility*[1], Simon Critchley wrote, "It is the deaths of those we are bound to through love that undoes us that unstitch our carefully tailored suit of the self that unmakes whatever meaning that we have made. It is in mourning and grief that we become ourselves when we acknowledge that part of ourselves that we have lost and which we will forever have lost."

His words have been echoing in my mind since Mother's passing because they ring true to me.

The true nature of life is that real people live and die, unlike Sherlock Holmes and Dr. J.H. Watson, the two men who had never lived; therefore, can never die. I tried hard to accept Mother's death in that context, but it was daunting and excruciating.

After a few months of a mental struggle, it dawned on me that I had to find a more tangible avenue to deal with this unimaginable loss that resulted in continuous depressive thoughts.

Hoping to find solace, I started writing by expressing my feelings and thoughts associated with Mother. I acknowledged that I could not remember every nuance of daily life, but to my surprise, my

---

1 **Simon Critchley**, *ABC of Impossibility* (Univocal Publishing, Minneapolis; 2015)

recollections, thoughts, and feelings began to fill several notebooks with rapidly flowing words.

I remembered it all, like a laser-sharp image snapped by a professional photographer. Those images have assembled to develop a story that I wished to tell.

This story is about my mother, who shaped my life with her will, but not her love, and my father, who led me to glittering success.

Unlike Father who had expressed his loving feelings to me from day one until his death, Mother had kept a secret about her behaviour towards her only daughter. Eventually, she would reveal that secret posthumously.

Seemingly, she had held a grudge against someone who had crossed her path, percolated the related anger and had victimized me, simply because she had the power over my life.

Now, I have decided to tell my story to the world.

If I don't, then it would continue to own me. I believe that by writing and sharing it, I have flipped the tables and regained control.

PART I

CHAPTER 1

$\mathcal{M}$OTHER AND HER $\mathcal{A}$LMIRA

Mother had an unrelenting will to win at all costs. She was obsessed with money, and without a doubt, she had been in love with herself. She hated my presence, detested my progress, and caused unimaginable pain in my life until her death.

I firmly believed that her death would end my life-long suffering. I was wrong. Posthumously, she revealed a devious plan she had designed to control my life from beyond the grave. That was her final victory.

With that, she would leave me heartbroken.

In December 2016, soon after hearing about Mother's passing, I felt frustrated, as I could not find an itinerary from Ottawa, Canada to Colombo, Sri Lanka, to make it in time for her funeral. Although such challenges are common for immigrants living far from their motherland, missing the last opportunity to see her devastated me.

In February 2017, nearly two months after her heath, I travelled to Sri Lanka to fulfill Mother's last wish: to place her ashes in the family grave.

Upon arrival, the familiar surroundings of the Katunayake International Airport greeted me, yet it felt different, perhaps because I no longer had parents to visit in that blessed land. My heart sank, and my eyes watered.

As usual, the airport was teeming with travellers, and the duty-free shops were bustling with eager shoppers seeking bargains on something international. I had no interest in any of that. I walked through the crowds with bewildering thoughts and exhaustion to meet my only brother at the arrivals lounge.

It was a great comfort to grieve with him.

On the second day in Colombo, I accompanied Brother to the funeral home where Mother's ashes had been stored until my arrival. A man with a pleasant smile handed me a small, round clay urn. The moment I touched the urn, I was transfixed. My thoughts were unfathomable. My knees felt weak and restless, and my hands trembled. Although I was surrounded by hot air in Colombo, I felt a chill down my spine; tears rolled down my cheeks.

All that glitter, splendour, and glamour Mother had flaunted during her life had materialized to this: *a handful of ashes in a clay urn.* I was holding the remains of Mother in my hands, and she was not complaining.

After picking up the urn, Brother and I drove in silence to the gravesite. The traffic in Colombo was horrendous. Seemingly, all commuters were in a rush and they constantly honked at each other, but for me, it was a welcome distraction. I held the urn on my lap and remembered always being on Father's lap as a young child, while Mother had preferred to hold Brother. Ironic indeed!

At the gravesite, the caretaker opened the marble slab of the monument that Brother and I had built to protect the remains of Father. I could see Father's urn at the bottom of the cavity, undisturbed since his passing. Brother reached down and placed the second urn on the ground. The new one touched the old as if it was meant to be that way. We both sobbed; it was the end of an era.

The hot air had become heavy and a mirage could be seen on the tar-paved road next to the cemetery. We stood side-by-side at the grave while the caretaker completed sealing the marble slab and cleaning the surroundings. A nearby tree provided a little shade to endure the heat and the grief.

I looked around for a distraction and saw a pair of tall white birds—perhaps Sri Lankan cranes—arriving from nowhere and had started to walk towards the family gravesite. The pair was in great harmony while stepping in unison. The pure white birds glowed in the shimmering rays of sunlight. An incredible sight!

Was it a sign that our parents were together now, in some mysterious abode? "I hope they are happy," was my singular wish.

We returned home filled with grief and exhaustion. After having lunch in silence, Brother spoke.

"Some time ago, Mother suggested that after her passing, *you* should have the first opportunity to go through her personal effects. She wished for you to select anything for yourself"

He then handed me a bunch of keys to Mother's large *Almira* (wooden wardrobe). Her suggestion surprised me, and I was curious about her intentions.

This set of keys had been Mother's exclusive property. She had always secured them out of sight; therefore, I had never opened her wardrobe. I felt reluctance rather than excitement at the prospect.

Mother's two-door wardrobe stood silently before me, with no indication that it would restrict my approach.

Torrential rain was pounding on the treetops and the metal roof of the neighbouring house, creating the typical sounds of a tropical storm. The downpour had made the surroundings gloomy; it matched my mood. I returned my attention to the keys I held.

I took a deep breath, inserted the key, and turned it while my hands were shaking and my heart was sinking. The key turned with ease and the right-side door opened with a gentle creak.

A neatly packed stack of clothing and other belongings of Mother greeted me. I exhaled.

Instantly, a familiar fragrance from her belongings touched my senses, evoking a flood of memories. It was the delicate fragrance of Cuticura soap mixed in with Pond's face powder. I had encountered this fragrance blend a million times during my life whenever I was around her.

I then opened the left-door of the wardrobe. It contained a stack of boxes and some books. I scanned the boxes that were labeled with handwritten notes. My heart fluttered with unusual vigour when I saw a box labelled 'To my daughter.'

I took the brass box, sat on the bed, and unlatched it. As expected, there was no note from Mother. She had constantly struggled to express herself during her life, which had led to many misconstrued encounters.

The box contained several items treasured by Mother.

The gold bangles she wore during weddings, which I had admired all my life, had been presented to me. I could not believe my eyes. Her wedding ring tied to Father's ring with a bit of string laid next to the bangles.

While caressing my parent's wedding rings, I cried for several minutes.

Among the glittering gold items, there was a package in a paper bag. I spread its contents across the bed. A delightful collection of hand-stitched samples of a variety of designs made a sparkling display. I remembered Mother telling me of winning first prize for a hand embroidery competition during her tenure at the Teacher Training College in Kandy.

I touched the pale yellow collection of fabric, knowing that her creative fingers might have spent many hours on these materials while attending to the details. Sadly, my lack of interest in her favourite craft had disappointed her; this might have been her final attempt to spark my interest. I decided that I would frame the collection one day to remember her dedication to the delicate art of intricate stitching.

It deserved a lasting view.

The very bottom of the brass box was lined with pure silver coins. I recalled her receiving this collection from my paternal Grandmother; she would have wanted Mother to present them to me. I was thankful for the valuable gift. I read the face of one coin: 1878.

Several books were packed next to the stack of boxes. Mother had been an avid reader. During my childhood, what I could remember the most was Mother either reading a book or being surrounded by colourful threads and needles while enjoying embroidery.

I picked some books from the stack. To my surprise, they were the books I had won in school. I was delighted and felt eternally grateful for Mother's thoughtful gesture.

Mother had appreciated my achievements? That was a surprise.

I continued my search. The pink handbag, Mother's favourite purse, was visible on her pile of clothing. I had gifted it in 19.., and she had taken it with her to the senior's home to protect her precious items: a few rupees given as spending money, her eyeglasses, the Sri Lankan identity card, and a spool of thread with a needle secured in it.

I had asked about the spool one day, and she explained, "One should darn the garments if they are not in perfect condition."

That was Mother, the perfectionist. She had left this Earth without her spool of thread and the needle! While hugging the pink handbag, hoping to feel Mother's warmth, I wept and prayed for her to be in a place with perfectly stitched garments.

The torrential rain had stopped, and a glimmer of sunshine peeked through the grey clouds; my inner strength improved; however, I would lose all that in the next few moments.

A stack of neatly folded sarees was visible in rainbow colours. During her prime years, Mother pranced in those like a peacock and dazzled onlookers. Who would drape these now? As the only daughter, I would automatically inherit them, but I did not wish to have them as my chances of wearing a saree in Canada were rare. I decided to find a suitable beneficiary who could appreciate them.

I touched her silk sarees and slowly ran my finger down through the stack. The feel of Mother's clothes made my heart flutter while comforting my sorrowful soul. Tears rolled down my cheeks, soaking the feelings of loss that were choking in my heart.

Suddenly, there was an end to the silkiness at my fingertips; something hard and rough pressed against my fingers.

I lifted the garments, and an old book with a hardcover emerged. On the cover, *My Life* was written in large, bold letters. I felt that I was holding a *time-lapse video* of Mother's life in black and white.

It was her journal. Had she hoped that I would find it among her thoughtful gifts?

I was reluctant to open it, as I imagined I might invade her privacy, but my temptation was intense which made me shiver.

The sun had set behind the large trees, making my surroundings dark and cool. The storm had passed, and I could view the night sky dotted with a few glimmering stars. Yet, the turbulence created within me after the unexpected discovery of Mother's journal made me feel like I had been abandoned on rough terrain during a merciless tropical storm. Tears rolled down my cheeks, and they found their way to the journal I held.

With my back against the wall, while holding her journal close to my heart, I sat alone in the darkness and let Mother's spirit occupy my mind and my body.

A few weeks after returning to Canada, I gradually built up the courage to read Mother's journal.

While debating whether she truly intended for me to find her personal writings, I waited for the right moment. First I thought that it had been her intention for me to locate her journal by being the first one to examine her personal effects. After deep reflection, I concluded that she had led me to her private thoughts to make her inner feelings known only to me; I wondered why.

Mother's trust to let me read her private journal was uplifting. But, her true intentions revealed later were unexpected and disturbing; they were selfish and cruel.

One Sunday morning, I sat by the window and started reading *My Life*.

By reading her journal, I hoped to find answers for many vexing questions that convoluted my mind, especially those about our troubled relationship. But, her written words generated more questions, instead of providing answers to those that troubled me the most.

The early chapters were cryptic and enigmatic, much like her life had been. Although, all my life I had sensed that Mother did not wish to have me around, reading about her hatred towards me in her journal after her death was unbearable; my heart fragmented into little pieces. I could not read on. I decided to return to it later.

It took me a lengthy period of time to make the final decision to read the rest of her journal.

She had left a journal filled with riddles for me to unravel, suggesting that she was determined to confuse me even after her death. She had plotted and unleashed a devious plan from beyond the grave, and her plan worked, because no one alive could verify any of the facts. To my greatest dismay, her most intimate thoughts were only disclosed in the final chapter of her journal.

A quandary had burdened my soul, and Mother's *coup de grâce* began to drown me in a whirlpool of sorrow.

To find solace, I began to re-evaluate my life experiences through her eyes, mainly to clarify a million little misunderstandings I had encountered with her. Perhaps that had been Mother's primary plan; she had expected me to return to our past for me to understand who Mother was.

It had been an enlightening journey that would lead me to an unexpected ending; forgiveness.

Mother had desired pardon from her only daughter; she would be victorious.

CHAPTER 2

𝒢ROWING 𝒫AINS

In order to re-evaluate my life through Mother's eyes, I had to start from the very beginning, to remind myself how she and I had interacted with each other. The memories were very fresh; they did not make me smile, instead, they still could make me cry.

It all started on a small island in the Indian Ocean.

I was born to an educated, upper-middle-class family in post-colonial Sri Lanka. According to the planetary arrangements at the moment of my birth (astrological horoscope), I was destined 'to go places' and receive great accolades.

Regardless of the astrological predictions, I had lived some part of my life with hardships. But, to its credit, I had been blessed with numerous kind people, many memorable encounters, moments of recognition, and pleasurable material possessions that a human would consider as a privilege. I had considered all those occurrences as small blessings that had arrived at opportune moments to fulfill my goals and dreams in life.

I was fortunate to have two parents in my life until I was an older adult, and because of their association for that length of time, I never had feelings of being lost in the world. But, from a very young age, I had noted that the love and affection I had received from Father had been comparatively much more than that from Mother. Those made me wonder whether I truly had two parents.

This revelation as a child was the beginning of the end of a loving relationship with Mother.

Mother was an accomplished lady in her own rights, but she had not given much attention to her two children. Instead, she consistently focused on her life. I could not comprehend her self-attentive nature.

According to many books I had read, a mother's nurturing was essential to the physical and mental well-being of a child. Dr. Phil, the TV personality, had said that deprivation of such essentials to one's children was a sign of a "cancer growing in the family"—much like the link between the subconscious actions of parents and the perpetuation of high-risk behaviour of their children.

There were numerous misunderstandings during my life, which led to disappointments and heartaches because of my strained relationship with Mother. Later, I had focused on the few bright lights she had shone on my life, though unfortunately, they were only sporadic dim flashes, much like the flickering of a firefly on a deep dark night.

Father, on the other hand, had been the beacon in my life. His focus had been on my education, in which he had combined the efforts of a mother and a father. He had envisioned that his daughter would reach the apex of the highest mountain.

Father's warm heart and warm hands carried me through when I was a little girl. He had provided me with the necessary strength to overcome the obstacles hurled at me or dropped in my path throughout my childhood by Mother, her siblings, and her parents. He had been my rock. I could not have had a better Father. I had wished that he would meet me on the other side to be a parent to me in many lives to come.

Although I had many unpleasant memories generated during my childhood, I also had been blessed with one redeeming positivity; a sibling, which I had considered as a privilege.

From the time I could walk and talk and had a memory of being alive, my only brother—who is one and a half years older than me—whom I referred to as Aiyah (elder brother in Sinhalese), had been my playmate and my companion during my childhood.

We had been inseparable.

I still vividly remember sitting with Brother on a pile of fresh carrots stacked in the front of the house during harvest season. We had many things to discuss while sitting on that carrot pile, and such conversations were considered private. As children, we were never bored with each other. He had been my friend, Brother, and my confidant. Seemingly, my joyful memories with him had filled the dark crevasse in my life created by the many negative effects from other members of my extended family.

In light of those wonderful memories, I believe that when we were children, together, Brother and I were happy.

It was my understanding that a child, from the start, would need to feel wanted and loved. They need to be nurtured by the affection and care. There is no replacement; it is the most important thing. If it was not right from the beginning, then everything afterwards is playing catch up—trying to make life better when it was not good. As such, childhood would mean much more than just the space between birth and the attainment of adulthood.

Through my teenage and adult years, I had this unusual feeling that I was constantly missing something in my life. Could that be the result of lack of affection through childhood? Had I been playing catch up?

After looking through my childhood memories, there had been a question that nagged me for a very long time: had my parents neglected me as a child?

If such had been the case, I believe it originated from my childhood living arrangements.

For nearly nine years of my childhood, my family lived in a house that belonged to my maternal Grandfather, where we had the company of the extended family.

The house had been crowded: four members in our family – Father, Mother, Brother and I—two maternal grandparents and Mother's youngest unmarried brother (*Podi Maama*), two servants, three cats, and one dog. Mother's two other younger brothers also visited frequently. It was a large house with six bedrooms, yet there were too many people, and their proximity made everyone irritable at most times.

I could recall discussions and arguments. I could also remember being lost in that crowd with very little attention paid to my well-being.

The home was situated in a historically valued town, about 17 miles from Kandy, the sacred city in the Island's central mountains. Several years before, that house had been built by a wealthy man, supposedly a judge in the local courts. It sat on a hill overlooking lush green cultivated land. After Grandfather's retirement from a school principal post, he had purchased this house from the judge.

The home had a beautiful flower garden in the front. A long flight of steps had been built on the left-hand side to reach the front garden from the main road. On the right-hand side, a tar-paved road had been built for vehicles to reach the two-car garage.

The front garden was extended in all directions, providing access to each of the three roads surrounding the property. Along the left side of the home, margining the fence, were several large fruit trees: *Laaulu*, *Katu Atha*, and Orange. On the back, the land was crowded with many fruit-bearing trees of banana, papaya, mango, coconut, jack fruit, while fruit-bearing shrubs such as guava, lime, lemon, and mulberry grew well among the trees.

All in all, this garden had provided the family with a variety of fruits, vegetables, and numerous spices useful for daily cooking.

The members of my extended family had lavished lifestyles. I could remember having visitors—some regulars and some from out of town, which happened to be passing through the village—at lunch or at dinner, almost every day of the week. The hired servants cooked for the family, cleaned the home, and tended the garden, enabling family members to enjoy their lives with pleasurable endeavours such as entertaining visitors or travelling for various reasons.

Grandfather was head of the household. In addition to owning this massive property with the family home, he also owned coconut estates in the south of the Island. In the vicinity of the house, he purchased several paddy fields and numerous lands to grow vegetables. With his potential unlimited income, he had the means to purchase more than one car for the family. Back in those days, he was known as the only man who had owned vehicles in the town or in any surrounding villages.

The villagers, therefore, had considered him to be a wealthy man.

The harvests from the land he owned were measurably large, and they were transported for sale to various parts of the Island, which resulted in accumulating great wealth. He gained respect from the villagers in his community because of his philanthropy and his willingness to hire many locals who did not have a school education to be employed elsewhere.

Unfortunately, his pleasant disposition was limited to those who worked for him and those who did not live in the same household. For example, he had never directly spoken to Mother—his only daughter—when she was a child or adult. Mother had been instructed to communicate with him through her mother, his wife!

I am not surprised that I do not have any fond memories of Grandfather. He constantly found reasons to quarrel with all. Everyone in the family had experienced the most difficult times because of this unpredictable man. Mother once described her father as a man with a domineering personality who was a ruthless disciplinarian, setting strict rules for his family.

I would call him a bully based on one mind-boggling incident that I could recall.

It was the celebration of the seasonal harvest; the Sinhala Tamil New Year. For this special day, family members would exchange gifts such as new clothes and other personal items. It had been customary for the parents and grandparents to gift children with toys.

A few days before the celebrations, Grandfather was out shopping the whole day. When he returned, I was playing in the sitting room with Brother while Father had been watching us play. That was when the incident occurred, which instilled a painful memory.

I was only four years old.

Grandfather had handed a package of toys to my brother and looked at me and said, "You don't get any toys from me."

I looked at Father, and he had sorrowful eyes, and he immediately carried me in his arms. Yet, that did not stop me from crying my eyes out. Father kept consoling me with kind words and had promised that he would buy a beautiful doll for me for the occasion, which he eventually did.

I could not understand what I had done wrong not to deserve a toy.

Had I done something to offend Grandfather, to make him treat me with cruelty? My question to father on this matter received no answer. But later in my adult years, I would learn that the contempt towards Father was directed at me by Grandfather.

Why would he hurt a child to get at his son-in-law?

Since that day, I had been in a dark place. Grandfather's cruelty to me at that young age had a lasting effect. I firmly believe that I grew up to be a woman who could not handle rejections very well based on this mental aberration.

Unfortunately, Mother's reaction to her father's cruelty towards her daughter was worse than her father's actions. She did not exhibit any concern for my distress; instead, she complained that Father paid too much attention and cared too deeply for me. Although I could not understand her narrative as a little girl, even at that young age, I wished I had a different Mother.

I never spoke to Grandfather again; in fact, I hid from him throughout my life in that home. I had feared for my life in his presence.

Several years later, Grandfather had died of chronic diarrhea, instigated by his inability to follow his doctor's instructions. Mother only cried a few tears while standing by his casket, but his wife had none to offer. His ashes were buried in his property, and a great monument was built in his memory. Eventually, one of his sons removed the monument to build an extension to the home, which he inherited from Grandfather.

I had never visited his gravesite.

It had been rumoured that Grandfather's third generation, who had eventually inherited the family home, had difficulty living in it because of a ghost who troubled the young family; the original house was then demolished. I wished that I lost my childhood memories in that rubble. Unfortunately, they had taken a life of their own and had followed me around.

My maternal Grandmother was a school teacher. While being employed, she gave birth to ten children. By the time I was born, most of her children had either passed away or had left home never to return, except three sons and her only daughter.

Much like the Grandfather, I had to believe that Grandmother also disliked my existence in that household. This thought was proven true based on one undesirable encounter I had with her when I was about five years old.

Because of my parents' occupation as school teachers, Grandmother was entrusted to take care of Brother and me for lengthy periods during the workweek.

One day, Grandmother had decided to read a book to us in her bedroom. Then, out of the blue, she recited a verse in Sinhalese while looking at me. The translation reads:

The female kind is dirty and gross, while the male kind is superior. Therefore, kill the female by thrashing them on a rock but praise the male by offering flowers and bowing your head.

At my young age, I could not comprehend the words well, but to my surprise, that verse stuck in my mind like an octopus with million tentacles, damaging the healthy neurons in my brain.

The feelings of disgust read in this verse came to haunt me years later. Perhaps her dislike towards females had originated in her mind because *her* mother had not treated her well. But why did she victimize me to release her stress? I still do not have an answer.

Now, I wonder whether Mother's disgruntled life might have sprung from a link to her rotten mother. I could only speculate.

Many years later, I would find out Mother's reasons to be spiteful and bitter; they would carry a mystery of their own kind.

Even before my grandparents adamantly made me believe I was an unwanted child, their youngest son, *Podi Maama,* jumped on the torturous bandwagon to insult me and damage my young mind before his parents.

He had been circling me like a soldier with a hand-grenade, affiliated to the enemy battalion, looking for the right moment to throw it at me. He had been a high school dropout; therefore, he had too much time in his hand. So, he trampled my life and took the cake.

Wouldn't it be wonderful if the first memory of every child's life was pleasant, as that would create the fundamental foundation for a child to build a life on? Unfortunately, my first childhood memory had been unfathomable because of this uncaring young man.

When I was about four years old, an unforgettable incident occurred.

On that sunny day, I was out in the garden playing with Brother, and I distinctly remember *Podi Maama's* question for me.

"Do you remember where you were born?"

I looked at him with surprised eyes. I barely understood the question, let alone have a sensible answer. I had to take my time to understand the question. With that delay, Brother responded, "I do, I do."

I looked at him and said, "I don't."

"See, your brother could remember, so you must be stupid not to remember your birthplace," he responded with a mocking smile.

I looked at Brother for his reaction, but he had none.

"We must have a nickname to indicate that you are stupid," *Podi Maama* continued.

"What should we call your sister?" He enquired from Brother. Brother kept quiet.

"We will call you *nothannagedara maadanwala*." (Translation: the one who does not remember her birthplace, which is *Maadanwala*.)

He started to laugh out loud. I was bewildered. Why was he laughing? I started to cry with all my might, not because I had understood the name he had assigned me, but because I did not like his attitude towards me.

I ran into the house, and Brother followed.

I had looked for Mother or Father for help. No one was there. Finally, I was able to locate Father, who immediately took control of the nasty situation. Mother was reluctant to address the damage her brother had done. Why wasn't Mother there to protect me from being ridiculed by her family?

I dare say I could never find an answer to this question.

Although I was very young, the associated memory had lingered, like a sticking plaster stuck on an open wound, which would be very hard to pull out until the day the wound would decide to shed it naturally.

What damaging effect his unwarranted ridicule had on me?

Apparently, I had developed a defensive mechanism to numb out and withdraw when faced with criticism or ridicule, and later to carve out a contingency mechanism to defend myself, to prove those who insulted me were wrong.

Why can't I defend myself at the moment of impact? I do not know.

Unfortunately, that was the first of many incidents I wished to forget; most had been related to the same man. He was relentless, like a disturbed, lonely wolf that could sniff out potential culprits to feed its avarice. Based on numerous undesirable encounters with him, I decided that he was my worst enemy among all those who had inflicted poison on my life.

Over several years, he would prove to be the enemy of many of his own family members; he eventually died alone, without having contact with his siblings.

Miraculously, those undesirable incidences of my childhood would eventually instigate Father to place his initial plans in motion to change our living arrangements by moving out of Grandfather's home. However, it would take several more years for its implementation.

Despite enduring a difficult childhood in a dysfunctional family, according to Father's account, I grew up to be a girl who liked to dance, read, write, and who had been blessed with an angelic singing voice.

My singing abilities during my formative years, as described by Father, could be corroborated by one strange incident that happened when I was about four years old.

Every day after lunch—which had been around 1:30 p.m. — everyone in the home had a habit of taking a *siesta* (nap), and it would, at times, stretch until 3:00 p.m. During this period, Brother and I had played in the sitting room without adult supervision. Sometimes, Brother also had a nap, leaving me to play alone. According to my parent's account, I had a difficult time sleeping during the early afternoon.

I had cherished the solitude at that young age; I had million little projects to work on.

On one of those lonely moments, I had roamed around the house, trying to keep myself occupied. I had ended up in the long hallway at the back of the house, which had an entrance to the garage. I had sat on the floor with my toys and started to sing.

According to Father, as a little girl, I had the habit of listening to the radio and emulating the singing of *Latha Mangeshkar* (a popular singer in India during that period). According to Mother, I could sing in perfect tune but with incomprehensible lyrics; I did not know Hindi.

That particular afternoon, I had been singing one of *Latha's* songs, and I had been in awe, much like what I would feel during a singing episode today. In that empty hall, the echo of my voice had enchanted and pleased me.

Suddenly, Father appeared looking for me after hearing my singing from a distance.

He approached me with caution, as if there was a looming danger close to me. Although his movements were very different than what I had seen before, I kept singing. I had not realized the reasons for his strange movements until he grabbed me and whisked me away from where I sat. I started to cry, wondering why he disturbed my singing. At that moment, I followed the direction of his stare.

A surprisingly unusual sight was seen very close to me.

A large reptile—an iconic snake—with an unmistakable pose: the rearing, hooded display with an intimidating upright posture, laid on the cemented floor enveloped in an eerie silence; a cobra had positioned very close to where I had sat.

I had no idea what I was staring at, although I was shaken by the display of the reptile because I had never seen one before. Father knew what the danger had been, which explained why he had whisked me away from the ominous scene.

Later, I would learn that this particular cobra had been living in the backyard of this ancient house for a very long time and had been considered the incarnation of the judge who had built the home. It had been understood that the judge had decided to stay around after his passing to protect his property.

After this incident, to dissipate my fear, Father informed me that the cobra was fascinated by my singing and loved the way I could enchant the basic instincts of its reptilian brain. But, since that event, Father became more mindful of my whereabouts during family nap time.

Now, when I reminisce about that incident, I realize the venomous cobra had uplifted my spirits, unlike those humans who had been identified as 'family'; ironic indeed.

There were many other awful childhood memories about that household that I would like to forget. Unfortunately, they have stacked in my mind, like a pile of old dusty books secured in a personal library, for which only I have the keys to enter.

Throughout my childhood, I had jumped over many hurdles to survive. But, after surmounting my childhood *battles*, a rude awakening awaited, as a *war* arrived later.

CHAPTER 3

SEPARATION

Since I had read Mother's journal, I continued to re-evaluate my life through her eyes. Then one morning, Father's face appeared before me, like I had seen it a few decades ago when he brought news that I was expected to attend an exclusive girls' school.

I was only nine years old when Father had decided to send me away to an all-girls' school; indeed with good intensions for his only daughter.

On that extraordinary day, an epic change was brought to my life.

I had excelled in a school entrance exam and was selected to study in the most prestigious girls' school in Kandy: the X Girls' College. The entrance criteria for this school were extremely difficult to meet. In addition to being a good student, one needed to be privileged with a substantial amount of money to cover the cost of attending over several years, since the school was privately run.

Evidently, Father considered the value of my education in this school above and beyond any inconvenience in his life for the years to come—the "out-of-pocket scenario." He was my hero.

In the previous year, when Brother was nine years old, he got selected to study in a boys' school in Kandy. It was the only time I could not follow him, and I had gone into a dark place with a sorrowful heart. I had cried all day long, missing Brother's companionship. I had refused to attend the small, local Christian school without him.

Father had a difficult time consoling me and had decided to send me to a school where I could find companionship among my peers.

With that decision, he had investigated possible schools for me. He exhausted all avenues to locate a good school that would provide me with the best primary education. Back in those days, the internet and its search engines did not exist, but Father was successful in finding the right school for my first step into the world of education.

One day, Father informed me that I needed to prepare to write exams on language and math. He then took an hour every evening after returning from work to teach me the two subjects and the nitty-gritty of the exam process.

After several weeks of teaching he said, "You are ready, and you will do well. You should envision being in a new school with new friends and teachers, wearing new clothes and enjoying your life."

I did exactly as he suggested.

To facilitate writing the exams, Father designed a "clipboard" using regular cardboard. He pasted a wonderful picture of Buddha on the opposite side, believing it would to bring me the blessings I needed to pass the exam. Taking an exam at that early age would make any child nervous, but I was ecstatic and full of confidence because I trusted Father and his directions.

On the day of the exam, I was ready to take on the world.

Father helped me don my socks and shoes because I still had to learn how to tie a shoelace. We travelled together to Kandy. I cannot describe how the day unfolded or the people we met along the way, as it happened a very long time ago, but I can clearly remember writing the exam, sitting among a large group of girls around my age.

I proudly used the "clipboard" and noted that none of the other girls had that convenience for writing the exam. I felt very special and great love for Father.

After the exam, we had lunch at the Devon Café in Kandy before heading home. Father did not ask me about the exam. He assured me that the results would be very good. He added that he would always love me regardless of the outcome.

When we reached home, we were surprised by a heated argument between Mother and *Podi Maama*. My pet name *Podi Duwa* (little daughter) was heard several times in the discussion.

Father held my hand in a protective gesture.

At that time, I did not know what the argument was about. Later, when I was old enough to understand adult communications, I would learn that it was a disagreement between *Podi Maama* and Mother on the efforts taken by Father to educate me in a school that required a large investment of family money.

Podi Maama had argued, "A girl does not need education, period!" He had suggested that I be sent to a local school with a minimum cost to the family, as it would deliver a curriculum similar to that of a prestigious girls' school.

The heated argument between the siblings was the last straw for Father.

He was compelled to reverse his decision to live in Grandfather's house. On that day, he had decided to build his own home. He had only agreed originally to live with Mother's family was to keep peace and fulfill Mother's wish: *not to live with her mother-in-law.*

However, this decision also would bring about more unexpected consequences that we would have to endure.

One month after I sat for the entrance exam, a letter arrived by registered mail with the return address, The Principal, X Girl's School, Kandy. After reading the letter, Father lifted me up in his arms and shrieked with joy while he twirled me around, and announced the good news. The time had arrived for me to leave home to step into a new world.

I wondered, *was Mother in agreement with Father on this decision?*

The accounts in Mother's journal detailed individual events that were of significance to her, but the details were sketchy on events that were important to me.

I could not understand her perspective as she was emotionally and physically detached and had limited involvement with my life. However, the snippets of her true feelings written into the details were significant. They shed light on several incidents to reverse my thoughts about her behaviour, while others sealed my sentiments firmly and took me deeper into an emotional hole.

In her journal, Mother had written about my success to study in Kandy; indeed, a surprise.

Her entry about it indicated that this life-changing event had been an important part of her life as much as it was in mine. Her account of my achievement in the journal read, "I did not expect my daughter to reach such heights as my son would, by getting accepted to study in a prestigious school."

Unfortunately, her words were sharp and detrimental to my soul. Seemingly, she had not condoned my efforts and the resulted success.

After reading the journal, I was disappointed. Very close to Mother's passing, she only acknowledged once that I had been successful in my life, although she always had her doubts about my abilities. Her doubts were unfounded, because with time, I was successful in my life beyond everyone's expectations.

On the other hand, Father had trusted my abilities to clear a path and achieve my goals in life. It had been a great opportunity for me to study in Kandy, but there had been significant drawbacks to that success too.

I would be separated from my family for a very long time. Eventually, that separation had an unexpected outcome for all of us.

The X Girls' College is located in the heart of the city of Kandy, overlooking Kandy Lake.

Kandy is a picturesque city situated on a plateau of the central province, surrounded by mountains. It is home to tea plantations, a biodiverse rainforest, and is famed for sacred Buddhist sites, including the *Temple of the Tooth* shrine.

One could reach this city—which is known for its historical significance and the well-preserved traditions—from the coastline *via* strategically carved roads in the rugged mountains. Kandy survived as the capital of independent Sri Lanka for over two hundred years, withstanding the fury of three European powers at the height of their prowess.

The city's heart is the scenic Kandy Lake.

It is surrounded by a paved sidewalk that is popular for strolling. It is outlined with a 'cloud wall' —an undulating structure to depict the waves in the lake. The sidewalk is shaded with various tropical flowering trees, including Cherry Blossoms bearing pink flowers, Araliya bearing white aromatic flowers, Rath-Maara bearing red flowers, etc. These trees and the 'cloud wall' come together to design a colourful garden around the lake.

The X Girls' College was founded in 1932 by a group of wealthy ladies who had the privilege of knowing 'royalty', and who had a vision for the future. With meticulous scrutiny, the school used a tedious selection process to maintain a quality of education that would sustain the reputation of the school. They had established a disciplinary environment for girls who were moulded to graduate as well-behaved young ladies.

I was fortunate to have had the opportunity to live in this beautiful historic city to receive my primary education. Although it was considered a privilege, I had to leave my family to live in the boarding house provided by the school because Kandy was too far to travel every day from home.

Until I started life in the boarding school, I did not realize that I was never happy in my home, with constant watchful eyes following me and intimidating me in a hurtful way. Yet, regardless of the difficult life I had with Mother and my extended family, the separation, at first, was very difficult, but in time, I started to enjoy my life in the new environment.

Seemingly, I was escaping a grip that held me from reaching for the stars. Since then, I progressed well, and I was over the moon!

The day finally arrived for me to leave home. I cannot remember feeling sad or happy, but I remember feeling grateful to Father for giving me the opportunity to make new friends. I also felt grateful to Mother for dressing me on my first day of school in a well-tailored taffeta frock with red polka dots on a white background, to present myself to the new community.

About a month before my first day, the school had sent a list of essential items for boarding and for attending classes. The list was very long. Mother got into action immediately. She went shopping and brought all the necessary fabric, and started stitching.

A pile of brand new clothes started to collect on a table. I can still smell the aroma of new fabric filling the air and hear the sewing machine in the background, like a restless bee buzzing while looking for honey in the garden. I also remember Mother sitting at the sewing machine and pushing the pedal while moving the fabric gently to complete her creative venture.

When completed, she monogrammed each item in red-coloured cross-stitch design.

I ran in and out of the sewing room to see what item of clothing would be stitched next. It was exciting, because both parents joined together in paying attention to my needs at hand.

I still feel very grateful for all that they did.

Father bought a new metal trunk, and he neatly arranged all of my clothes in it while checking the list with a pencil. Mother ensured that the list of toiletries was checked in: baby soap, powder, cream, hairbrush, toothpaste, a toothbrush, and a small box containing my earrings.

My school books were bought the next day, and Father covered each book with a brown sheet of paper, and on it he wrote my name and grade in neat bold letters. All things were ready. Then, I placed my favourite doll and her accessory box on top of the pile of items packed into the trunk.

To this day, the fact that I left home when I was a child to live with strangers is unbelievable. I was still a baby, attached to my dolls.

It was the beginning of a new era.

The school hostel was situated at the top of a hill, overlooking Kandy Lake. It had two separate buildings: one to house very young girls in Primary School (Junior Hostel) and another for teenagers (Senior Hostel).

The matron of the Junior Hostel, where I was assigned, was an older woman, who was well known to many in town as a strict disciplinarian. She wore round, thick glasses and looked at me and smiled. I was scared of her from the moment I saw her large peering eyes through her concave glasses, thick like the bottom of a glass bottle. I decided to try never to encounter this lady or become the recipient of her disciplinary actions.

She took my parents and me around the hostel and emphasized what *not to do* in each locality.

We visited the dormitories first with its rows of identical beds—they looked like hospital wards. The beds were well settled with colourful coverlets tucked at the foot-end with decisively made pleats. The dining room had long clean tables with meticulously arranged place settings. Bathrooms were expected to be shared with the group of girls in each dorm room. The study hall had been furnished with rows of tables for the children and a table set at a higher level for the on-duty teacher.

At the end of the tour, she took us to a visitor's room in front of the building and informed us that a visitor must sign a book before meeting a child. Only those visitors registered by the parents were permitted to enter the premises.

At that moment, I understood my predicament of being in such a regimented place. I felt as if I was going to be locked up for a very long time.

I did not know the gravity of this situation until I came of age. For over nine years, I had to live a regimented life that was structured according to strangers. That made me skeptical about my future to be happy and free in the real world, outside the walls of this establishment.

I was right.

In the end, I would emerge as a young adult who was expected to face the real world after being secluded. As I suspected, my first experience of facing the real world was daunting.

Indeed, in the real world, people do not have a regimented life that follows a strict timetable for each of their daily activities. But in the boarding school, all activities within a given day were associated with a ringing of a bell:

6:00 a.m. - The wake-up call;

6:30 a.m. - Study before breakfast;

7:00 a.m. - Breakfast;

7:30 a.m. - Start walking to school after an inspection by the matron: cleanliness of clothes, shoes and the length of one's finger nails;

1:00 p.m. - Lunch (some free time—finally—after that);

3:00 p.m. - Snack time in the dining hall;

3:30 p.m. - Participate in various sports activities to be held in the school playground;

5:00 p.m. - Bathe and prepare clothes and shoes for the next day before heading to the study hall; and

7:30 p.m. - Dinner would be served.

After a long day of following the ringing of bells, time would arrive to gather at the foot of our beds. Here, we would follow meditation instructions by the matron to help us fall asleep.

Who needs help to fall asleep after such a tedious day filled with activities? Every single evening, my head would hit my pillow, and immediately I would see dreams.

I remember having a dream each night where I floated into a world without rules.

Although the structured, regimented life was not easy, living in the junior hostel was memorable. I met a variety of children from all walks of life. Eventually, I would learn that the majority of them were born to privilege.

Among all the rich and the famous, I also located some like-minded girls. We became friends easily, as we had to depend on each other's care and affection for survival. We were all in the same predicament; we had no parents to reach out.

I made a few true friends who have kept in touch with me to this day. My life in the hostel was bearable because of those valuable friendships.

As children, we played with dolls and studied together. We held hands during our Sunday morning guided walk around Kandy Lake; the only outing we had as children.

Regardless of caste or creed, we ate the same food and slept on identical beds while growing up under the same rules. One future day, each girl was destined to encounter a varying society outside the walls of the hostel. This was true whether the child was born to an aristocratic family whose members may never have had to work a day in their lives or to a family of a merchant who had to work 24/7.

From what I heard, later in life, the effects of our lives within the walls of the boarding school had impacted all of the girls in a most unexpected but remarkably similar manner.

That had been the truth for me too; I did not know how to live a normal, non-regimental life outside of the school walls.

Yet, the education I received from this school was unparalleled. I carried it with me into my future to meet the competitive world. I believe that Father made the right decision for my future, and no matter what was written in her diary, I am grateful for all that Mother did to enable me to live among rich children, without feeling left out or disadvantaged.

But eventually, I would learn that during this lengthy period of separation from my family, Mother had planned her life according to her own will with no regard for her duties as a mother.

Mother's behaviour confused my young mind. Perhaps the separation from Mother would have enabled me to reach my goals without interferences.

School holidays in Sri Lanka were divided into three sessions. Three weeks in April to celebrate the Sinhala and Tamil New Year, one month in August for annual processions to pay homage to the *Tooth Relic of Buddha*, and three weeks in December to celebrate Christmas and the dawn of the New Year.

Father took Brother and me home for each holiday and brought us back to school on time. In between times, at least once a month, Father visited me and enquired after my health and my progress in school. He did not miss a single parent-teacher meeting.

Unfortunately, I cannot recall Mother visiting me during those years.

Each time Father visited me, he told me that Mother was busy taking care of matters at home; she had sent her love instead. I was surprised by her absence but did not question her motives for staying away.

In her diary, Mother had written: "Three times per year, my children came home for their holidays, which ended my holidays because I had to attend to them." *How strange*, I thought. Did Mother believe her children were a burden to her, denying her the freedom to enjoy life?

I think that she appreciated her solitude.

There was one unforgettable incident that still festers in my mind. One year, all children in the Junior Hostel were permitted to go home for a long weekend in May. I was twelve years old and was one of the two girls left behind in the empty dormitory.

Father came for a visit when I was in distress. He took one look at me and decided to take me home, although it had not been discussed with Mother for consensus. When we arrived, Mother went into a rage, and harsh words were directed at Father. I sat in a corner and felt helpless. She demanded an explanation for his decision to bring me home. Father's decision exhibited his loving-kindness towards his child.

Therefore, I decided that Mother's fury was unpardonable.

That incident made me feel like a rare baby elephant that was rejected by her mother. Her behaviour that day changed my perception of her and diminished my self-worth.

As a result, I saw life from another viewpoint; I had been abandoned to survive on my own.

With that experience, I lost the ability to trust people, I found solace in books, and the family cat became my best friend.

Mother had written: "After the birth of my daughter, the attention of my husband was withdrawn from me and directed at her. That saddened me greatly. I was angry. She took away everything that I deserved." How could a Mother be so careless as to reject her own child based on unfounded reasons?

I could not comprehend her immaturity and apparent callousness. That day, I decided to move forward, leaving behind all negative feelings in my mind. With that resolve, for a brief moment, I felt strong.

But that strength only lasted until I hit puberty! The vulnerability associated with this transformation engulfed my life with a vengeance. Mother had no offerings to help me.

I had no choice but to take charge of my feelings and my life, and move forward.

So I did.

$\mathcal{B}$ROKEN $\mathcal{H}$EARTS AND
A $\mathcal{B}$ROKEN $\mathcal{D}$OOR

Change is the only constant in life. This known natural phenomenon is inevitable.

Mother had scribed in her journal about an event that changed all our lives. That event was a result of a notable change that Father had implemented: our move out of my maternal grandparents' home to a new home that he had built in Kaduwela.

Kaduwela is a tranquil little village situated about 24 miles from Kandy. It is surrounded by ranges of mountains, which also was part of the village; many small houses were visible on various locales on the green slopes of the hills. One of the mountains proudly exhibited a beautiful waterfall. People in this village lived peaceful lives, but much like in any other small town on the island, everyone knew everyone else's business.

The land Father inherited from his mother was spacious and had been a great asset to our family. Most of all, I was thrilled about this new living arrangement, because my paternal Grandmother also lived on the same property in her own home behind ours.

The new home was gorgeous, and it had five bedrooms, a patio, a beautiful dining room, a decorative porch, and a wonderful space to cultivate a flower garden in the front yard.

Finally, I was offered a private room, and that was extremely rewarding.

From the outset, Mother's time had been extensively spent to beautify the home and develop a flower garden in the front, which she had shaped into a large star. Mother used all her resources to bring plants from around the Island, specifically from The Hakgala Gardens, which was famous for flowering plants suitable for mountain climates. Eventually, the 'star' had blooms of gardenia, dahlia, bougainvillea, shoe flower, carnations, jasmine and many other tropical flowering plants.

She carefully selected rose bushes of varying colours and planted those along the path from the gate to the flight of ascending steps leading to the star garden. Her designs brought an enchanting look to the new home.

Her efforts and the outcome had become the talk of the village.

She then extended her green thumb and planted many fruit trees in the surrounding land, adding value to the property for years to come. On any given day, we were able to pluck ripe fruits that were ready to eat for breakfast or lunch: papaya, banana, a variety of mangos, pineapples, and avocados. She also planted many spices in the backyard: cardamoms, lime, lemon, ginger, garlic, cloves, and peppercorn.

Seemingly, she had reproduced the garden from her original family home and then some on this new property.

Her planned garden also had coffee trees. She planted those along the property line, mimicking a fence. Behind the house, the garden extended far down towards the paddy fields, and that part of the garden was crowded with jackfruit, breadfruit, coconut and king-coconut trees.

She planned the location for each plant and gave instructions to the hired local men to do the landscaping and planting. I am proud to say that Mother was organized to her highest capacity during this venture, and if she were to be more organized than that, her DNA would have unravelled.

On the upper part of the property, Father had been responsible for establishing and maintaining a vegetable garden, which provided carrots, beans, cassava, pumpkins, and various leafy greens for salads.

Because of the lush and productive land, my parents did not have to buy many groceries.

After moving to this new house, every time I returned home for school holidays, my primary action was to visit Grandmother. She had lived in her house for all of her adult life. As a single mother, she had brought up her only son, my father, and educated him well, since my paternal grandfather had passed away when Father was an infant.

Her home was simple but had been elegantly decorated. She was a clever lady who knew how to stretch a rupee and live a comfortable life. She was one of the very best cooks I had the privilege to encounter. Her specialty was Sri Lankan sweetmeats. The spices used in her products, such as cardamoms, cloves, and ginger, had rendered a signature aroma to her home, which captured my senses every time I entered it.

During our holidays, she would prepare all three meals for a given day and would end a perfect meal with homemade sweet treats. She took advantage of our short holidays to demonstrate her love for her only two grandchildren.

She was a major part of our lives and the greatest Grandmother to both Brother and me.

Yet, Mother living close to her mother-in-law would bring detrimental effects to our family, and the created disharmony would gradually damage my relationship with Mother.

In Sri Lanka, the celebration of a daughter's coming of age is a special event filled with many traditions.

In my case, fortunately, the activities were kept within my immediate family. These celebrations would entail a variety of rituals. Sri Lankan parents believe that presenting their daughter to society as a woman at an auspicious time would bring a better marriage and a better-married life for her with many children. The gifts the daughter would receive during the celebrations were considered as a sign of things to come.

I had been in the junior hostel playing with my friends when I noticed physical changes. Based on questions I had raised to the matron, she declared that I had reached puberty. My parents were contacted, and they immediately arrived to take me home.

Since then, the procedures that were followed by all those around me were strange and mind-boggling.

After helping me get dressed for travel, I remember Mother covering my body from head to toe with a white cloth and escorting me to the car where Father was waiting to take us home. I was informed that the covering was to prevent any male from laying an eye on me in my vulnerable condition, and it was also to prevent me from being tempted to look at one!

After arriving at home under a steamy cover on a hot and humid day, Mother locked me in my room for four days. No explanations were provided, and none were requested.

Brother was brought home from his school hostel to celebrate the occasion. Soon after arriving, he had rushed to the locked door looking for me, hoping to speak with me. He had no passage to the room and was surprised. He knocked on the door and asked,

"What are you doing in there?"

"I have no idea," I replied.

"Could I come in?"

"Mother may not like it," I responded.

No more questions were asked after Mother instructed him to stay away. During those four days, I was kept under lock and key, and my meals were brought into my room. I sat on the bed and enjoyed my downtime by reading some books. I was taken out of the room for bodily rituals; each time, Mother made sure no male was in the vicinity.

I did not have a bath for all four days, making me feel very uncomfortable.

On the fifth day, supposedly at an auspicious time based on the planetary arrangements, a woman came to release me from bondage and bathed me while chanting some strange stanzas. At that time, I could not understand the meaning of her words, but later, I would learn that the verses contained advice on how to prepare for married life and motherhood.

Unfortunately, the purpose of chanting on that day was not served, as I had no clue what they meant!

After the bath, the woman dressed me in brand new clothes and took away all of the clothes I was wearing. She even took my hairbrush, toothbrush, and any other personal items, like my earrings, which I had worn during the closed-door event.

Mother then presented her newly crowned 'woman princess' to the family, cleaned as a new penny and dressed in a bright-coloured dress. Instead of being thrilled to be the center of attention, I felt like a decorated plum pudding displayed for sale. The feelings of uncertainty for my future probably would have been etched all over my face.

Brother was delighted to see me after his several failed attempts to peek through the keyhole of the locked door to get a glimpse. He presented me with a gold chain that had been selected and purchased by our parents for the occasion.

I was happy to see Father after the long and restricted period. He looked at me with a Cheshire cat grin and some tears in his eyes. My parents presented me with new clothes and gold earrings to wish me good fortune for the future. That moment was overwhelming, as I was self-conscious to have their eyes on me. After the rituals were complete, I enjoyed a special meal with my family to end the celebrations.

I was relieved that the undesired focus on me was over, and I was hoping to return to my old self. However, as a budding woman, a new set of rules had surfaced. Mother's instructions for the rest of my life were not what I had expected: *no physical contact with Father, Brother, or any other male until my parents would agree to give my hand in marriage to a suitable man.*

Although her instructions were neither carved in stone nor explicitly verbalized, they were insinuated every time she thought a man paid attention to me. Indeed!

The day after the celebrations, the unexpected and unwarranted incident, which Mother had scribed in her journal, occurred.

My paternal Grandmother asked me to visit her at her humble home. After a brief discussion on my current status as a woman, she gifted me with a 24k gold coin to commemorate my coming of age and to wish me a prosperous and happy life as a woman.

I looked at the shiny gold coin resting on my palm. I was exhilarated. I hugged Grandmother and noted that her eyes were watering. She kissed me on the cheeks and said, "You are my little daughter. I took care of you when you were very little. I want you to have the best life, the best education, and a good man to take care of you."

I could not fathom the true meaning of her words at that moment as I was fascinated by the shiny object on my palm. Much later, I came to realize her kind words and was perplexed.

I ran into our home while tightly holding the gold coin in my palm, like a clam protecting the pearl in its slime. With pride, I opened my palm to display the treasure to Father. He was thrilled and surprised by his mother's kind and appropriate gesture.

He forgot that I was no longer a little girl. He hugged me with joy before asking me to show the gifted coin to Mother. I was reluctant for a moment but decided to follow Father's suggestion.

Mother was in the bedroom reading a book. She looked at the coin and looked at it again, then looked into my eyes and said, "This is not real. Your Grandmother was trying to bribe you with a dud." I did not believe her words as I was old enough to realize the coin's true value.

I returned to Father, and he assured me the authenticity of the coin and informed me that it had been a gift from my great-grandmother to her daughter, Grandmother. He also said that I should always treasure this coin and regard it as an heirloom. I was happy and decided to secure it in my purse.

Unfortunately, Mother had not perceived Grandmother's generosity kindly. Soon after, all hell broke loose.

I was putting away the precious gift when I heard someone scream, and it was coming from the direction of Grandmother's house. I heard Mother's voice as if she was talking to herself. I was too nervous to approach.

After a few moments, I heard a loud bang mixed in with the screams, and with that, the dog started barking frantically, and the cat swished passed me to hide. It sounded like a heavy object was being pounded on the wooden door of Grandmother's house. I ran to inform Father of the commotion. He hurried to the back of the house to investigate.

An unexpected scene had unfolded.

Mother was striking the closed wooden door of Grandmother's home with an axe! She was hysterical, and her voice was screechy; no one could comprehend her words.

I could not believe my eyes. I felt thumping heartbeats and butterflies in my stomach. I realized that Mother had just lost her self-respect and dignity. She failed to maintain her composure; she behaved in a most un-ladylike manner in front of her family.

It was ironic that her unacceptable behaviour was exhibited on a day when I was looking for a role model as I blossom into a woman. Brother did not wish to observe Mother's bad behaviour. He kept to his room and did not come out for hours.

What made Mother lose her mind was a mystery to me.

By the time Father released the axe from Mother's tight grip, some damage had been done to the door and the adjacent wall.

Mother ran back to the house while rashly screaming from the top of her voice. I was in tears and was paralyzed by this unexpected event. Father calmly put the axe away and examined the damage.

Grandmother did not come out of her home. I ran in and found her in tears as she sat on her favourite chair. I hugged her shaking body and comforted her by putting my cheeks on hers and sharing the tears that were rolling down her face.

I was certain that the golden gift from Grandmother triggered Mother's anger. At that moment, my heart broke; it bled with sadness and despair.

Grandmother's gesture was to wish the best for my future. Therefore, I tried to rationalize Mother's outburst: did Mother not wish me a bright future or was her mind too clouded to see the true nature of the gift that would bring me good fortune through Grandmother?

Father quietly withdrew to his office room, and an eerie silence blanketed our home; a vivid contrast to the past celebratory environment.

I decided to speak to Father, hoping to find some solution to the problem. I suggested that I return the gold coin to Grandmother and let Mother know about it. He vehemently opposed the idea and explained that the gift I received was from a woman who had a golden heart, and I deserved it. I decided to bring the suggestion to Mother, but she did not respond to my suggestion, instead, she rudely continued to read her book.

I was lost and confused.

I could not enjoy the golden gift anymore; Mother stole my joy. Most of all, I could not understand her motives to steal my joyful moment. I wanted to forgive her, but it was harder than I had imagined.

Since the coming of age, for some unknown reason, Mother refused to stitch any clothes for me. Perhaps she wished me to be independent, or perhaps her dislike towards me reached a higher level after the gift from Grandmother. I could only speculate.

Mother had written in her journal of this unfortunate event, which brought disharmony to the family during an occasion that should have brought joy and togetherness. "A gold coin for my daughter and a bag of silver coins for me; I deserve the best. Not my daughter. My son should have received a gold coin. I lost my temper that day, and I may have caused damage to my family. But I firmly believe that my daughter was not the deserving one for inheriting such treasures."

After reading her entry, I questioned whether Mother had ever loved me. At that moment, another question popped into my mind: *Who was I to her?*

I could not recover from the mental disruption caused by Mother on that day. We parted a few days after when I had to return to school. I could not utter a single word to Mother before departure; I could not thank her for arranging the celebrations on my behalf. I believe that she understood my reservations; therefore, she did not try to speak to me either.

Unfortunately, she never apologized for her actions. For many years to come, we remained strangers. Father or Grandmother did not utter a word on this event ever again. They knew some things about Mother that were oblivious to me and Brother.

Perhaps they forgave her based on that knowledge.

Unfortunately, I did not have sufficient time to resolve several major issues with Mother before her passing, and this particular incident was one that I could not bring myself to discuss with her. She never spoke of it either. She took the secrets surrounding that incident to her grave.

After Mother's passing, I read in an article published in the local newspaper, Ottawa Citizen: "*Not resolving conflicts can have surprising consequences. If you don't deal with your mom (and dad) by resolving conflict, you're going to carry those same patterns into your future relationships, whether that's with your friends, partner or boss.*"

I examined my relationships with those who came close to my heart, and I realized there had been incidents that were ridden with conflicts; perhaps some could be related to this particular incident. Yet, I had become strong to initiate and carry on with very fruitful relationships in my life too. I am thankful for those. I decided to apply the saying, "Instead of being in a tug of war, just drop the rope," which enabled my chances to develop good relationships with many friends and associates.

I thought of Mother as a woman with her "own wounds and hurts," born and raised in a different generation with different values, family relationships, and issues.

I had to forgive her for my own peace of mind.

After I became a young woman, I was transferred to the Senior Hostel. My dormitory had ten other young women, and I was fortunate to have some of my close friends in the same premises.

The Senior Hostel was situated on a beautifully landscaped grounds filled with a variety of mature trees and bushes. It was a stone throw away from Kandy Lake. My bed was next to a large window with silky sheers that overlooked the front garden and the lake beyond.

Every morning, I only had to look through the window to experience the tranquillity of the surroundings marked by a thick layer of mist that floated over the lake. With the rising sun, the fragmentation of the mist was admirable and memorable, which would eventually clear to reveal a small island in the middle of the lake, just like a scene in a movie.

I was at peace.

My life changed after I moved to the new location, only because there were new rules, agendas, and a new matron, but the same routine continued day-in and day-out for the rest of my hostel life.

The only major difference I admired was the new addition to the list of outings for the boarders. We were scheduled to attend a Russian ballet when it came to town. As a group, we saw great movies such as *The Sound of Music, My Fair Lady,* and *Poseidon Adventure.* But the security was tighter during those outings. They were much more pronounced and stricter than when we were at the junior hostel.

We were closely monitored.

The Sunday stroll around Kandy Lake continued all through my senior years. I no longer held hands with friends but enjoyed their company as young adults. I noticed the difference in my perception of the world; the flowers looked more beautiful, and the men I saw on the streets paid more attention to me, and I returned their favour.

One time, there was a strange incident of the appearance of a 'showman' under the bridge we passed. The girls who witnessed this incident spoke of an 'ugly item' on the man. I was inquisitive about that 'ugly item,' but never had the courage to ask about it. This unexpected event led to the cancellation of a few regular Sunday walks.

The discussions among my friends also changed from dolls to real-life incidents. One of my friends had met a boy during the school holidays, who was interested in having a relationship with her. This notion was taboo in the hostel. Therefore, she decided to keep the relationship a secret. However, another girl in our hostel could not keep the secret under wraps, and the coupled girl was expelled.

No one spoke of the incident again, and no one dared to have a relationship with a boy after that.

I once read that when one reaches puberty, every emotion is considered different from those that surfaced in your mind before; hormones are responsible for all changes. Understanding those emotions and feelings were important to reach maturity. For that, the environment needs to provide encounters to materialize emotions such as intimacy with others.

Unfortunately, the environment I lived in did not have this capacity.

The only male we saw around the hostel was the gardener. He was old and was constantly in the burning hot sun. The only other males who entered the premises were two old men who brought clean laundry weekly in separate bundles with name tags. No one was allowed to speak with them.

Then one fine day, the old man was accompanied by his teenage son. For some girls, it was a vision to embrace. They spoke of that young man till the cows came home. It was obvious that we had been famished and parched for intimacy.

As young adults, we lived in a very unhealthy environment that was unsuitable for emotional growth.

The final years of my hostel life were devoted to studying and preparing for a better future. Some of my friends did not pass the Grade 10 Ordinary Level exams and had to leave school. I missed them very much, but I was determined to be happy and focus on getting good grades in the Grade 12 Advanced Level exams.

I did not have much time to think of Mother or her issues. Father continued to visit me, and much later, Brother accompanied me home for school holidays after he was old enough for the task.

After writing the Grade 12 exams, I said goodbye to my friends. It was difficult. We were sheltered from a normal life during our formative years, but we knew how to survive. That was our prerogative.

I graduated from school with grades required to enter any one of the universities on the Island. In Sri Lanka, several universities were operated under the British system. I sent my application to the university closest to my home and the best in the Island.

After leaving school as a young adult, I expected my childhood to be over. Yet, the child in me lived on, searching for answers to questions about Mother and her relationship with me during my childhood.

To add insult to injury, the world I encountered outside the school surprised me and confused my sensibilities. Soon, I realized that I needed to learn many lessons to survive in the real world, those that were never included in my school curriculum. To make the transition more joyful, I had to learn those skills very fast.

Trying years were about to meet me; those would be demanding, unsettling, and unforgettable.

Through them all, Mother followed me like a living rain cloud.

As Boris Pasternak wrote in[2] *My Sister Life and The Zhivago Poems*, "A mother's love or witches' curse, only time will tell."

---

2 **Boris Pasternak**; *My Sister Life and The Zhivago Poems* (Translated by James F. Falen; Northwestern University Press, USA; 2012)

CHAPTER 5

ℱELICITY

It was the year the Island was officially renamed Sri Lanka after abolishing the name Ceylon. After leaving high school, I was anxiously waiting for the selection process results, to be admitted to an undergraduate program at a local university. It was a long wait, seven months to be exact. I imagined that such a lengthy period of time living with Mother as a young adult would help me to understand her personality and her disposition towards her family.

Unfortunately, I was right; that understanding would lead to the permanent damage to my relationship with Mother.

Mother had not written much about this period in her journal; she might have considered that as insignificant and worthless. For me, however, it was memorable.

Naturally, my parents were still working full-time and had very limited time for me. I had to decide how I could employ myself for this lengthy period of leisure. I planned to learn a new craft, read as many books as possible, and most of all learn more about my family, especially about Mother.

As usual, Mother did not make my life easy, and I felt I was invading my parent's privacy. It was apparent that some adjustments—physical and mental—were necessary after a regimented hostel life. Although *freedom* was at my doorstep, I was not trained to recognize or embrace it. I was looking for a structured life that had been familiar to me.

I constantly felt that my life at home was unproductive.

Brother had left high school a year prior; unfortunately, he did not have many employable prospects. Mother was disappointed with his situation. She had spent a large amount of money on his education at a privately run school in Kandy.

After leaving school, Brother rarely appeared in our lives. I could not fathom his absence as my parents were unwilling to share any details. I only had one brother, and we were the best of friends; my parent's silence on this matter was unacceptable. I missed him greatly.

Two months after I left school, I received a letter from Brother, explaining his current status. The return address was a P.O. Box number. My heart sank. I tried to understand what that meant.

"He is at a temporary residence in Colombo, and he will be following accountancy courses at the Aquinas College in Borella to find employment," Father explained.

I wished that he would come home to spend some time with the family and discuss his future. I wrote and begged him to consider a visit. But he did not, and I was devastated.

Mother had written in her journal: *My son had a great potential to reach major heights, but he was not fortunate. He was deprived of the education that he deserved due to the lack of good teachers in the privately run school; I did my best to provide him with a path. I have very little faith in his future. I feel as if I have failed him and failed myself.*

Soon after Brother's decision to stay away from the family—according to Father's account—Mother's behaviour turned worse: intolerable and irrational. She continued to teach at the local school, but her enthusiasm for life seemed to have vanished. She did not tend to her star garden as before, and bare patches started to appear. She did not speak of Brother at all.

She hardly spoke with me.

Unfortunately, Father also kept to himself. Since my coming of age, his close association with me had diminished; it had become more formal, and that saddened me greatly. Perhaps he also was concerned about the future of Brother.

I was left alone to deal with my emotions, and I felt extremely vulnerable.

The days dragged on, and I was bored at an Olympic level. From time to time, I visited my paternal Grandmother, who had aged rapidly over the years. Mother was not pleased with my attachment to Grandmother. Seemingly, she considered my regular visit with Grandmother as a hindrance to her own peaceful existence. I could not comprehend her thought process. But to maintain peace, I decided to visit Grandmother when my parents were at work.

Father's relatives lived in the vicinity. However, I never saw them, because Mother had prohibited any visits from them, even to see Grandmother. According to Mother's rule book, Father had to visit his relatives in their homes but did not have the opportunity to entertain them at ours. Perhaps they did not like Mother and preferred the arrangement anyway.

I longed for some company.

After about three months of despondency, I asked Mother for her permission to learn how to cook, as I had no opportunity to learn this craft while I was at school.

"Why do you need to learn how to cook?" Mother asked.

"Because won't I need to know at least the basics in cooking, in case I would not have access to cooked food?"

Answering her question with another question was not successful. She became defensive.

"You will have domestic help to cook for you, just like I had all through my life. Besides, you will cut your fingers using a kitchen knife, and I will have to take you to a dispensary to dress the wounds."

Her reasons as to why I should not get involved in the kitchen activities were not acceptable to me, but it was her kitchen, and I preferred not to rub her the wrong way.

Yet, Mother had made sure that three times a day I would have wonderful meals: hoppers or string-hoppers for breakfast, delicious curries with rice for lunch, and simple meals such as coconut roti with fish or egg curry for supper. I constantly wondered how such meals could be prepared, and whether I would ever have an opportunity to learn how to excel in this craft.

But Mother had made her decision. The result of her decision was devastating. I remained oblivious to any culinary skills; the consequences of Mother's neglect of not encouraging her daughter to learn how to cook would haunt me with a vengeance. I did not see that coming.

I was naive to believe Mother's assurance that domestic help would be freely available to serve me.

A young girl named Biso worked in the kitchen during this period.

She arrived one day with her father when she was five or six years old. Her mother had passed away, and her father—a poor farmer from a distant village—could not support his only daughter. Mother had been more than willing to take Biso in and train her to do household work. A small salary had been agreed for her services, and since then, Biso had lived with us. She followed Mother's instructions without a single pushback; Mother must have loved that very much.

Biso was a great companion for me during my lengthy leisure.

She spoke only a few words other than answering my questions, mostly related to the family cats, *Loku Haamine* and *Hinni Haamine,* or her daily routine. Nevertheless, she was a great comfort for my lonesome life.

I sometimes sat and watched her efficient hands prepare vegetables for cooking or pounding soaked rice in the wooden mortar to prepare the batter for breakfast hoppers. She was like a little red ant on a mission, moving hither and thither to complete her daily tasks.

I imagined how Biso slaved over the hot stove for most of her day while I enjoyed the wonderful aroma streaming out from the kitchen. She had rosy cheeks each time she emerged from the kitchen after cooking, but she never complained. I was unhappy that she had to work in a kitchen in her youth, without future prospects.

I silently wondered what her thoughts would have been on this subject.

I also wondered how Mother treated Biso when no one was around. Since Biso was reluctant to speak, I had no way of knowing her day-to-day dealings with Mother. I hoped that Mother was pleasant to Biso and provided her with, at least, the bare necessities of life.

Once Mother suggested that I hand over my old clothes to Biso, and I was more than happy to comply. Since I did not have any sisters, I considered Biso to be my adopted sister. Since then, Biso was well-dressed, and she appeared to be happy to wear my clothes.

Time passed without notable incidents or excitement.

I had nothing to do. I was fed well, and no one interfered with my daily routine. Yet, I was restless because of the uncertainty of my future. I could not find any specific reasons why I should depend on my parents to support me if I could not be successful on my own. My hope to enter a university provided me with a reason to wake up every morning and face each day.

One time I thought of shopping to eliminate the boredom because I was certain that activity would have kept me engaged and happy. But that was not possible without Mother's permission, as all local shops in the village were situated along the bus route.

The road leading to our home from the bus route was long and curvy, and I could not venture out on my own. For the same reason, many locals also left the family alone, unless there was a specific reason to visit the house.

The ground around the home had a dense growth of large and small trees interspersed with shrubs. The only colour around our home was green; no other colour had a chance to paint the surroundings.

At dawn, I would wake up and lazily lay on my bed to listen to the jungle greeting the sun. From a distance, I would hear the *cock-a-doodle-doo* of a rooster, and just outside my window the unpleasant sound of crows inviting each other to find a suitable breakfast. I would cover my head to dull this unpleasant noise.

Every day the same sounds woke me up; the monotony was unbearable.

Each day at dusk, I would sit in silence to listen to the sounds of nature ending a day and wondered whether what I heard at dawn would be reversed; indeed, that would be true, day in and day out.

In the greenery surrounding our home, hundreds of birds such as parrots, kingfishers, woodpeckers, and many others lived emulating a man-made sanctuary. A few snakes and some lizards also lived on this land, but humans were a rare breed.

Without a doubt, we were secluded and isolated in a land that belonged to exotic creatures.

Sometimes, I listened to the birds. They were entertaining, but I hoped that a cobra or a large lizard would appear to create some excitement. That would be rare because the family dog would bark like a maniac if any of those creatures approached the home, signalling the potential danger. So, the creatures stayed away, which made it a safe but lifeless place to live. I craved and wished to associate with people who were of similar age— in my opinion, Kaduwela was a ghost town.

Then one day, I encountered felicity; at least, that was what I imagined it could be.

As a general rule, the daily newspaper was delivered around 9:00 a.m., under Father's name to a nearby shop. This was a prudent arrangement as no one was at home to receive it. My parents then picked up the paper on their way home. Since my return from the hostel, my parents requested home delivery. Father had informed the delivery company that I would receive the paper at the door, but strangely, no one informed me to take care of this task; I presumed this was an oversight by my parents.

One morning a knock on the door alerted me.

I was not certain whether I should open the door as my parents did not provide me with instructions on this activity. I decided to investigate. I took the time to unlock the door.

A young man with a pleasant smile greeted me.

I had never seen him before, but I smiled back. He was about 5'5" tall. He had dark curly hair and healthy tanned skin. He wore a plain blue short-sleeved shirt and a pair of brown shorts.

Mother would have described him as "just another man," but I thought he looked smart and attractive.

Who would have thought that a young woman who grew up in a well-respected school would be swayed by a single encounter with an unknown young man; but, there it was. I felt as if a life-altering moment had been placed at my door.

This must be a special day, I thought to myself.

Since my experience with men, young and old, was limited, I decided not to speak to him. After all, Mother would not have anticipated me having any association with a man after her clear instructions at my coming-of-age ceremony.

He handed me the newspaper. I was happy to know the reason for his arrival at the door. I acknowledged his presence, took the newspaper and turned to the door to close it behind me. Then he spoke.

"Have you finished your schooling?" he asked.

"Yes, I have," I answered. I might have looked surprised.

I was certain that I was blushing. He blushed too. My heart started to beat like a drum played for an Indigenous Rain Dance. It had a beautiful rhythm to which I could have danced in harmony. I was not certain whether the excitement was because of his interest in knowing my status or the unknown thrill of being alone with a young man.

The admiration in his eyes was very clear, as if I had come down to Earth from heaven. I closed the door before he could utter another word. I stood there for a moment to return to Earth before taking a look at the headlines.

At that moment, the excitement in my young mind was unfamiliar but bubbly and beautiful. My stomach churned, and my toes twirled. It took only one moment to outpour the powerful emotions, suppressed for many years, like a bubbling fizz of a pressured bottle of soda. I had to work very hard to curb my joy and recover from the thrilling morning to face my parents in the afternoon.

I thanked my parents for having the paper delivered for my reading pleasure, but the details of the delivery were not revealed, as I thought it would prevent the paperboy from earning some money. My parents were happy that I appreciated their gesture, and that was the end of the discussion.

However, I was not clear on how the next delivery should be handled. I thought about it at length. I needed to make the right decision, and most of all, I had to make it on my own.

The next morning the boy arrived at the door, keeping to his schedule. It was a pleasure to see him, but I was determined not to respond to any of his questions this time. I smiled with the expectation of receiving the daily paper.

A moment passed by, then instead of the newspaper, he handed me a beautiful pink rose.

I looked at him with wide eyes, and his eyes were planted on mine with a wonderful gaze. My legs felt weak, and my heart was enveloped with unusual warmth. The world around me disappeared for that unexpected moment, and surprisingly, my hand stretched towards his to accept his rose. He blushed with me. The universe connected us in a blissful moment.

He handed the newspaper next, but it slipped out of my hand and fell on the floor. He smiled with sympathy and picked it up, handing it back to me. We could not speak, we only stared at each other for several minutes, and then suddenly he ran away.

Words were not necessary, I thought, *because the pink rose spelled out his feelings beautifully*. At that moment, I had realized that I was capable of comprehending the language of affection of a young man. I was exhilarated!

I stood at the door while my hand was shaking like a feather in a morning breeze. I took the rose to my nose, and it smelled wonderful. The fragrance of that rose reminded me of sweet honey complemented by berry notes, mixed in with the unusual aroma of spicy herbs, a mixture of anise, basil, fennel, and lavender. The fragrance from the rose woke my senses with enthusiasm. I followed him with my eyes as far as I could see, then he passed through the gate and was gone.

Numerous questions rushed through my mind, overpowering it, like floodwater clogging drainage during a tropical storm: what was his name, who could be his family, how did he know who I was, and why was he a paperboy in this particular village?

I did not have any answers to a single question, and I dared not ask my parents.

Yet, he has answered the most important question: *was I an attractive young woman*? His unspoken answer kept me occupied for months to come. As Rumi, the 13th-century Persian poet and gifted wordsmith said, "Love without words has more clarity . . ."

That evening, Mother had noticed I was playing with my food and was not paying much attention to what she had to say. She became suspicious. I sensed a storm had started to brew on the horizon.

That night, the dilemma in my mind overwhelmed me until the next morning: *meet the boy or not to meet the boy*! I tossed and turned all through the night to make my decision. Finally, I decided not to answer the door to receive the paper.

The dawn of another morning had arrived with chirping birds and slanted rays of sun kissing my closed eyelids. I felt sadness in my heart because I had realized my decision not to meet the boy had been made to avoid any aggressions from Mother.

Unexpectedly, my decision on this subject would alter the future of many people.

Later in the morning, I found the newspaper on the porch. I was sad, but I needed to protect the dignity of the boy and my self-respect. Most of all, I had to avoid the brewing storm in Mother's mind that would drown me in sorrow.

I firmly believed that my decision was fair and prudent.

Although I had decided not to meet the boy again, my mind had opened to a new and delightful world. I began noticing pleasant activities in my surroundings. Seemingly, the boy had woken the sleeping beauty in me.

After spending many years with suppressed feelings in the confines of the school hostel, this one encounter with the opposite sex seemingly opened the flood gates to a world of imagination with a delicate touch of reality.

The most significant and joyous experience I had was my reaction to the flute music that I heard every evening. I did not know who held the flute. I imagined a young man in love with a sweet girl, was playing it as a mating call. I felt that he included me in the sweet melody because of the warm feelings awakened in me. I was delighted to be in this imaginary light, although I had not experienced romantic love before.

Exactly at 6:30 p.m., from the surrounding mountains to the valley below, the soothing sounds of flute music reached me and wrapped me in a silky musical blanket. It was fluid. It was air. It was continuous without any clunky stops. It was enchanting. The haunting melody excited me with a mellow poetic feel, rousing the inner goddess that was waiting to see the beauty of this world.

I sat on the veranda each evening in anticipation, and the flutist never failed me for all of the days of my lonely existence. I suddenly had become a poet. The words that were stagnated within me started to flow like a colourful ribbon obeying the force of gravity, after it had been thrown into the air.

I painted that 'man' with a silver brush,

Come feel my soul with a golden touch . . .

Since then, I happily immersed myself in a poetic sea without having any fear of drowning.

Based on my firm decision, after the second encounter with the paperboy, I did not meet him again, but I wondered how he was. I wondered whether he waited longer each day, hoping to see me. After a few weeks, I did not hear a knock on the door, but I always found the paper at the doorstep.

Somehow, I did not have any further interest in that matter. I no longer needed to find reasons to live. I was living. I wrote poems almost every day. My life had become pleasant after receiving the pink rose from the young boy.

Then soon after, in one horrific moment, Mother took all that pleasure away.

Unfortunately, the paperboy had expressed the distress to his brother, which he had experienced after his brief encounter with me. Perhaps he expected more for his life from me. He had withdrawn himself from the family. Gossip had travelled through the grapevine and landed in Mother's ears faster than a speeding bullet.

On that Saturday—a bright, normal, warm day—all normality came to an end.

My family had just finished a delicious breakfast prepared by Biso. As usual, Father was getting ready to run Saturday errands. I sat in a comfortable chair on the veranda to read *Rebecca*. Then, Mother started a discussion with Father, and I did not like the sounds of it. Father was calmly providing answers to questions raised by Mother, but the discussion was growing in momentum, which eventually led to an argument between the two. *What was the disagreement now*, I wondered.

Suddenly, Mother ran out of the room with a cane in her hand and headed to the kitchen.

The wailing sounds of Biso and the unpleasant sounds of the brush of the cane on her clothes made me sick to my stomach. Mother was beating Biso. Father did not come out of the room, but when he had realized the gravity of the situation, he came to me with teary eyes. We both had the most difficult time understanding the unfolding event but did not have the courage to save Biso from getting hurt.

I now know that not taking action to avert a dreadful outcome was wrong.

I came to know from Father, Mother's knowledge of my encounter with the paperboy during her absence made her furious. She wanted to punish me, but Father disagreed with her specific suggestion: Father should enforce the punishment. Unfortunately, he had decided not to reveal the details of the suggested punishment to avoid my potential bitter feelings towards Mother.

Since Mother could not punish me, she hurt the girl. Biso did not deserve to take any blame for my actions in life. Besides, I could not identify what crime I had committed by speaking to the boy.

I decided that Mother had a distorted mind.

I wanted to confront Mother, but the respect I felt for Father stiffened my whole body. Father had a guilty and helpless look about him as if it was "damned if he did, and damned if he did not," and he left home, not to return until that evening. I could not face Mother. Grandmother consoled Biso and me, and that aggravated the situation.

Mother had created a mental pain in me, and I wished that she would disappear from our lives forever. I decided to forgo my meal for that evening, and I felt miserable the next morning.

In her journal, Mother's accounts on what she had experienced as a child shed some light on her mental status. She wrote: *My mother was always in anger after the death of my eldest brother from pneumonia and the disappearance of the second brother from home. My second brother was an introvert to its true nature; he was never seen outside his room except to eat his meals. In his room, he constantly read the Christian Bible while wearing a cross around his neck. This behaviour enraged my father.*

After an unforgettable confrontation between my father and brother, my brother left one day to borrow some books from the British Council Library in Kandy and never returned. A letter arrived a few days later, mailed from Kankesanturai, the northern tip of the Island in the Jaffna peninsula. He thanked my mother for her caring during his childhood and wished her well. He did not write about our father. There was no explanation for his departure, and we did not hear from him since then.

Ten years later, a local newspaper printed a letter found in an apple crate—during the period where apples were imported from Portugal—which informed the family in Ceylon that he was now being held in a prison, and that he regrets his decision to leave the Island. My mother fainted after reading his letter and has been bitter since then. The anger she felt for my father had extended to me, as I was the only girl in the family and the only one who would not confront her. I endured a bitter and sad childhood because of my mother's distressed life.

From the moment Mother beat Biso without a valid reason, I had difficulty feeling any love or empathy towards her. I concluded that some dreadful events happened during her childhood might have poisoned her personality. Yet, I hated her for being the lawmaker, jury, and judge presiding over our family because, in all accounts, her judgment was grossly skewed.

I no longer had any interest in living with Mother. I called a close friend in Kandy, asking her permission to live with her family for a few days. She was delighted to have my company.

Father was happy that I had decided to stay away from home for this period. As I was about to leave, Mother came to the door, but she did not provide her opinion; Grandmother cried a few tears.

I hugged Biso, and she looked into my eyes with tenderness and despair. I wished that I could have taken her with me.

One week later, Father wrote to inform me that I had been selected to enrol in an undergraduate Science program at the University of Peradeniya. An acceptance letter and an enrollment document package had arrived. I returned home a few days later, and to my disbelief, Mother had already started to stitch garments for my new adventure!

According to Father, Mother had regained enthusiasm for her own life after my success.

To everyone's surprise, she had extended an olive branch to me too. I was delighted that I had been the source of Mother's resolve, but I was not certain how long it would take to change her mind. In the past, I had observed a pattern in Mother's behaviour, and I was skeptical, but to keep peace and harmony in the family, I decided to play the game to comply with Mother's rule book.

Even after experiencing Mother's horrible behaviour, Biso remained with our family because her father did not return to take her home after she reached puberty, although that was the original agreement. After her father's demise, by default, Mother became her guardian until my parents found a suitable partner for her in marriage. As an orphan, her life was at the mercy of Mother.

She did not have a chance to be happy, like a cat in hell without claws. I was very sad.

By the time she reached a marriageable age, she had a bank account with a small amount of money—leftovers after her father's consistent withdrawals—but my parents assured me that she was provided with many items for her new life as a young bride.

My heart burns with sorrow, even to this day, when I think of the moment Biso had to endure such cruelty because of me. She was truly helpless. I have gifted her many personal items without Mother's knowledge. Yet, I felt the deep guilt instilled in me.

I was certain that she knew my feelings. Yet, she behaved and worked as if nothing had affected her. Not surprisingly, she was as silent as the grave on this subject until her departure at marriage. She had left our family while I was attending the university, and I did not get the opportunity to wish her well or to get to know her future partner in life.

Some years later, I inquired after Biso's whereabouts from Mother, but she did not wish to reveal any information. Seemingly, Mother did not wish me to meet with Biso after her marriage. I often wondered why. To this day, I continue to search for her, but no one seems to have any leads.

I will not give up my efforts until I die.

Several years later, Mother spoke of the paper delivery boy. I was surprised. She informed me that he was in an accident. He was delivering the newspaper using a van that belonged to his friend. One day, as usual, he had stepped out of the van and headed to the trunk to pick up the load for delivery. At that moment, a passing vehicle arriving from behind had hit him.

He had died instantly.

After hearing the details of this death, I felt a deep sadness. Although I never met him after that wonderful encounter, I considered him to be the star in my youth when he gifted me with the pink rose. He will remain a star in my life, as I still believe he taught me the first lessons in love that brought felicity to a lonesome girl.

I felt miserable that I could not offer any help during his short life; I wondered whether he would meet me on the other side.

CHAPTER 6

A Monumental Loss

The day my paternal Grandmother tripped and fell on the concrete floor between our home and hers led to incidents that resulted in further damage to my relationship with Mother. Grandmother broke her left leg at the knee, and when Father hoisted her up, she could not stand. According to Father, the broken piece of her leg looked like the seat of a chair, perpendicular to the rest of her body.

She never walked again.

Two weeks before her unexpected fall, I had left home to enrol in the science undergraduate program at the University of Peradeniya.

Grandmother was in tears when I said goodbye. She wished me all the luck in the world. She was certain that she would witness my marriage soon after my graduation, although she had previously insisted that I consider marriage before my university education. She assured me that she would be in the front row to see me in my wedding attire.

She had many hopes for me. She had many wonderful dreams about her life with me. All her dreams were shattered when she fell on that tragic day.

I rushed home after I received a message from Father. Grandmother was resting on her bed and recounted the events that led to the fall.

At dusk, she had stepped out with her walking stick because she had heard the dog barking. She always had the instincts to investigate as she had lived alone for a very long time before Father built his house on the same property. When she rapidly turned around to return home, her walking stick became entangled in a crack on the concrete floor and unbalanced her. When she tried to regain her balance using the stick, it had broken, making her fall to the ground.

Mother informed me that Father's attempt to take Grandmother to the local hospital was fruitless. She had requested Ayurveda medicine for the broken leg. I had to believe Mother's account on this, based on the history of Grandmother's treatment choice for her injuries. I sat on her bed and spent ample time trying to convince her that she needed hospitalization if she wished to walk again.

She promised to make a decision soon, but to our distress, she never did.

I left home with a heavy heart as Biso had been assigned to take care of Grandmother instead of a hired nurse or relatives who would be willing to help. My parents could not care for her because of their careers, and I felt helpless. I promised to visit her soon, but my undergraduate program got in the way.

In my gut, I knew that unless Grandmother was taken to a hospital, the result could be fatal.

In our lives, one can never be sure of what a day brings to pass.

The day I started the undergraduate program, the deepening current of my life swung in a pivotal way. In a twinkle of an eye, the whole course was changed, as if a little mountain brook would pause and turn to a new direction to gather strength for the long journey towards an unknown ocean.

I visualized a new, fruitful path ahead; I gracefully stepped in.

The first time I saw the grandeur of the buildings, the lush green foliage, flowering trees surrounding the University, and an enthusiastic crowd of students who seemingly were having a great life, I felt invigorated and excited.

This institute invited me with open arms.

I felt like a bird freed into its natural environment after being caged for years. I spent the day wandering through the paths, stretching in many directions among the enormous buildings; I encountered many young men and women who roamed just like me. I sensed that I belonged to something larger than myself. I embraced the order in perpetuating chaos and the unity amongst the diversity. Finally, a purposeful life had commenced.

I confess: my university life as an undergraduate had been the best.

The University of Peradeniya is a state university in Sri Lanka, which was established as the University of Ceylon in 1942. It is situated on a site that touches the lower slopes of the lush Hanthana mountain range, about three miles from Kandy. It is famous for its natural beauty. The Mahaweli River flowed across the campus in a northerly direction, enhancing its attractive landscape.

Its picturesque surroundings had inspired many of Sri Lanka's intellectual leading playwrights. As this institute holds a central position in classical university education, it has become the setting for many dramas, films, songs, poems, novels, and other cultural works in Sri Lanka.

In general, Sri Lankans consider being accepted into this prestigious university a privilege. Probably because it provided not only an unparalleled education through eight different faculties—which have employed some of the best professors in the country—but was also generously endowed with well-designed surroundings and a unique, sophisticated, and attractive environment to inspire and encourage a young mind.

I considered that surroundings a paradise. My memories of attending this university are vivid and delightful. For more than four years, I enjoyed all that it had to offer.

Among the numerous positive aspects of my university life, there was one thing I wish to erase from my memory: the cruel ragging (identified as hazing in North America) conducted by the seniors on newly enrolled students (fresher).

One particular incident still haunts me today. A new female student's dignity had been robbed by the physical abuse and torture she endured during ragging by three senior students. Later, the victim jumped off the residence balcony. The severe brain damage that resulted from this fall had caused her untimely death. I was deeply saddened by it and felt distressed over it for several years.

Another disturbing incident—inflicted on a student enrolled in the medical faculty—was exceptionally cruel as it resulted in him becoming disoriented for several months.

A group of senior medical students took the Fresher to the "morgue" that housed the cadavers for medical and scientific studies. The activity started at midnight. The boy was asked to wear a pair of gloves, walk into the cold and dark morgue alone, count the numbers in a row of cadavers, select the number five, force open the mouth, and drop a toffee into it.

The seniors stood outside the building.

Other than being scared to walk alone into a dark morgue, what other reason would have made him nervous? He had no reason to anticipate any unexpected activity that would create unimaginable fear in him either.

But the seniors had a nasty plan to stress the newcomer.

One senior boy, who had been hiding undercover on a table next to the assigned cadaver, suddenly jumped up and spoke in a deep and eerie voice once the toffee disappeared into the mouth of the corpse: "What about meee?" The junior boy fainted and was hospitalized for trauma.

I was fortunate. The ragging inflicted on me was relatively mild.

I was asked to sing songs because a rumour had spread among the seniors that I was a professional singer. I merrily complied until they got fed up, as I knew all their requests by heart. Another time I was forced to jump up and down fifty times on one foot while reciting, "I am lucky" because the seniors had come to know that Mother had bought me seven pairs of new shoes to attend university. I was grateful for Mother's generosity but resented her action after the tenth jump.

Mother had the ability to cause distress from a distance, even when her intentions were honourable.

On the first day at registration, senior students asked each fresher to wear the clothes inside-out to meet the staff. While walking to get registered in ridiculous-looking outfits, one boy—who was three times my height—approached me and asked me to hold an umbrella over his head. It was not raining. I thought that suggestion was funny. I was curious about his intentions to pick me from a large crowd of girls. Later on, I would learn that he had approached me because he hoped to make an alliance.

After the umbrella incident, the boy returned to visit me for several days at the residence. I brushed him off, and I had no clue why I was that ruthless. Later, I understood the reasons. I constantly thought of Mother's instructions at my coming-of-age party.

My conclusion: I had been brainwashed.

While all the other girls enjoyed the attention from the boys and most found good partners to spend time with, my thoughts compelled me to stay away from boys. I decided to focus on my studies instead.

That was an unfortunate decision.

I was assigned to the Wijewardhana Hall, a girl's only residence. It was a hop-step and a jump from the Science Faculty. When I arrived at the residence hall, I was pleasantly surprised by a few of my fellow schoolmates. I managed to spend a fair amount of time with India, as she became my roommate for a period of time.

Compared to the girl's school, as expected, the social environment at the university was rather unusual. Seemingly, girls and boys who were educated in various schools—some in mixed schools while others in either all-boys or all-girls schools—had different approaches to life.

I started to learn a new way of living; many new lessons had to be learned quickly for survival.

The undergraduate program started with a heavy workload, but I enjoyed every minute of it. Compared to the difficult life I had before, it felt like I was encouraged to jump into a whirlpool to find a hidden treasure; I joyfully concurred. I had to follow chemistry, botany, and zoology for credits to advance to the second year of the program.

My life was focused, and it was interesting beyond my expectations.

At the end of the first semester, three months into the first year, I took time off to visit my family.

I was sad to see the condition of Grandmother. She was sleeping in the same position that I saw her last. She was clearly dying, trapped in some pained transitional state. Her face and body had taken on a skeletal appearance. I regret my long absence, but I knew that she would understand the reasons for my delayed visit. Her eyes had a lost look within her stilled body. She could not hear much, but she heard me when I spoke.

What do you say to a loved one when you know your words could be the last? Do you choose your words carefully, speak with your heart, or carry on with the everyday conversation about your life and the weather? I wanted to shout out "I love you" for the whole world to hear. I was choking with tears, but I needed to give Grandmother a chance to speak. I needed to hear her voice.

I stood next to her bed and held her hand. Her fingers felt small in mine, and her skin was like a dried leaf, rough and wrinkly. Tears swelled in my eyes, rolled down my cheeks, and had landed on her hand.

"Don't cry for me," her soft words brought solace to my breaking heart. Her dimmed eyes couldn't see my face, but she knew my distress; she always had.

"I'll be with you all the time. I will always be looking over you. If you need me, just call and know I'll be sending you my love," she uttered with difficulty.

I thought of all the times I had called on her when I was upset. Every time, she filled me with encouragement and wisdom. She had loved and lived with passion. I was scared to lose my beloved Grandmother, but she had no fear of death. Seemingly, she was ready.

Father informed me that during my absence, Biso had tried to wash Grandmother, but she was unable to make her sit to carry out the task while in bed. Grandmother was physically strong and unusually tall for a woman who grew up on the Island. Therefore, I understood the difficulty that Biso had faced.

Unfortunately, Mother did not wish to help, and Father was too soft-hearted to carry out the task on his own mother. I was furious but helpless. I knew that Grandmother's time on this Earth would be short unless help would arrive.

I suggested that she be taken to the hospital.

A stretcher was brought in to transfer Grandmother to the vehicle. When lifted from the bed, she did not make any sounds, as if she had already left us. Her clothes were soiled, and a pungent aroma filled the air. Biso was crying in a corner of the room. I needed to be strong as Father was not in a position to provide instructions.

Mother was nowhere to be found.

At that moment, when Grandmother was taken out of her own home, the stories she shared with me about her life flooded my mind.

As a young lady, Grandmother single-handedly established a business that attracted regular customers and a dedicated clientele. She must have had a potent elevator pitch to make this happen; there was no foggy sense for her marketing capabilities. By the time she retired, she had accumulated a sizable wealth and purchased several properties in the vicinity. Her wealth helped with Father's education and his future family.

Through her business, she had served her community and had become the best Sri Lankan sweetmeats provider (sweet edibles made with local ingredients according to ancient recipes) for the village folks during her time. Eventually, on one side of her shop, she had established an eatery to serve her sweetmeats, and she had become the first owner of such an establishment in the district.

Grandmother had always been an energetic and self-reliant individual.

She fought battles in her life: enduring the early death of her husband, bringing up a boy as a single mother, running a successful business without a support system, and singlehandedly maintaining a household. She never re-married.

She would have hated being carried on a stretcher, leaving her home of nearly sixty years. Even those who did not remember her fierce individualism would pity the condition she now found herself in. I felt her feelings of distress in my own heart; I knew that her passing would only be a matter of time, which would change our lives forever. But we had no other option. Father accompanied Grandmother to the Kandy hospital.

That was the last time I saw her alive.

After Grandmother was taken to the hospital, I left home without uttering a single word to Mother. I decided that it was better not to face her that day as I was certain that Grandmother was the topic I needed to avoid discussing with Mother, because I did not comprehend why Mother had not allowed Father's relatives to attend to Grandmother.

I instructed Biso to be strong and assured her that Grandmother would be taken care of in the hospital, but I could not control my tears until I returned to the university.

The change of scenery helped me carry on with my daily studies.

The workload in the second semester of the first year was brutal. Students were eager to receive good grades as the last term exam results would determine the acceptability for an honours program, which would run for three more years. I was confident that I could reach that threshold. Yet, carrying on with my studies with sad feelings about Grandmother was like pulling a cart without wheels on a gravel road.

Then, surprisingly, some help arrived out from nowhere; at least, for a short while.

It was a June day in Peradeniya. As usual, the day was bright and sunny. I returned to the residence hall for lunch, and after a quick wash, I went to a chemistry laboratory for the afternoon session.

Suddenly, I noticed that a young man, whom I had not seen before, was following me with his eyes. I intentionally ignored the attention as I was already late for the session. I walked across the grassy quadrangle and crossed to the laboratory.

"Hi, I am Chip," an unfamiliar voice interrupted my walk.

I turned and faced the man who was monitoring me. *"Chip, what kind of a name is that?"* I thought.

He introduced himself. "I am a third-year student. I live at Jayathilaka Hall."

I realized that this was the gent's hall across from the Science Faculty, and it was the closest to Wijewardhana Hall, where I lived.

He continued, "Would you like to discuss your study materials with me? I could be of some help because I had already passed first-year chemistry."

At that moment, I realized three important points: a. He knew I took chemistry classes; b. surely, no crime would be committed if I would discuss chemistry with a senior student, and c. I had not spoken a single word yet!

Finally, I smiled. "That would be great," I replied.

He pointed to a bench under a large tree close to the Science faculty and said, "I will meet you there at any time convenient to you." I agreed to meet him at 5:00 p.m. after the laboratory session.

We met once a week to go through chemistry lecture materials. We became great friends, and he provided me with pointers that were helpful for my year-end chemistry exam. We kept our meetings brief and only discussed chemistry. Then one evening he had decided to change the course of our relationship, and said,

"Would you like to take a stroll along Lover's Lane tomorrow? I hear that it is beautiful in the evening."

Lover's Lane was situated alongside the bank of the Mahaweli River. It was understood within the university community that only lovers are permitted to stroll on this 'sacred' path. It was not difficult to locate the historical significance of this legendary path.

In an article written by an alumnus read: "The lure of the legendary lover's lane was such that I felt an acute desire to hold the girl's hand and stroll down this path of love, talking about anything that comes to mind."

I was pleasantly surprised by Chip's invitation, but I did not have the courage to accept his offer because my mind rushed directly to Mother. I hated disappointing my friend, but that was it; I considered him only as a friend. That ended a great friendship. Since that day, he kept his distance, but he came to visit me before leaving at the end of his three-year program.

Seemingly, he was relieved to leave the campus.

A few years later, one of his friends informed me that he failed his finals but was successful in getting a teaching post in the central province. I was sad to hear about his failure to graduate from university. He deserved better. Several years later, he appeared on a local television program to discuss competitive boxing in high schools.

Although he had changed much, I recognized his kind face.

I received an urgent message from Father on Grandmother's demise when I was getting ready to sit for the end of the first-year exams with only two weeks left to study.

I rushed home to attend her funeral. Her remains were transferred to our home in a decorative casket. Grandmother looked peaceful. On a normal day, her silver hair would have been tied into a knot at the back of her head. In her coffin, her hair was loose and was placed along both sides of her body. Her long silver hair reached far down below her knees.

Our home was filled with people who had arrived to pay their last respects.

While some of those I had already met, many others were strangers. Father informed me that the strangers in our home were Grandmother's relatives. I was eager to meet them, and I was anxious to see Mother's reaction in their presence. Surprisingly, Mother did not react to anything that day. She was absent from the scene altogether. I stood beside the casket and silently prayed for Grandmother to attain *Nibbana* (Nirvāṇa in Sanskrit, the ultimate goal of the Buddhist path).

As Grandmother's casket was hoisted by Father and five other pallbearers to take it to the burial ground, for the first time in my life I saw Father burst into tears. His emotions were raw and justified. He was an only child, and the woman placed in the casket had given him life and had taken care of him without the presence of a father. I prayed for him too.

I cried till I could cry no more. A deep sadness had enveloped my body and my soul.

On the day of the funeral, to my greatest joy, Brother managed to return home. Unfortunately, he arrived after Grandmother's remains had been taken to the burial grounds. He missed the opportunity to view Grandmother for the last time. He expressed his distress and sobbed with me.

Grandmother's final departure from our home created an abyss in my life. I knew that the love and tenderness I had the privilege of experiencing had left with her. Her remains were buried in one of her properties, about a kilometre from our home.

After the funeral was over and the crowd had departed, Mother demanded that all properties inherited by Father be handed over to her, for the difficulties she had to endure while Grandmother was bedridden. Anyone who was alive during this particular period knew that Mother did not serve Grandmother when she needed help.

But no one spoke against her demands.

Since the day of the funeral, I accompanied Father to Grandmother's gravesite during my infrequent visits to Kaduwela.

Little by little, the flowers that had adorned her gravesite withered, much like the memories of her in the minds of those close to her.

To this day, my childhood memories of Grandmother are still fresh in my mind, and they comfort me during difficult times.

She had lived for eighty-two years.

I returned to the university residence soon after the funeral. India was sympathetic towards my loss. I spoke of the funeral and Grandmother much that evening. She was all ears. I was lucky to have an attentive friend during this period. Naturally, I was exhausted and felt lost in this world. I might have fallen asleep instantly.

. . . The room door opened a crack at a time. The movement of the door garnered my full attention. Suddenly, Grandmother walked through the partially opened door.

She was dressed like a queen.

A silky white jacket covered the upper part of her body. It had full-length sleeves, and the edge of each sleeve was frilled and decorated with thin, delicate lace. The bottom part of her body was covered with a beautiful garment with floral print. As usual, her silver hair was tied into a bun and a golden hairpin held it together. A joyful smile carried all the way to her eyes; both eyes were healthy and shiny.

She slowly walked to my bedside while carrying a misty glow around her body. She bent towards me and gently caressed my pinky finger like a silky flower, and I felt a current run through my being . . .

Grandmother's touch felt real, and it woke me from my dream. I realized then that India was shaking my body while sitting on my bed. I was in a daze.

"You might have had a dream. Try and get some sleep," she kindly suggested. She then dragged her bed close to mine. I closed my eyes, knowing that India was right next to me in case I needed her to rescue me again.

She later said that my blood-curdling scream awoke her at 2:00 a.m.

Soon after India went back to sleep, I might have fallen asleep again. Surprisingly, the dream that awoke me continued. Grandmother was standing next to the partially opened door. One of her hands was placed on the doorknob as if she was getting ready to close it. Her smile was comforting to my lost soul.

She waved at me with her free hand, and then, she was gone.

I knew that Grandmother came to say goodbye to me that night because neither of us had that opportunity. She could not have left without a proper goodbye to her little granddaughter. Since her passing, she appeared in my dreams to warn me of many potentially dangerous or harmful events coming my way.

I truly believe that she had been and continues to be my guardian angel both in her life and in her death.

I sat for the end of the year exams two weeks after Grandmother's passing. I was satisfied with my performance and hoped that the results would get me into the honours program.

Soon after the exams, I returned home for my holidays. I knew that the home front would be very different without Grandmother, but I had no choice; our home was the only residence where I could enter at any time. Father greeted me at the porch with warmth. I was certain that he was happy to have me home after the loss of his mother.

I walked in with Father and immediately smelt something burning. I looked at him, and he had the same sensation. When we reached the back of the house to investigate, we could not believe our eyes.

There was a great bonfire behind Grandmother's home.

It was obvious that Mother was instrumental in the act. Mother's movements confirmed that she was continuously throwing items into the burning pile. I was stunned to see that Mother was burning Grandmother's belongings! I tried to run towards the fire, but Father pulled me back.

Mother had decided to get rid of Grandmother's belongings on the day I had been scheduled to arrive at home.

A trail of black smoke reached sky-high from the fire, depicting a message being taken to Grandmother in heaven. Soot filled the surroundings, and the smell of burning materials was unbearable. Father and I stood transfixed and heartbroken. We did not speak, but we were in great sorrow.

Later that day, I stepped into Grandmother's home. The place was deserted, and the space that had been active and alive for many decades now stood in silence. Any evidence of her living had gone up in smoke.

Suddenly, I sensed the presence of someone. A cloud-like movement startled me. I decided to leave. Perhaps Grandmother had come for a brief visit to investigate, but was unsettled to find that the familiar items had disappeared.

Burning her prized possessions was not acceptable to me; it was simply spiteful. A donation to charity would have been a better choice.

To my greatest surprise, after destroying Grandmother's possessions, Mother did one good thing that pleased me greatly. She saved all of Grandmother's jewellery for Biso for her dedicated service to

Grandmother. I later learned that my parents had delivered them to Biso as a wedding gift when she departed their home as a wife.

After attending Grandmother's funeral, Brother lost contact with our family again. I wondered how he was faring in his life. No one informed me of his status, and I decided not to press on this matter any longer. I had to move forward on my own.

After spending one month at home, I arrived back at the university residence hall to start the second year of my undergraduate program. To my great joy, I was successful in all three exams. My name was on the Honours Lists that was posted on each department's bulletin board: chemistry, botany, and zoology.

It was wonderful to have a choice.

I had to select one subject. I selected chemistry. The path to my future appeared solid, and I stepped on it with a firm foothold. It felt right.

Much later, I would understand why I had selected the chemistry program over the other two; the universe had a plan for me to meet my fate.

A month later, Father received a letter from the Department of Education informing him of his promotion to the principal of a school in a distant town. He decided to take the position. I was overjoyed for his success, but leaving Mother alone at home for the first time in their married life frightened me greatly.

I had several questions that needed answers. Among those, two were very important: would Mother be able to maintain the home with Biso and would she have an unpleasant reaction to Father's departure by taking his promotion as a personal defeat?

I did not have any answers, and I decided to let the future unfold on its own accord. Father left home at the beginning of the school year to start his new career as the principal of Bambaragama High School.

I decided to wait and see what path Mother would take after that.

When I returned home for a visit during my first holiday in my second year, Mother had already demolished the front of Grandmother's home. Several men were at work reconstructing and converting the old home into a large kitchen. Grandmother's bedroom had been converted into a storage facility for paddy from the fields my family owned.

Mother had, in effect, wiped out all traces of Grandmother's existence. Since then, Mother had become the master and the mistress of our home.

Strangely, Mother's journal had no entry about Grandmother's life with her. I was not surprised. Most certainly, I was glad that she did not print any unwarranted comments about her mother-in-law.

For me, Grandmother's death had been a monumental loss. Gradually, I realized that no one could fill the void that she had left, and I started to focus more and more on my education to find contentment.

With the progression of my university education, I had become defiant towards Mother's interferences. She might not have expected that but she might have realized that I had started to protect my personal space.

In addition to Mother's past negativity and her interactions with everyone around her, I had seemingly created a vacuum in my heart with respect to Mother because of the way she neglected to help Grandmother. That emptiness brought sadness to my life.

With that, the minuscule amount of affection I had towards Mother disappeared.

Over the years, Mother sold all the properties that Father inherited from Grandmother and pocketed the money. It was the moment of truth. When I looked back, I had realized that Mother cultivated and enhanced the property value of the land from day one, because she already had this plan in her mind.

Following Grandmother's death and Father leaving home, Mother created an unimaginable chaos in our lives. Mother's spiteful behaviour towards Father's progress brought disgrace to our family.

How could a Mother disgrace her own family and be that heartless to her own daughter?

With great hopes to find the answer to these questions, I continued examining her journal, although I could not find much pleasure dipping into Mother's personal thoughts. The details were sketchy; speculations created more confusion in my mind.

I believed that instigating confusion in my mind was part of Mother's devious plan when she left me to find her journal.

Seemingly, despite all the money accumulating under her belt, Mother was still not happy. Eventually, I would be shocked to find out her indignity to create a dreadful blueprint for my future; she had an unbelievable desire to drown me for good.

Perhaps she was looking for happiness through my unhappiness; was she successful?

CHAPTER 7

DISCRIMINATION AND HYPOCRISY

After getting selected for the Chemistry Honours Program, I started my second year with great enthusiasm. I had the confidence that I was well on my way to graduation.

Yet, stepping on a few rough patches along the way was inevitable. One of those stood out: Mother had the audacity to create an unexpected scene to make my mind as rough it could get; it was infuriating.

That year, twenty-two students were selected to specialize in chemistry: five women, including myself, and seventeen men. On the first day, we arrived on time, and for the first time, the twenty-two strangers met in front of the chemistry lecture theatre.

There were no introductions or pleasantries to break the ice. I observed each student that I would interact with for the next three years and realized that individuals in this group were driven to succeed. I was stunned to be amongst them.

The diversity within this group was as clear as the colours of a rainbow. With time, it was evident that lines were drawn between people and groups based on their size, shape, colour, and social standing.

In the group, I had found friends, foes, and thieves. There were singers, dancers, and some socially withdrawn individuals. What irked me the most was the annoying male characters looking for mates; they spent more time befriending girls while lectures were in progress. There were praises, insults, and ignorant remarks directed at each other. I embraced them all. To me, that was nothing new; I had experienced that already in the girls' school hostel.

One of the most notable memories was how one man attempted to distract me during the very first week. He disrespectfully criticized my clothes and my reluctance to speak with men. Yet, that did not deter me from maintaining my composure or the direction that I wished to take; such attempts made me more determined to reach my goal. No one had the power to distract me because the picture in my mind for my future was very clear.

I was on fire!

The Sri Lankan society consisted of a few culturally diverse ethnic groups.

Sinhalese were the majority, while Tamils were considered a minority. There were also Portuguese and Dutch Burghers, and Malay communities, who could be traced back to past colonial establishments or foreign traders who had visited the Island. However, during my formative years at school, I had not been privy to numerous cultural, ethnic, political, linguistic, or religious aspects of Sri Lankan people.

There, I was only exposed to Buddhism, and the language of operation had always been Sinhalese, except during English class. The school did not have any girls from other minority cultures, so I did not have an opportunity to learn any other language or nature of the other cultures. My parents were not politically inclined; we did not discuss such subjects during dinner time or on any other occasion.

In contrast, during my second year in university, I had the opportunity to make acquaintances with a variety of men and women: Sinhalese, Tamils, and Burgers with varying religious backgrounds of Christianity, Hinduism, Buddhism, and Islam.

I understood that I had been presented with a minute cross-section of the multicultural and pluralist society in Sri Lanka. For the first time in my adult life, the university environment enabled me to understand the impact of mixed cultures and varied privileges in our society.

One day, a male student remarked, "Sri Lanka is a cultural boiling pot, and with a little spark, there will be an explosion." I did not comprehend the gravity of his words until much later, when his description became a reality.

When I heard those ominous words on the potential dangers associated with a pluralist society under tension, I became inquisitive.

I read literature: since Sri Lanka had regained its independence from the British Empire in 1948, relations between the Sinhalese and Tamil communities had been strained. Based on rising ethnic and political tensions, starting in 1956 and intermittently throughout the upcoming years, riots erupted in several parts of the country. As a result, the formation and strengthening of militant groups advocating independence for Tamils had been evident.

At the beginning of my second year, there were no visible signs of animosity among the Sinhalese and Tamil students that I regularly mingled with. Although there were rumors of favoritism by some ethnic professors towards their respective groups, there was no concrete evidence to prove or disregard such allegations.

Then one day, the percolating anger beneath a well-concealed surface broke loose, and the reality of the divisive nature emerged with crystal clarity.

It was a Wednesday at 4:00 p.m., the day before our scheduled end of the second year laboratory exam—*a titration of a solution*.

(A **titration** is a technique where a **solution** of known concentration is used to determine the concentration of an unknown **solution**. Typically, the titrant [the known **solution**] is added from a burette to a known quantity of the analyte—the unknown **solution**—until the reaction is complete.)

After attending the final lecture for the day, students were heading out to their respective residence halls. Then, one man who was panting and sweating, appeared before the two women I was walking with and said,

"Do you know the concentration of the stock solutions for the lab test for tomorrow morning's exam?"

All three of us looked at the man with wide eyes.

"That is supposed to be a secret, is it not?" I asked.

"Yes, only the professor in charge would know that," one woman in the group agreed.

"Yes, but I heard that some of the Tamil students have been given the answer to that question by one of the Tamil professors," the man insisted.

We were speechless and looked at each other in amazement. *That cannot be true*, I thought. If it were the truth, it would be truly unethical and unacceptable. But, there was no corroborative evidence to prove the allegations. We decided to keep it quiet, yet the man with the message was relentless. He ran around to spread the word.

By the time we reached the residence hall, some other men had arrived to meet with us at the entrance, expressing their views on the noted calamity. Since there was nothing anyone could do to remedy the situation, we thought that finding the answer in advance would not be necessary if we had a good understanding on how to conduct the titration.

We were unhappy, but we were more determined to carry out the experiment in good faith.

The laboratory exam was held as scheduled, and we noted that some of the Tamil students completed their experiment way ahead of the allocated time and left the premises, while the rest of us were hard at work to complete the task on time. I completed the exam to my satisfaction.

When the results were published, it was clear that those tipped off by the alleged Tamil professor had failed, and they were disgruntled for being placed in this situation.

What had gone wrong in that process was a question on everyone's mind?

Later, the mystery of the 'misunderstood concentration' was solved. The Sinhalese professor, who was in charge of the laboratory test, had learned about the leak on the eve of the laboratory exam. Overnight, he had prepared fresh stock solutions by changing the original concentration; those who trusted the Tamil professor therefore, had failed the exam.

The unethical behavior of the Tamil employee was detrimental at two levels: the relationship between the Tamil and Sinhalese students soured, and the reputation of the employee was tarnished forever. Strangely, there was a bright side to his devious action—a leak of any kind was never encountered during the rest of the program.

This incident was my first experience with the pre-existing ethnic problems in the country.

The lack of understanding between the Sinhalese majority and the Tamil minority stretched to greater lengths over several years. Ultimately, many years later, the disharmony between them would lead the country to a civil war that lasted for more than twenty years. It attracted undesired international attention.

Although I had not directly experienced the tragic effects of this turmoil, the civil war profoundly affected my personal life.

Unfortunately, it had inflicted much pain on all people living in the island and had caused destruction to the land.

With that unpleasant incident, second year exams were finally finished.

Soon after, I returned home for the year-end holidays. The change of scenery was needed after a long and tedious process of studying and sitting for exams.

I arrived with happy thoughts, but as I entered through the front gate, an awful smell overwhelmed my senses like a bag of excreta hitting my face. I could not figure out the source of the stench, which became more pronounced as I walked through the front door.

Father's absence was immediately felt as there was no one at the door to greet me. I wondered what Mother was doing.

I continued to the back of the house in search of Mother, and very soon, I came upon an unexpected scene: a barnyard full of poultry. The source of the smell that was sensed from the gate became apparent; a chicken coop had been constructed next to Grandmother's former home.

Perhaps Mother needed a new occupation to fill the void created by the absence of her family members.

The chicken coop was massive, and it housed nearly fifty hens and a few roosters. Feathers were flying in the wind, which also carried that horrible smell. I love all animals, including birds, but mother's chicken coop certainly was not a petting zoo.

I located Mother inside the coop, collecting the daily delivery of eggs into a basket. Seemingly, productivity had been great. When she emerged, she was covered in dust and feathers and smelled like a farmer who did not have a moment to refresh.

"Oh, you are home!" she exclaimed while picking out feathers from her hair.

"Could you take this basket and empty it into the egg cartons I have lined up on the counter?" she asked.

I followed her directions and found a series of eggs ready for delivery. She had developed a business with a local shop, and it had become a successful venture. Mother was always industrious, but I did not envision her being a chicken farmer while attending her day job. She was truly into it.

Mother had named her fifty hens with individual numbers. This made sense to me, as Mother was a math teacher, and she was comfortable with numbers. She even knew which one had delivered the eggs for a given day. It was fascinating how she figured out such details because to me, all the hens looked alike.

The next morning, a rooster woke me up at 5:00 a.m. I was always an early riser, but that was an annoying wake-up call during my holidays. I was under the impression that to compensate for the smells and the rude sounds from the birds, I might receive a good breakfast with eggs. How wrong I was.

No one was allowed to eat the eggs from the home coop; they were only meant to generate revenue!

To add insult to injury, I was distressed to learn that the cleaning of the coop had been assigned to Biso—as if she did not have enough to deal with. The home industry was booming, and mother seemed to have found a source of happiness.

Unfortunately, her happiness did not last. A two weeks into my holidays, Mother noted that the coop had become infested with rats and various parasites, such as mites. The snakes in the area also had a field day swallowing eggs. One time, a few hens were killed during a vicious attack by a cobra. Seemingly, the local snakes had passed on the message to those in the nearby villages, because eventually, Mother could not find any eggs in the coop.

E.B White wrote in his article "The Hen" in 1944, "Chickens do not always enjoy an honorable position among city-bread people, although the egg, I notice, goes on and on."

When Mother no longer found eggs in the coop, she could not find the purpose for the hens' existence. By the time Father arrived home for his holidays, the coop had been dismantled, and a few men were hired to clean up the mess.

Mother decided to sell all of the chickens instead of killing them for family meals. I was glad. I could not have eaten birds that had been living among us. I was happy that the environment was cleaned and disinfected for all concerned.

After dismantling the chicken coop, it was clear that Mother was depressed. Since it was still school holidays, Father decided we should take a trip as a family to cheer her up and to spend time with me. As Brother was still away, only three of us planned to make the trip, but Mother made a surprising decision.

She invited one of Father's male cousins, Piyal, to join us for the vacation.

Piyal was a student who used to attend the English and math classes held by my parents. I had met him on several occasions, and he was more than ten years older to me. After graduating from a local Central School, he moved to Kandy to follow a profession in policing. At times, he visited our family while off duty, and it was always a very short visit, but he frequently brought some Maliban brand biscuits and bananas as a gift.

I was curious why Mother suggested Piyal join our family holiday, but as usual, no one questioned her, and she got her way.

Back in those days, both my parents were eligible for benefits offered by the Education Department in Sir Lanka. They received free annual train tickets for themselves and their families; therefore, the dates for our holiday were fixed, and the plan was to travel by train.

I was excited about the selected mode of transportation, but without Brother, I knew it would not be as thrilling as travelling together to Colombo when we were children.

This family holiday's destination was the historical sites at Anuradhapura.

Anuradhapura is renowned as one of the oldest inhabited cities in the world and is considered a sacred place on the Island. It has been declared a UNESCO World Heritage site and is part of the cultural triangle. Although my family had visited this city twice before, it still had special places for us to discover.

I was thrilled to visit it again.

Anuradhapura is in the dry zone of the Island. For survival and food cultivation, rainwater had been collected in enormous reservoirs built by the past ruling kings. Numerous lakes are spread across the area; they help to cool the air during the hot season.

The most notable architectural designs in this city were the variety of *Stupa* (Pagodas) built by Sinhalese kings to preserve Buddhist artifacts. The serenity and calming nature around each stupa were memorable. My favorite spot to feel this was in front of the stupa *Ruwanweliseya*, built by the great King Dutugemunu, who ruled the Island from 161 BC to 137 BC.

The day for our travel arrived. We left home in the early morning and travelled to Kandy to board the Yaal Devi train, which crossed through the city of Anuradhapura in the northeast, heading to the Jaffna peninsula in the north of the Island.

As usual, Mother was well organized. She prepared a hamper of food and drinks, along with clothing for a weeks-worth of travel and for our stay at a local hotel.

We reached our destination on a warm sunny afternoon and settled into a comfortable hotel. After dinner, we decided to stroll along one of the lakes, Kala Wewa.

I enjoyed watching the sunset over the vast body of water, spreading its largess into a grateful sky. Rich hues of red blended with orange, purple, and crimson were visible. For a moment, the sun sat at the edge, as if it looked over the earth stretching out its magnificent rays to everyone below. My spirits soared at the sight as I was transported into a timeless existence. I imagined the protective and comforting blanket I would hug after this wonderful outing.

But, I would soon realize that for Mother, the reality surrounding this family trip was vastly different from what I had imagined.

Unfortunately, the events that unfolded from that moment were unforgettable for all the wrong reasons. They would create havoc in my peaceful mind, further distancing me from Mother.

To my great surprise, Piyal started to pay more attention to Mother. Father became agitated by his unexpected behavior and Mother's juvenile demeanor in Piyal's presence.

I decided to walk with Father along the bank of the lake, giving him an opportunity to speak. He was silent at first, but eventually, some sorrowful words started to flow like a river. A rumor had brought Father's attention to Mother's lifestyle during his time away from home.

The presence of Piyal during our family vacation had confirmed his doubts. I was disgusted.

I did not anticipate that one of Father's relatives would betray his trust. Most of all, I did not believe that Mother, who had been authoritative in providing directions for my life, could be hypocritical. She had been adamant that I behave like a perfect lady after my coming-of-age. Indeed!

Mother had demonstrated that she could not practice what she had preached.

The vacation was ruined, and we returned home a few days earlier than scheduled to have a family discussion, but mother refused to accept any scrutiny. We all knew that Mother's reputation was tarnished forever. Piyal disappeared from our lives, and I could not have been any happier.

A few days after returning from the trip, Mother's behavior became intolerable. She flew into a rage that blew the roof off our sheltered lives, and then she went into self-isolation. One morning, though, she emerged from her hiding. She looked like a gas-filled balloon about to explode. She stood in front of me and said,

"I wish you bad luck in the world to find a husband just like your father. I hope you never feel happy with the man who marries you."

She had become the tyrannizing Wicked Witch of the East. What possessed her to cast a bad spell on me? How could she blame me for exposing herself to ridicule? Besides, what was wrong with Father? I felt I would be fortunate to have a partner like Father, who was gentle and kind.

I stood like a statue, but my eyes started to water. I decided to stay calm. When I did not react to her foreboding wish, she became angrier. She started to scream with a loud shrill from the top of her voice, hoping to provoke a visceral reaction from me.

"Did you know that the planetary arrangement at your time of birth was the reason that I could not have any more children?" she screamed.

"You are not blessed to have younger siblings!" she continued.

I rushed out of the room before she could hurt my feelings any further.

Mother did not have scruples or self-respect, but she had an evil soul to blame me for the disharmony in her life and the disgrace she had brought to the family. I did not understand her world at all. I was left in a dark place, pondering her betrayal, her hypocrisy, and most of all, the heavy burden she placed within my heart.

It seemed she was fixated by some past events or incidents that impacted her personality profoundly. She appeared to be stuck in between innocence and some unknown terrible place. It was clear to me that not even her marriage or motherhood could offer her an acceptable escape from her past.

Much later, I would learn from her journal that my instincts about Mother's past were undeniably accurate.

That day, I saw Mother as an emotionally fragile woman rather than a spiteful and evil human being who was filled with rage and held a grudge against all of humanity. She did not know how to respect anyone around her. Most likely, it resulted from a past event that had been inflicted on her.

For the first time, I was worried about Mother's emotional well-being.

I could not eat or sleep. I was swept away by the winds of infidelity of Mother and her hurtful speculative remarks about my future. I had hit emotional rock-bottom. I packed my books, said goodbye to Father, and left home. Yet again, I buried myself in my books to escape the realities of my family drama.

One of Mother's journal entries detailed some distress she had experienced. The entry was recorded a few years after I had been born:

I lost my third child, a wonderful little boy, because of a tumor that had obstructed his normal growth. He lived only for seven days. This resulted in surgical menopause and the terrible aftereffects that I had to endure for the rest of my life. No one could understand the agony of my loss and the physical and mental

*discomfort I endured due to menopause at a very young age. I
was only thirty-four years old.*

*It is all because of my daughter, who did not have the blessings
to have younger siblings. She should not have been born to this
family to cause mental and physical problems in my life. She
was not a blessing. . .*

In my mind, the accounts in her journal had no merits as her
own family had damaged her long before my birth. I pitied her for
her misfortune and her inability to see the realities of life.

Unfortunately, she viewed the world through a prism contami-
nated by bubbles and inclusions, and the most distorted view she
saw was me.

Life is a like a chain, and each link of that chain would impact
the next. What was the first link of Mother's chain that made her
vulnerable to life's woes? I had a mystery in my hands, but I did
not have help from my family to solve it.

Only after Mother's death, in her journal would she reveal her
secrets to me, and only me.

The third year of my university program started as scheduled. I
embraced it with open arms. It was hard to learn advanced chemistry, but that took my mind away from the gloom and doom at
home.

There were no exams at the end of the third year, so during the
last semester, I decided to explore the 'good life' offered to me by
my wonderful university. That decision was most helpful to forget
the distress I experienced in the past through Mother's behavior and
avert further hurtful encounters with her for the rest of the year.

I took a day trip up to the Hanthana Mountains with a group
of friends. This range is a favorite destination among the mountain

hikers in Sri Lanka, especially for the university students who live around them.

The mountain range consists of seven peaks that stretch all the way from Kandy to the town of Galaha. The freshwater springs on the western end of Hanthana feed the waters of the Mahaweli River, and the tributaries of the river separate the individual hills of the range.

The scenic view from the top while looking down at the campus was breathtaking and panoramic. We spent the day walking, picnicking, and singing, returning to the residence refreshed and ready to take on the world.

The second avenue I explored was joining others to enjoy the cultural performances seen around the campus.

Performing arts was a recognizable activity available to university students. The *Ghandara Sabhawa* (A Cultural Society) produced a variety of dramas. The street dramas created by student groups were also very popular. It was enjoyable to view the creativity of fellow students. I was grateful to be part of the soothing environment where students lived a life as if nothing was wrong. I blended in effortlessly.

The most entertaining performances presented were at the Sarachchandra Open-Air Theatre on campus. This theatre had unbelievable acoustics and could accommodate a large number of people. It had been built according to the architectural style of ancient Greek theatres, where the entire audience was above the stage while the performance area was a sunken pit. It was the only one of its kind in the country.

Once every week after dinner, I joined friends to attend dramas at this theatre, affectionately known among students as the *Wala* (in Sinhalese, it means a 'sunken pit').

I cherished the songs and the dramatic acts in all presentations at the *Wala* and enjoyed each moment I spent with my friends, sitting on the steps under the night skies of the theatre. The air was full of laughter and joy.

We created memorable moments to preserve the university life within our hearts.

We had a month-long holiday at the end of the second semester of the third year. Students enrolled in the Chemistry Honors program were expected to work on this holiday, as they were assigned to conduct research outside the university premises.

I was assigned to the Rubber Research Institute (RRI) in Colombo. While boarded at a family friend's home, I commuted on foot every day to conduct research at the RRI. It was a welcome break away from my family.

I enjoyed learning about the chemistry of natural rubber. At the time, the natural rubber industry in Sri Lanka was second only to the tea industry, which supplemented the local economy. The research I conducted would be valuable to the country.

After my working holiday, I avoided visiting my parents. I did not wish to have my mind twisted with insults and disharmony before the commencement of the last semester. I returned to the university residence directly from Colombo and wrote a letter to Father explaining the reasons for my decision not to come home for the holidays.

Soon after, I received a letter from Father informing me that he had made a decision to retire from his post. He had explained that it was not his time to retire, but it was time for him to come home. I believe that Father had sacrificed his career to preserve harmony in the family.

He was always a noble man who thought about everyone else but himself.

In his retirement, he had decided to learn carpentry. He detailed the list of tools he had already purchased and a small list of projects he intended to start. I was very pleased that he had a predetermined plan for his retirement.

I went home at the end of the third year and noted that Mother had re-established a good relationship with Father. I was delighted.

Since Brother had decided to live in Colombo away from the family, Mother's approach to life was to do as she pleased. She went to great lengths to preserve her rights to achieve this goal. On most occasions, she saw me as a hindrance to her progress, but, unfortunately, with or without my participation, she was not successful in her pursuits.

She remained an angry and sorrowful woman for the longest time.

Along the way, I learned to avoid Mother's aggression: any time her claws and needles came out, I stepped away to protect myself and let her walk through life. She resembled a tiger waiting to pounce on her prey. I was happy and content, but she was not. She had a hollow pit in her soul, which she constantly saw as a place to brood and gather venom.

I let her.

After experiencing many difficulties in my life with Mother, I never forgot to pray for my family that they might find peace, because I wished to have a peaceful relationship with all my family members. Yet, based on my life experiences with Mother, I had been speculating whether peace was real or whether that was just a hopeful thought in a human mind.

By the time I finished my third year in university, Mother was still looking for that sweet spot in her life. She continued to suffer since she could not see any light at the end of the tunnel.

I, on the other hand, was looking forward to my fourth and final year at the university to fly out of the thorny nest and find my own sanctuary in life.

Finding a sanctuary had been on my mind for a very long time, but I knew it would be a far cry based on the life I had lived. Eventually, I realized that I needed to find a life path to forgive Mother and myself if I were to reach that goal.

This remained the most difficult venture, as Mother continued to obstruct my efforts towards a sanctuary more often than I had expected.

Yet, I was optimistic about continuing my efforts to find this sanctuary. During my final year of university it almost worked out. Thanks to Mother; however, several years later, I realized that a sanctuary is not a real place on this Earth.

It was an illusion; I had to learn to accept this reality.

CHAPTER 8

Mother's Resolve

In the fourth and final year of my Chemistry program, I was ready to blaze my trail. I could picture a clear path to the finish line. My tranquil mind was primed to accomplish all tasks successfully and dash to the end, but chaos replaced serenity, and my trail was obscured by a rude intervention that forced me to take a detour through a difficult terrain.

However, when I was looking for a way to get back on track, Mother surprised me with her generosity; that was a momentary bright spot in our relationship. Yet, her journal entry revealed her true sentiments of her decision to help me, still, I was grateful.

The impending calamity started with the political intervention on the university educational system.

One year before, the presiding Vice-Chancellor (VC) had been appointed by the Prime Minister of Sri Lanka. Unfortunately, the newly appointed VC did not have the students' best interest at heart. So, the students vehemently objected to this political appointment, and this mistrust of management led to the creation of student political groups.

Many meetings had been conducted, focusing on a possible strike. These groups created an unsettled environment. Eventually, the scheduled discussions between the students and VC collapsed, and the student leaders instigated riots.

To my disadvantage, I had very little interest in university politics or even political activities in the country; the turmoil sprang out from nowhere; therefore, unpleasantly surprised me. I should have had an inquisitive mind in this regard, which would have prepared me to face an unexpected political disharmony.

On the 10th of November of that year, the riots had spread across campus overnight, and by next morning it had reached a flash point. Tear-gas had been released by security personnel near the University Senate Building. In order to regain control of the premises and subdue the uprising, the VC closed the university for all sessions.

Early morning that day, although Sri Lanka was *not* at war, I certainly felt like we were.

I was awakened by a loud banging on the door by the warden at an early morning hour. She sternly said, "All students have been asked to vacate the premises immediately. This is a mandatory order by the VC."

Since my roommate India had graduated from university in the previous year, when the evacuation order arrived, I was alone in my room. With the final year exams rapidly approaching, closing the campus was an unwelcome shock, and I felt helpless.

I opened the window to investigate. As usual, at 9:00 in the morning, the fog had lifted, and the sun was blazing down. Galaha Road, the street facing the window, was buzzing. I was under the impression that the students were out and about to attend their daily lectures; they did not appear to be in a hurry, and I was skeptical of the news about the university's closure.

However, the moment I turned away from the window, I realized that the crowd of students moving willy-nilly on the road had started to run towards the Senate building. Some were shouting incomprehensibly. I could not identify the reasons for the noted exodus either.

That's when I heard an approaching rumble; it terrified me.

I returned to the window. The rumbling was getting louder and louder, and a series of large, armoured trucks manned by policemen carrying long rifles rolled down Galaha Road.

A question rushed to my mind: Are we at war?

The heavy artillery moved ever so slowly. They looked like monsters that had lined up for a battle. Seemingly, the police had taken charge of the campus, and regular vehicles were no longer allowed on the road. The environment had changed dramatically; a potential war zone had shattered the idyllic scene I was used to seeing through my window.

I ran to the entrance of the residence to gather more information. Many residents were already there. Looking towards the Science Faculty, I witnessed a smoky sky, making it difficult to discern any activities on the horizon. It was clear that dark clouds were lingering above the high hills of Hanthana. Slogans were bellowed out, followed by an eerie silence that had spread among the students crowded at the door. An uncertain future loomed.

It was time to leave.

I considered two options: Walk along Galaha Road to catch a bus from the Galaha Junction or stay in my room and wait for some assistance.

I did not have to wait too long to decide. The Warden had been making rounds, providing the necessary instructions. She had requested that small groups of girls congregate in the hallway and suggested walking to the Galaha Junction together. She prepared us for a rapid exit, in case of an emergency, which meant leaving all our personal belongings behind. However, many in the group decided to take notes and books as everyone had been preparing for exams.

I decided to pack my study materials into a cane basket.

Five female students joined me. We discussed how we should escape without attracting the attention of the police. Since we had not committed any crime, a direct attack from the police was unlikely. Yet, the possibility of a random attack was imminent; we decided to be cautious. When we stepped out to the road—although vulnerable—we were ready to survive together.

Soon we realized that we weren't alone in this unfortunate venture. Rows of students were heading towards the Galaha Junction, hoping to find transportation out of the campus. At the end of the walkway, we turned left onto the Galaha Road. We started walking towards the junction, two-by-two, with our heads down.

Police were scattered around the area but were not paying much attention to the pedestrians. The absence of armoured vehicles on our road gave us peace of mind as we walked.

It would take us twenty-five minutes to reach the junction.

We were about to cross a narrow, old bridge when we heard a few gunshots. From the level and the direction of the sound, I presumed the shots were fired close to the faculty of Arts, and fortunately, it was far from our current location. We could hear the loud voices of frightened people as the events unfolded. Some men ran past us, and down the road towards the junction; we ignored the running crowd and maintained our slow pace.

We knew that the environment was becoming more dangerous by the minute.

When we started to cross the bridge, another series of armoured cars headed towards the campus; they began crossing the bridge along with us. During their slow movement on the narrow bridge—with soldiers sitting on each side of the armoured vehicles—the barrels of their guns almost touched us on the sidewalk.

It was a terrifying few minutes.

We kept our heads down and continued to walk. It felt like we were trespassing on occupied territory. My heart was pounding. Strangely, the book basket became my strength for that moment; although the weight of it seemingly increased with every step. I kept moving with the group.

After crossing the bridge, we could see the Galaha Junction at a distance, and I saw a familiar figure approaching us. Father was on foot along the Galaha Road. I was terrified as his safety in this unsettled environment was uncertain. He walked fast and met with our group, recognizing me among them. My eyes teared with joy and sorrow.

He immediately took my book basket and put his arm around my shoulders to assure my safety; we walked fast to find a bus.

Father was at work when he heard the news on the radio and had decided to get me. I was ever grateful for his thoughtfulness. Although I was an adult, in his mind, I was still his little girl who needed protection.

He was always my rock.

We arrived home safely, and Mother, as usual, was critical about Father rushing to help me and complained, "All other students went home as soon as they heard of the riots in the campus, and I cannot understand why you did not. "

What did she know about the terrifying moments I had endured? She did not understand the fear that had gripped me until I painted a detailed picture of the event.

The riots on campus had escalated after we had left. It had reached a tragic point when a first-year student was shot dead by the police.

A week later, a local leading news magazine published an article on the tragic incident. "The brutal police attack on students spread across the country like wildfire. Trade unions, school pupils (nearly 4 million), political parties came to show their anger against the brutal attack on innocent students and to protest against the Prime Minister. The Vice-Chancellor was removed from the post."

The university was closed for three months, and the fourth year of my program was stretched to a fifth calendar year. The uncertain future was unsettling.

Unfortunately, after that eventful and tragic day, the tranquillity that I admired the most in this university never returned in its entirety. Closure of the university because of student uprisings became the norm for years to come.

Finally, as scheduled, the university was re-opened after three months. Although I had developed mental and physical readiness for the exams before the riots, the sudden closure had been disruptive. However, I had used the break successfully to prepare for my exams.

Surprisingly, Mother's kindness nudged me to reach that success.

My home life during those three months was unusually pleasant and productive. I woke up early every day and studied for nearly two hours before breakfast. The delicious breakfast prepared by Biso kept my strength to spend more time studying after my meal. I took small breaks to play with two cats and six kittens and to bathe the dog. I had chats with Father whenever he was free, and he always provided useful advice with kindness and love.

During this break, the most notable difference was Mother's behavior—it had been an unexpected happy time. Seemingly, she had changed her mind about me being around, which took me by surprise.

Mother frequently invited me to accompany her to travel to Kandy. On many of those occasions, we did some serious shopping, and then we walked around Kandy Lake, having wonderful chats while eating *Wade* (spicy doughnuts) from a famous vendor named

Hotta, who had an outlet by the lake. Frequently, she treated me to special lunches at Devon Café.

The time I spent with Mother during those three months was memorable and peaceful. I wondered, *what changed her mind?* Yet, out of respect, I did not enquire about her reasons to treat me with love.

It was interesting to find an entry in Mother's journal in this regard. She had written: *My daughter surprised me greatly when she gained entrance to the University of Peradeniya. One day, she will make us proud. What happened to my son is partly because of my decision to move him from one school to another with the hopes of providing a better school environment. I have given up hopes for him to achieve his full potential, but my daughter would have the potential to take care of me as an old woman. I needed to support her to gain her trust and affection. I am hoping that she will one day understand why I treated her differently than my son. I wish that day would come before we part our ways.*

Mother's intentions were clear; she needed my help when she moved into her elder years. Yet, I was happy that she understood my efforts and supported them in her own way.

Strangely, fate would take us both in opposite directions; the result would be vastly different from what she had expected.

I returned to the university residence to complete my program with a peaceful mind. Although I did not have time to socialize, in the back of my mind, I felt lonely as all students were very busy, even to have a quick chat to break up the tedious task of preparing for exams. It was crucial to be at peace and keep to a strict schedule to complete the preparations.

I missed India's gentle encouragement to take a break for a proper meal or to have a good night sleep. Now, on my own, I did not want to spend time making such decisions, believing that I might lose valuable studying time. Being alone in my residence room was very stressful and made me feel helpless.

Then the unimaginable happened!

Two weeks before my final exams, Mother exhibited an unusual kindness to her only daughter. Her generosity at that most needed moment would carry me over to the winning post; my heart fills with warmth even today when I recall her offer.

Mother arrived with Father and suggested that she wished to keep me company during this difficult time. At first, I was skeptical, but with Father's assurance, I agreed that Mother's presence would certainly help me to study well.

Soon after, just like a roommate, Mother moved in with me.

For the first time in my life, Mother's gesture brought light into a dark and narrow tunnel that I had to traverse slowly but efficiently to get through my final exams. She took care of me. She made sure I slept enough and ate well. She travelled daily to Kandy and brought me delicious food from the Devon Café; the sear fish and fried rice were my favorites.

I realized that it took me many difficult years to find Mother. With her love and care, my confidence grew rapidly, resulting in an inevitable outcome. It was a win-win situation for me and my family. Finally, I had demonstrated my abilities to Mother; seemingly, my efforts had impressed her.

Mother's loving-kindness to lend her hand at this critical juncture nudged me to forgive her for many undesirable encounters I have had with her in the past. To this day, I look at those two weeks as the best in my life with Mother because, unfortunately, there were not too many circumstances hence forth.

After my final exam, I ran to my room and threw a bunch of papers that were spread across my study table up in the air and shouted, "Finished!" and Mother laughed out loud and shared my joy. After taking a moment to calm down, I gathered my books and papers and stored them in boxes. Mother helped me to pack the rest of my belongings.

The day after my final exam, Mother and I celebrated the end of my university life by visiting the Royal Botanical Gardens—situated across from the campus—to see the Orchid House. Mother loved blooms of all kinds, but the variety of orchids displayed in the enormous greenhouse fascinated her. I bought her a Kandyan Dancer orchid plant to add to the collection in her star garden at home. She was thrilled. We travelled together to reach home before noon. I could feel that Mother also felt relief after going through the tedious process with me and taking care of me.

For the first time in my life, Mother exhibited her wonderful side; she was selfless for my progress in life.

After arriving home and receiving a warm welcome from Father, I felt like I was released from bondage. I looked forward to my newfound freedom. Mother's new attitude towards me certainly sprinkled sparkles on my plans; like kindling on a newly lit fire. She enriched and energized my life for a brief period of time.

I was elated to be home but, Mother's unusual love and attention towards me did not last very long.

It was clear from her journal that she appreciated the efforts I took to educate myself, yet her change of heart soon after returning from university puzzled me. For me, the reasons for her eventual change of heart did not matter, because at my time of need, her love was real. It was joyful.

However, I did not anticipate her attention to my well-being would be short-lived and temporary, but so it was.

After a week of family discussions on what my next step in life would be—for which no one could find an answer—I decided to end the chatter by stating the true facts: to make any future plans, I need to know whether I had passed my final exams. With that note, we agreed that we should take a short vacation to celebrate our family reunion.

This time, only three of us, Father, Mother, and I would enjoy a holiday together.

The destination: the waterfall, which was visible from our home, on the face of one of the surrounding mountains.

During the past several years, we discussed the waterfall and wished for a closer look. This was the first opportunity that we were able to make firm plans to visit it. We realized that the trip would be challenging.

According to our neighbors, a direct route to the site was available, but we had to climb hundreds of steps and go on lengthy walks across villages and ravines. Since we had not attempted the noted route before, it would be an adventure. We all looked forward to the change of scenery and quality time together.

On the day of the hike, at dawn, the three of us set out on the new adventure.

The sun slowly rose on the horizon and gradually illuminated the surrounding mountains, exposing their bold silhouette. The mountain peaks appeared as a green line at dawn, and below those peaks, the supporting rocks looked like giant hands holding the peaks in place.

I imagined how the slopes would be a home for so much life, a foundation for trees and shrubs, grass, and ferns. With the blue sky above, ever lightning as the sun rose, I felt like it would be a good day; it was a memorable day.

Mother had packed a light lunch with fruits and drinking water for the day. Each of us had to carry our own lunch bag. Father prepared us for unexpected weather and delays by packing some hats, an umbrella, blankets, and flashlights.

After a steady climb through most of the morning, we reached a plateau close to midday.

While we sat in the shade for lunch, we realized that our family dog had followed us all the way. We were surprised, as Biso had been asked to secure the dog. He was panting with exhaustion and was expecting us to provide some food, any food. We decided to share ours, and he flopped under the tree, seemingly not to move again. Just like us, this was his first trip to the mountains, and he was not in a happy place. After resting for a while, he disappeared. We anticipated seeing him later at home.

Soon after lunch, we continued our journey. From the plateau, the path towards the waterfall ran through a tea estate. The lush green tea bushes were not the friendliest to pass through as they were prickly and crowded, but their flowers blossomed in pure white and dotted the green mesh of woven bush tops. The tea flower did not have much of an aroma, but they were a pretty sight.

I picked a fresh one from a cluster and placed it in my purse as a memento of our hiking holiday to the mountains.

As the stony footpath through the tea bushes was narrow, we had to walk single file, which added extra time in reaching our destination. By the time we reached the peak of the mountain, the afternoon sun was hugging the horizon.

As we ambled along the mountain path, we heard an unusual humming sound vibrating in the air. It sounded like a swarm of bees. With each step towards the fall, the buzzing sound became louder. We rounded the corner and uncovered the source of the sound: it was the whirring waterfall. It plunged into the depths of a paradise-blue pool.

As we began to get closer, the whirling became growling and rumbling.

We gasped in astonishment at the full view of the waterfall. From home, we could see the same waterfall as a thin white line during the dry season and a thicker and wider spread during the rainy season.

From afar, it looked like a silver-tear track on the wrinkled face of the mountain. The close-up was surprisingly different. Water spurted over the rocks, spilling eel-like over the ledges. The clarity of the Caribbean-blue water was fascinating. Its clamorous passage at the foot of the mountain, threw up bubbles of spray. They sparkled uneasily in the dying light.

After throwing a blanket on a flat rocky area, we decided to immerse ourselves in this fantastic view. The receding daylight was still supportive of our decision.

Mother surprised us by bringing out some snacks: bananas and lemon puff biscuits. The small, sweet snack felt like a giant tree set in front of a hungry elephant; we gobbled them down. That made the brief rest even more enjoyable.

The view of the waterfall from where we sat was fascinating. The cascading fall joyfully swished over the rocks. It was thundering down into the pool like a gigantic water spout. When it toppled into the pool, it foamed at the bottom. The rest of the pool was as clear as cellophane, allowing us to see down into the rocky bottom. Fronds of forest-green plants waved gently in the depths.

The scene was picture-perfect, so we decided to take an even closer look. We slowly climbed down along a footpath, probably made by other visitors. The pool spray was refreshing and encouraged us to dip in without fear, but we did not dare.

We stood under the waterfall to cool down, but it was catacomb cold. It immediately gave us goosebumps. We ended up quivering and shivering on the bank. The sweet smell of nectar from the tropical flowers perked up our spirits, but we needed to warm our bodies.

Fortunately, we were able to have a hot cup of tea that Mother had brought in a Thermos flask, and it was Godlike after experiencing the cold, wet spray.

Just then, the rays of the setting sun caught the watery slide, giving it a trance-like quality. It turned to glitter, like shreds of silky silver. The sparkling of its spray was magical and created a filmy mystique above the pool, dazzling us with its beauty.

The sun was about to set, and we did not wish to be around the waterfall after dark. We decided to return home by taking a route through the villages in case we needed assistance in finding our way.

We headed home with joyful feelings and chatter among the three of us, describing each one's experience competitively. It was memorable.

The noise from the waterfall subsided as we walked away and became a distant humming again. I ventured one look back over my shoulder. The willowy waterfall flashed silver one more time. Its soul-swelling magic followed me all the way home. The darkness was falling, and our flashlights guided us to the nearest village.

As we turned a corner into the village, familiar flute music captured my attention, bringing back the youthful memories that had enchanted my life as a teenager. I was inquisitive to find the mystery flute and its player.

Could it be possible for me to meet the player who had delighted my youth? I simultaneously felt a shiver down my spine and warmth in my heart. I asked Father whether we could try and locate the flute player. Without asking for a reason, he agreed. We set off along the path towards the foot of the mountain range, literally following the sound of the flute music.

We saw a small mud hut in the middle of the thinly populated village.

Buildings constructed out of the mud and other natural materials were considered primitive; the building of houses out of these materials became rare during the 20th century. Locating a mud hut this close to the tip of the mountain; therefore, was remarkable.

We finally reached the source of the flute music. A man holding a flute sat on a small, elevated veranda in his mud hut. He was enjoying the setting sun while converting the world around him into a musical arena.

A small kerosene oil lamp rested on a wooden table beside him. The flickering flame of the lamp swayed to the music, creating a magical flame dance to match the tune. The dim light from the lamp barely supplemented the fading light of the setting sun. But the man with the flute seemingly had greater power to light up his surrounding with his music.

I held my breath and walked slowly towards the man.

The music filled the air like the nectar from wildflowers, soothing and enchanting. The flute music was very much the same as I heard as a teenager. It was fluid. It was air. It was smooth without any clunky stops. The efficiency of the player was remarkable. I finally had an audience with the man who had given me such joy during my lonesome adolescence and youth while waiting for the opportunity to attend university.

At that moment, I was transfixed; he was either a double amputee or had been born without legs.

I did not wish to clarify this matter instead I was delighted to meet the man. I was certain that regardless of his physical conditions, he was a person just like any other man. His life's purpose was no less than any other human's. He was fulfilling his life's dream through his music and continuing to entertain others.

He was gifted.

I was fortunate to be up close with this musician. He was about forty-five years old. A scraggy greying beard climbed his face like last year's raggedy vines after a severe winter. The lower part of his body was covered with a ragged piece of cloth, but his upper part was bare. His eyes were closed, perhaps to focus on the notes he played.

I was in awe of his presence.

For me, meeting the flutist was like a kid meeting Kermit the Frog for the first time in real life after watching him for years on *Sesame Street*. It was surreal. I felt like I had been teleported to a different planet, where I had the opportunity to feel and touch a being in that imaginary place. He was at peace with his flute in hand until I appeared face-to-face in his mellow surroundings.

The music stopped, and he looked at me with surprised eyes. He had a gentle stare. I smiled. He smiled back.

I spoke first, "That was wonderful flute music. I could hear it all the way down in the valley from my home. When I was younger, I used to listen to you every evening." He appeared pleased by this information.

"How did you find me?" he asked.

"I came upon you by accident. We were visiting the waterfall, and I heard your music at the point we entered your village."

My parents slowly approached and greeted the man. He was happy to see people. Seemingly, he lived alone.

"I am glad you like my music," he said.

"How did you learn to play the flute?" I asked.

"I learned it on my own during my childhood. Flute music is my only comfort in life. I was born without legs. The flute and its music gave me a reason to live. I am unable to work, and my only source of income is this land. My brother helps me from time to time to cultivate it and sell a part of the produce."

He offered us to sit with him and have a cup of tea. We were grateful for his hospitality, but it was getting late. I sensed that Mother was becoming restless. She appeared angry and displeased; perhaps she was tired and was anxious to return home. I could not blame her, it was a long day, but I could not leave without providing some help to the man who had soothed my senses, unknowingly but effortlessly. I needed to ask.

"I would like to offer some money, if that would help you. Would you agree?"

"No, I have plenty for my life. I am in good health, and I am happy with what I have. What more do I need?" he responded.

Rumi's words rushed to my mind:

[3]*You were an ascetic, and I turned you into a singer.*

You were mute, and I turned you into a bard.

Within the universe, no one knew your name or any sign of you.

I sat you down and made you the revealer of secrets.

He revealed a secret: *A contented mind needs very little to survive.* His capacity to enjoy music made his mind peaceful and happy. Seemingly, he needed nothing else.

Was that a chance encounter with a prophet?

A thought crossed my mind. Perhaps I was prompted to be ready for my future by opening a spiritual channel, where I could feel contentment even during a time of few privileges.

We reached home after midnight. Our dog, who had returned much earlier, greeted us by wagging his tail incessantly.

I could not fall asleep as my mind was filled with new and fascinating memories: a scenic waterfall, whispering sounds of flute music, and a man without feet who was filled with joy through his music. Though my mind raced, I had a very tired body, and I eventually dozed off before dawn.

---

3 **Kabir Helmiski**, *The Pocket Rumi; Rubiyat*, (pp1247 Shambala Publications Inc., 2001)

The next morning, Mother's list of questions on the flute music and the flutist were long and exhausting. Later, I discussed the chance encounter with the unknown flutist with Mother without any reference to the experiences I had as a teenager regarding the paperboy and the flute music.

She listened to the details but had no response of any kind.

I concluded that she had never heard the flute music before, although we had been living in the same home; her world never matched mine.

Several years later, I thought of the flutist and his joyful minimalist life when I was forced into a similar life. Because I loved music, I was able to feel plenty within my poverty; music made me to reach contentment. The flutist already knew this secret, and I was fortunate that I had the opportunity to experience his prophecy first-hand.

Someone said there are no coincidences in life; everything happens for a reason. Indeed, the paperboy and the flutist placed a stepping stone in my life path that lifted my soul and nudged me over. I was grateful because they both had helped me to face my destiny with courage.

Yet, no matter whom I had met during my journey in life or what lessons I had learned, my story would end in the most unexpected and undesirable way. Unfortunately, even a prophet could not have predicted that.

Mother's generosity and kindness offered during this period was like a sporadic glimmer of light that helped me to find my way out of darkness. Yet, soon after, she changed her heart about her daughter; it was swift and hurtful.

Eventually, Mother took the power to determine what my future would be; it was unexpected.

CHAPTER 9

*I*NFATUATION

The results from my final university exams would not be published for several months. I felt I had earned a time-out for pure relaxation without any obligations. The hiking trip to the waterfall and meeting with the flutist was a real-life adventure. Now, I was ready and looked forward to curling up with as many books as possible on any subject other than chemistry.

But, Mother seemingly had her own plans for me. The discussions around the dinner table disclosed Mother's thoughts about my future; a marriage. I did not expect her eager desire to change my life; perhaps she meant well. Yet, I was determined to be financially independent before marriage. I hoped that Mother would not provoke Father.

Fortunately, Father had other plans.

A few days after the hike, he had contacted the Education Department's Director for the Nuwara Eliya District, requesting an interview for me with the hope that I would be considered for a teaching position.

The Director had exhibited a great interest in meeting me after Father had promoted my credentials well. The Director had confessed that chemistry graduate teachers were in high demand for rural areas, and even before graduation, he was willing to offer me an interview.

I was wondering how I should approach my first job interview. Father instructed me to be myself and assured me that it would go well. His words always gave me strength and confidence, and I braced myself to face a new challenge.

The interview had been scheduled for the last Thursday of July.

I woke up early that day to begin the three-hour journey to the city Nuwara Eliya. Mother was extremely supportive of this opportunity; she suggested that I wear a saree for the interview as that had been the traditional attire of a Sri Lankan school teacher.

She lent me a beautiful saree and helped me drape it. For me, wearing a saree was a novelty that I liked. I was satisfied with my reflection in the mirror, but travelling while dressed in a saree would be most uncomfortable, so I braced myself to travel without any complaints.

Mother's enthusiasm for my new opportunity was not a surprise as she was extremely supportive while I prepared for my final exams. However, she would express her true feelings about my progress in the coming days in an unexpected manner.

Father and I headed out at dawn after drinking a cup of tea; it was too early to have breakfast.

The prospect of securing my first job was exciting, and wanderlust elated me on my maiden journey to Nuwara Eliya. I looked forward to an adventure in the hill country and a visit to its main city. While on the road, Father oriented me by willingly detailing the historical background of Nuwara Eliya and its surroundings.

"Nuwara Eliya is a city situated on a plateau about nineteen hundred meters above sea level, under the shadow of Sri Lanka's highest mountain known as the Mount Pedro at twenty-five hundred meters. This city had preserved the colonial past of Sri Lanka; it was mostly developed during the British rule of the Island between 1815 and 1948. During their occupation, Nuwara Eliya was a retreat for the ruling class," he detailed.

Father informed me that visitors had nicknamed this city *Little England* because of the climate, flora and fauna, and as some of the names of the streets and the buildings were similar to those in England.

According to his account, the biggest park in the city had been called Victoria Park, and the lake was named Lake Gregory. The Tudor-style red brick house in the city had been an old post office, and the half-timbered building with flags was the British Grand Hotel. The ruling class had established a racecourse and a golf club within the city.

Father had been to Nuwara Eliya when the British ruled the Island. During those infrequent visits, he had heard the passing sounds of horse carriages and the honking of olden day motor cars on well-paved roads.

He informed me that in comparison to those days, Nuwara Eliya was now considered as an abandoned town like that in the wild-west with empty taverns, vacant wooden barns, and bare roads. Only a few new hotels were available to accommodate the needs of tourists who were looking for cooler weather after having spent time on a steamy coastline.

After hearing Father's descriptions of his experiences in Nuwara Eliya, I looked forward to exploring this city more than facing my interview.

After being on the road for about an hour, Father decided to stop for breakfast at a little hilltop cafe. By that time, we had climbed to an elevation close to two thousand meters above sea level. The climate was very different from the tropical Indian Ocean coastline; it was cool, like a European spring or autumn.

We sat at a table overlooking the slopes of a mountain range. Our view was captivating. Our server was also the owner of the café. He set the table; the cutlery and crockery he brought to the table were extremely cold to the touch.

Luckily, the authentic Sri Lankan food served was piping hot, aromatic, and delicious. We had string hoppers with Dhal and fish curries, sweet bananas for fruit, and a wonderful cup of Sri Lankan tea with boiled, freshly harvested milk.

"Fresh as you can ever get it. I just milked my cow in the backyard," the owner bragged.

After breakfast, we travelled along the mountain roads. They were narrow and wound through the rugged mountains. The hairpin, elbow, and Z bends of the mountain roads made me sit at the edge of my seat and concentrate on balancing myself during stomach-churning twists and turns. It was a steady climb, and I refrained from peeking deep down to the bottom. Still, the scenery at eye level was rewarding.

I was impressed by the breathtaking beauty of the hill country. It had everything a tourist would like to see: the terraced tea gardens, fruit and vegetable gardens, and cascading waterfalls. At that elevation, the breeze was cool and brisk enough that anyone could catch a cold.

I wrapped myself in a shawl to keep warm.

After reaching an elevation of six hundred meters from the coastline, the tea gardens were in their full glory. Healthy green tea bushes covered hundreds of acres on the mountains, looking like a massive well-kept garden. The bushes were manicured and pruned to keep them waist-high. The 'green carpet' was dotted with people plucking tea leaves and collecting them into baskets strapped to their backs. The plucked leaves would be processed in one of many tea factories visible across the mountain landscape.

That day, I had my first experience with the appetizing aroma of Ceylon tea spewed from the exhausts of the tea factories. The flavors of tea mixed in with the crisp, cool mountain air. It was invigorating to experience the beauty of this Island blending in with its economy in action.

We arrived on time at the sleepy little town of Nuwara Eliya. I was introduced to the Director, and Father left me to carry on with the interview.

The Director was a tall man with strong shoulders; he wore a blue suit and a tie. He sat behind a large table on a comfortable chair with a backdrop of a wonderful collection of books neatly organized on a wall-shelf. He faced me from across the table and looked intently at me through his thick eyeglasses. I was nervous about facing this powerful man, yet I managed to keep my thoughts well in place to answer all of his questions.

The Director administered several multiple-choice questions to test my knowledge of chemistry. He was satisfied with my answers, and the interview ended within thirty minutes.

Soon after the interview, I was offered a post at the local Central School to teach chemistry. I was grateful for the opportunity, and I was courteous towards the authority. Indeed, I was eager to serve my country by educating students who were in desperate need of a chemistry teacher.

Father was very pleased with the outcome and suggested we tour the town.

We spent the rest of the morning exploring the sites of the city. Experiencing the ancient lifestyles from a bygone era was like peeking into a lost world. After the tour, we had lunch at the British Grand Hotel. It was fascinating to see that the hotel's interior retained the architectural marvels of the British era while modernizing the culinary delights to fit the current local practices.

Father was in a very good mood, so he ordered all they had to offer on the lunch menu.

On the return journey, Father was talkative. He spoke about my abilities and how my future would shape up to make the family proud. Yet, neither one of us had any notion how this achievement would bring daunting changes to our lives.

When we reached home, naturally, I expected a warm embrace from Mother, but she did not have a good reaction to the news at all. She reverted back to her past practice of rationing her praises for my achievements and did it sparingly.

It was only much later that I would learn about her true feelings about my success, and it would make me cry.

A new chapter in my life was about to unfold.

In early September, I was expected to start work as a school-teacher. Yet again, I had to live amongst strangers. Father actively looked for a suitable place for me to reside. He finally decided on a home owned by one of his distant relatives, the Thisera family.

Mother packed my suitcase, this time with many sarees, mostly from her collection, for my new adventure. I was thankful for her generosity. Two days before the school year commenced, I travelled with Father to meet the Thisera family and to get settled. On the way, Father briefed me on the parents of this family.

The father of the Thisera family, Da, was the head of the household and had been a wealthy man. He apparently made his fortunes through his lucrative private bus company in town before the then Prime Minister of Sri Lanka, S.W.R.D. Bandaranaike nationalized public transportation.

According to locals, Da was a fair-minded man with a killer business instinct, which led to his wealth. After losing his business; however, he had turned to alcohol while looking for some pleasures in life. He was still very wealthy because of the properties and tea estates he owned.

The mother of this family of eight children, Mama, was distantly related to Father. Unfortunately, she had passed away in her prime, and I did not have the privilege of meeting her.

She had left their children—four girls and four boys—to a father who did not have time for them. Her untimely death left the children without a good authority figure to provide suitable directions for their education. Their wealth had spoiled them further, leading some of them to destructive paths in life.

Upon our arrival, the eldest daughter of this family, Akki, received us with a gentle smile. Father would have anticipated meeting with the head of the family, but he seemed satisfied with the reception. After a cup of tea, Father left me with Akki to get myself settled in with the new family. As usual, he wished me the best. As he walked away, I watched him with a heavy heart.

I felt that he was releasing me, a little at a time, to find my own way in life.

My new residence was situated on a hilltop overlooking the road to the neighbouring town. This house was substantially spacious and decent. One could walk around it to view the gardens with blooming tropical flowers. Several little, private outdoor gazeboes with garden seats, umbrellas, and decorative tables surrounded the home.

The house had a massive front porch. There were two entrances to the house from the bus route. One entrance had a flight of steps and the other a tar-paved road. They had been beautifully built on either side of the wide front lawn covered with silky, white sand. The architecture of the front of the house exhibited thoughtful planning of the home and the substantial wealth that enabled its existence.

The edge of the sandy front had been secured with a metal guard railing where various flowers bloomed and swayed in the cool mountain air.

That afternoon, after settling into my private room, I stood next to the guard rail and observed the picturesque, tranquil scene to the mountain range that surrounded the property.

The sun sets early in this hilly-country. At dusk, when the sun was disappearing behind the hills, I remained at the railing, soaking in my new surroundings. The colour transformation in the sky might have depicted the changes that were coming in my near future.

I shuddered at the thought of it but hoped for a better independent life.

That evening during dinner, Akki briefly introduced me to the other family members and many others who lived in the house. It was exciting to meet a new family, but at the same time, it was puzzling why all of them—except the youngest daughter who was attending school—still lived in the family home, although they were adults who were much older than me.

Akki introduced herself first as the eldest daughter of Da. She had been married and had a child but had left her family to return home because Da could not run the household after Mama's passing. Da had been instrumental in getting her marriage dissolved for his own selfish reasons. To my surprise, Akki had accepted her predicament and was seemingly living a contented life.

The second daughter, Lola, was a very attractive young woman. Eventually, I would learn that she had gone to a deep foreboding place and had been diagnosed as suicidal. In time, I realized she was perpetually depressed, continuously cried, and had tantrums like a child. She never got out of her bed. This behaviour was due to a broken engagement with the love of her life because she had consented to it against Da's wishes. Da had rejected the man because he belonged to a family of a lower class.

It was heartbreaking to learn that she was now wasting her life away in bed, while Da kept looking the other way.

The introduction to the third daughter, Sheela, was most alarming. She was about twenty-five years old. Da had a skin condition that needed daily treatments, and he had chosen her as his caretaker. She followed him like a sick puppy while attending to all his needs. Surprisingly, no one in the family had an issue with this father-daughter relationship. Later I would learn that she slept in her father's bedroom to attend to his condition, and there was only one bed in that room.

Da had a hand in disrupting the lives of three of his daughters. My mind was numb. I thought of Father and how he was a gem. I even thought of Mother. Even with having a difficult mother, I thought that my life was far simpler and better than the life of these three women.

I sincerely felt sad for all of them.

The introduction to the males in this family was memorable, mainly because it was distressing to learn that the youngest son was confined to an asylum due to a mental illness and only came home for short visits during a given year.

The eldest son, Sunil, took care of the family-owned tea estates. The other two sons also were introduced to me: Don an overseer at a local construction site and Erick, who is responsible for the financial management for the family.

It was surprising to learn that none of them had a steady job, and all were bachelors. Perhaps the family had enough money to keep the boys happy.

Later that evening, I was introduced to the household staff. The cook named Ensa, who was about fifty years old; the housemaid named Mary, who seemed to be in her forties; and the gardener named Banda, a teenage boy. The servants' quarters were separate from the main house. Though they had been employed by Da, they were given clear instructions from Akki.

I was happy to meet Ensa, and seemingly, she had the same sentiments for me. She was a very pleasant lady with chubby cheeks. Mary, on the other hand, was not very pleased to meet me. I wondered why. Perhaps she did not like that I was related to the family who employed her. I dismissed the negative thought that crept into my mind. I was certain that she had her own reasons for her behaviour and had every right to feel anyway she wished.

To my surprise, there were three boarders in this house too: Susila, a tea factory worker; Dilini, a student at the local school; and Gamini, a young man who worked at a shop in town. After meeting all of these people, I was anxious to know how many rooms were there in this large house, as each boarder had individual rooms too.

Altogether sixteen people, including myself, lived in this home. *Wonderful*, I thought, *as I can never be lonely or bored now.* It was obvious that Da was still a businessman.

The experiences I had with the Thesera family over the months that followed were unparalleled.

I entered this phase of my life as a naive young woman, and to my greatest joy, I emerged at the other end after spending three months of my life as a school teacher and as a woman who knew how *not* to complicate her life. As they say, if you wish to complicate your life, do it for a very good reason; I could not find one.

My life remained simple.

However, the mental aberrations I passed through during those three months might have changed my attitude towards men altogether.

The day arrived for me to start my teaching career. I woke up early that morning since I had limited ability in draping a saree. After a great battle with it, I managed to drape it, and it closely resembled Mother's end product. I took my handbag, which I had borrowed from Mother and a notebook, and walked out to the tar paved path to the road towards the school. The school was within ten minutes' walking distance.

It was a glorious day; my opportunity to become an independent woman finally had arrived.

I first met the principal of the school. He escorted me to the staff room and introduced me to the science staff, which consisted of one man and one woman. The man was in charge of all general science classes, and the woman was in charge of classes related to biology.

Indeed, I was badly needed by this school. I was happy to oblige too.

The school bell rang, and I met the students in one of my chemistry classes. The variety of students greeted me with enthusiasm. I introduced myself, and they did too, but naturally, I could not remember all their names, and I did not wish to try it on this very first day.

To my surprise, one boy stood out like a pillar in this student community. He came forward and introduced himself as Sujith. I was not certain why, but he touched my soul as if we had met before. I dismissed that notion at once. The day ended with satisfying feelings; I was very productive. These keen students learned chemistry for the first time in their lives.

I looked forward to the next day.

Akki was diligent in providing all the necessities to make everyone's life comfortable. As a result, under a large set of florescent lights, a wooden table had been set in a spacious, airy room. This table was for those who need to prepare for the coming workday or complete their homework for school. The table was meant for six people, but on that evening, when I was getting class notes ready for the following day, only two were seated: Achala, the youngest daughter, and me.

Then, the unthinkable happened.

Don, who had been introduced to me as one of the sons of the Thisera family, arrived and sat across from me.

I wondered: as a land overseer, what preparations did he need for his next workday? He must have a purpose to take a seat at this table. I ignored his presence, but I sensed that he was making every effort to garner my attention. I had enough papers to read that evening to keep me occupied; therefore, my attention to those seated at the table was limited.

However, in one unexpected moment, he caught my attention, and to my surprise, he winked at me from across the table.

I thought for one moment. What could that mean?

I had not learned the language of a wink yet, and his unspoken words were a mystery to me. I ignored his gaze and tried to look away as he was a total stranger to me. Yet, his unusual stare created a fluttering in my heart and made my mouth feel parched. He held me in his gaze for what felt like an eternity. That moment was strange but memorable. I was naive and young, and I felt he was a master of this process.

I looked away as soon as I felt my face flush.

That very first unexpected interaction with Don changed several lives in the coming days; most of all it changed my perception of men.

Could he be a man who played both ends against his majesty's middle or a man who was as slippery as an eel? I had no way of knowing the answers to those questions, so I decided to let him be and carry on with my work.

I would learn that the locals categorized Don as a handsome man with good fortunes.

He had a dapper, military mustache and manful peppered stubble. He also was blessed with Viking good hair, bristly eyebrows, a hawkish nose, defined cheekbones, and a concrete jaw. His almond-shaped eyes were on fire with a passion. He moved with leopard-like grace. He wore adventurous and ritzy clothes. An earthly scent swirled around him.

Sure, I could categorize him as handsome too, but his approach towards me that evening indicated a demanding and authoritative demeanour to fulfill specific neediness. To me, his behaviour was repelling. Don's wink lifted my guard like I was donning a protective epee mask. I wondered what his intentions were.

Was that an infatuation?

How curious it was that the banalest of truths—human beings are complicated and nuanced, and their inner lives and motivations are rarely fully known—remain among the hardest to swallow.

This was true to its core about Don.

I contemplated on Don and his existence in this small community during the coming days, and I would realize how unfortunate it was that his good looks had been his enemy and demon.

A week or two went by while I committed my life to teach. I thoroughly enjoyed the service I could render to those students who were eager to learn. I prepared answers to all questions raised by the students, and I spent my evenings designing and drafting my teaching notes for the upcoming day.

I also enjoyed spending time with Akki, as she made it a habit to keep me company during lunch after school. After some time, she became relaxed and spoke freely with me of her past and her family, which she'd had to leave. She explained that she was forced to take the reins of running this massive home for Da and leave her child behind. I wondered why she did not have the will to decide against Da for the sake of her child.

Yet, out of respect, I decided not to probe.

As time went by, I had several opportunities to have wonderful chats with Ensa during her time off from kitchen duties. After a few heart-to-heart discussions, she treated me with affection and respect and began to divulge the unusual incidents surrounding this household. I was stunned to know that Mary, the housemaid, had been involved with Don. Ensa was not clear on the nature and the extent of the liaison, but I kept my questions to myself.

The evening after I learned about Mary's alleged liaison, Don sat at the table again. This time I was alone. I ignored him as before, but he spoke with a deep voice to garner my attention.

"I think you look very smart and beautiful." His words were bodacious.

At that moment, my spirit was lifted, and I had an out-of-body experience. Mary's face flashed across my mind. I looked right at Don and said, "Thank you." I sensed that he wanted me to continue speaking, but I was determined not to encourage him. I continued with my work, ignoring his stare. He left the table with no further comments.

I was relieved.

The next morning, I headed to school on time, but I realized I had company as I walked. Don had joined me on my walk to school. I was not certain of his motives until he spoke.

"Would you like to go into town with me during the weekend? I can show you the sites, and perhaps we could have some lunch?" he spoke casually.

"I will have to think about it. I certainly would like to see around town, and I am sure you will be a great guide since you have lived here all your life."

"Alright, I will wait for your answer, perhaps in a day or two?"

"Yes, I will speak to you later after I discuss this matter with Akki, if you don't mind?"

"No, I don't' mind."

I turned to the path toward the school while Don stood on the road; I could feel his eyes on me all the way down the path. As soon as I entered the school grounds, Sujith appeared in front of me.

"Madam, may I speak with you for a minute?"

"Yes, indeed."

"Madam, I know that man."

"What man?" I asked.

"Don Thisera," he responded.

"Surely, that cannot be a surprise because you both live in the same town."

"But I know something that you might not know about Don," he stated with an eager voice. I stopped and looked at him. I was certain that I had a surprised look on my face.

"Don is known to many *married* women in this town, including my mother," he said in a disgusted and sad voice. I could not understand his motive to discuss Don with me, but I realized he might have seen Don walking with me to school.

"I am sure Don is a very popular man among women because he is rich and good-looking. Why should I perceive an illness in his associations?"

"I am sorry, madam, but he is not a suitable man for you to be associated with because he has a reputation of being a homewrecker, a man who would sleep with any woman." After dropping this bomb, Sujith ran as fast as he could.

I felt weak and sad. Could this be true?

I spent the day teaching chemistry but avoided further encounters with Sujith. Later, I realized that Sujith's disgust about Don was justified. I heard through the grapevine that his father had died of cancer a few years ago, making his mother a single parent. Perhaps Don might have taken advantage of the vulnerable situation of this woman to fulfill his desires.

Sujith had mustered his courage to let me in on this nagging secret. I was pleased that he was comfortable speaking with me, even though he had only known me for a few days. Perhaps, he was attempting to save me from a tragedy. If such was the case, I should have been thankful for his thoughtfulness.

The time passed by. Then, I received my very first paycheque for my services as a schoolteacher. I was over the moon.

I looked at the numbers; it was 520.00 Sri Lankan rupees (about CAD $40; I had been paid the salary of a graduate, although I have not received my certificate from the university yet). It was my very first fortune, and I felt that my financial freedom was slowly approaching.

In that joyful moment, I decided to visit my parents during the upcoming weekend to spend some of my fortune on them. Before then, I had to deal with Don's invitation to join him to "paint the town." I thought about the suggestion at length, but Sujith and

Ensa had provided me with enough reasons to decline his offer. Finally, I decided not to accompany him, though I was not certain how to reject his offer without revealing the reasons for refusal.

While in my room, I was still holding my first cheque in my hand and admiring its contents that I heard a knock on the door. It was Akki. She smiled and said, "You are welcome to visit the town and the surroundings with Don this weekend. He will treat you well." I could not hide my surprise, and she continued, "Don asked me for my permission."

"Thank you, Akki, but I need to visit my parents this weekend, so could you give my message to Don?" She was disappointed, and I was surprised, but I had made up my mind.

With that rejection, I thought that Don would never approach me in the future with another invitation. I was wrong; his next invitation would greatly surprise me.

Saturday arrived with good weather. As usual, Father received me warmly with open arms. After dinner, I discussed my very first fortune and asked what Mother and Father wished to receive from me as a gift for all their support in my life. That was when Mother became inquisitive.

"How much did you receive for the month of work?" she asked.

I immediately regretted being truthful. How could a daughter know that her mother would be jealous of her very first, small fortune? Mother went into a rage. At first, I could not find the reasons for her reaction because her attitude towards me and my achievements improved after she witnessed the efforts I had taken to complete my university education.

Unexpectedly, my first salary turned back the clock, and the distasteful pattern of her past behaviour re-emerged, like a poisonous tropical flower that would bloom with an attractive colour and scent to lure an insect, and suddenly snap shut to capture the innocent victim.

Father looked at me with sympathy. He did not utter a single word about Mother's reaction to my small fortune. Instead, he said, "You have done well, and I am proud of you. We could open a bank account for you so you could deposit a small percentage of your income every month. That way, you will always have money for your future." I nodded in agreement.

The next day, the truth of Mother's reaction to my fortune surfaced.

When Mother arrived at the breakfast table, I noticed her eyes were swollen; she must have been crying. I felt sad. Once Mother sat down, her mood instantly changed from mournful to anger.

What had caused this visible transformation in her was a mystery to me. When Father was about to stand after finishing his breakfast, Mother spoke.

"I thought your brother would earn more money than you ever could". I could have earned more money than you if I had opportunities," she continued. "I do not wish to have anything from you because my son will buy something nice for me one day when he earns enough money."

There it was. It was always a comparison of my achievements with Brother's. This time, the comparison had extended to her income as well.

I always thought that Mother had a sweet voice, but on that morning, she appeared to have fixed a steel cord in her throat, for her voice reverberated as if it could cut through my soul.

I felt sad. My small fortune had brought back that hateful demeanour in Mother.

An article I read suggested that normal or healthy mothers are proud of their children and want them to shine. But a narcissistic mother may perceive her child as a threat. Among many reasons, a mother can be jealous of her daughter's accomplishments and education and even the young girl's relationship with her father. That day, I witnessed all these sentiments in Mother's expressions.

My small fortune was tucked away in my purse when I left home. Mother did not appreciate it. Father wished me to save it. I travelled with a heavy heart. Although I was heading to a stranger's home, I felt happy to leave the unpleasant surroundings.

Don was at the door when I returned to the Thisera residence. Strangely, I was delighted to see him.

The disrespectful attitude of Mother made it easier to entertain respect from a total stranger; such thoughts cannot be far from the instinctive nature of an average human mind.

Based on this realization, I made a decision that day: without fear, I should entertain the affections of a man.

Mother's advice on how to be a perfect lady, hitherto etched in my mind, dissipated. I took charge of my life, and Mother lost her ability to influence my decisions.

At that moment, I felt like a bird that had been freed from its cage, looking to indulge in ripe and rare fruits.

Yet, deep down I felt that I had the wisdom to make right decisions. But I still wondered, was I in control of my own destiny? Did my life unfold according to what the universe had mapped out for Mother's interventions? Or was it simply my fate?

Those questions now come to mind, because the 'rare fruits' I found later in life, turned out to be bitter to my palate; they eventually would make me sick. Mother would ensure that the sweetness of those would be suppressed.

So I concluded that my fate was controlled by Mother.

CHAPTER 10

$\mathcal{T}$HE $\mathcal{F}$IRST $\mathcal{M}$ARRIAGE $\mathcal{P}$ROPOSAL

Could a young woman, employed as a schoolteacher for less than four months, influence the lives of those around her? I presumed it would be impossible, but to my surprise, I was wrong.

After Mother's cruel expressions about my first salary, although I wished to act defiantly against Mother's instructions with respect to men, I decided to find happiness in my work. I was cautious.

Yet, the events unfolded since then made it very difficult for me to avoid attention from some men in the Tisera family.

During my candid conversations with Akki, my influence on the lives of many individuals in that home became apparent. I supposedly have changed several lives. That was her impression; it certainly was not mine.

According to her account, I had changed Don from a sworn social butterfly to a homebody. I was told that he had not yielded to anyone's suggestions in the past. Although I saw the change, I did not wish to take any credit for it.

After this revelation, I started to notice that Don was everywhere I was, and he attended to my most intimate and minute necessities. How I could take credit for this change was beyond my comprehension, as I had not desired his attention or requested a change in his lifestyle. However, Akki willingly bestowed this honour on me day-in and out.

Apparently, he has become obsessed with the idea that he could win me over to make me his life companion. I assured myself that if such a change was seen in Don, it was not intentional on my part. I presumed that it was his decision.

Then there was that beautiful Lola. At first introductions, it was clear that she was unreachable by anyone in the family; therefore, was considered a "gone girl." It was an unhappy reality for her family. After my associations with her, which consisted of casual conversations, she had decided to get out of bed. One day, she put on some makeup, a beautiful dress, and suggested that she and I go shopping. That was a remarkable recovery indeed.

To my joy and surprise, everyone credited me for being instrumental in releasing her from her unfortunate situation. Perhaps I could take half credit for this change because in reality, she had to make that decision for herself. I was informed that she had turned 180° after seeing me as an independent woman.

The responsible eldest boy Sunil was the next on the list. According to Akki, he started to spend more time at home after I became a boarder. She had the pleasure of his frequent participation in household activities. He spoke with me only a few times, and we understood each other's position in this household; I did not have any regrets that our encounters were infrequent.

One day, I was reading a book under a garden umbrella, and Sunil appeared behind a large sitting room window. His silhouette in the window did not register as anything unusual.

The repetition of this incident, however, made me curious. Eventually, he started to circle me like a vulture looking for a roadkill. I felt uncomfortable. To add insult to injury, in light of the unusual actions of Sunil, Don had taken a greater interest in me than before.

Since then, my life with the Thisera family became more complicated, because Don has embarked on a sibling competition to win me over.

The family categorized any changes I had instigated as positive, although some changes certainly created chaos in my life. I was happy that, inadvertently, I had converted someone's life for the better.

It was humbling to hear their praises in the true sense of the word.

However, I refused to take responsibility for one particular change they claimed I had had my hand in; Mary's distress. Mary informed me that she was planning to leave the Thisera household unless I left first. My presence had caused her mental distress because Don's attention had been withdrawn from her, and she was squarely placing blame at my door.

I sat with her to explain why Don could not have made such a decision because of me, but she would not hear of it. She had become sick and frail. Although her associations with Don were not known to me in its entirety, I knew that she had a strong attachment to him. I refused to take the blame for her situation. A few weeks later, she left the household. No one spoke of her departure, and a new maid was hired; life went on.

Then, a bizarre incident happened.

It was clear to me that Da ignored my presence from day one. I suppose he had accepted me as another boarder who had brought a little income to his family. One evening at dusk, I was relaxing and enjoying the sunset at the railing, that overlooked the beautiful mountain range. Suddenly, I realized that I was not alone. Da had walked to the railing and stood next to me and smiled for the very first time.

After a few minutes, he addressed me with caution, using a soft and affectionate tone. He enquired after my parents and my family background. I had nothing to hide. I felt that he appreciated my candour on this subject.

His follow-up question shocked me.

He asked whether I had a special man in my life and if my parents were looking for a suitor. I was silent at first as I could not understand his motive for the enquiry, but then I answered his questions: No, I did not have anyone special in my life, and please communicate with my father if you would like to know what my parents' plans are for my future. He smiled and walked away.

I stood in silence and was in dismay.

The sun had disappeared behind the dark, rugged mountains, and a crow sat on the railing and crowed. It took flight as soon as I paid attention to it. There was an unusual chill in the air that evening, and I shivered. I decided to write a letter to Father:

17th October 19--

My dearest Tha (father),

I hope all is well with you and mother. I am keeping well and enjoying my duties as a school teacher. I am grateful to you for encouraging me to take this post. It is a service to the children and a useful and profitable venture for me.

I write to let you know of a strange encounter I had with Da this evening. He was bold and direct. He enquired after you and mother and asked the most bizarre question; he was inquisitive to know whether my parents were looking for a suitor for me. Why do you think he asked this question? I would like to hear your thoughts on his attempt to extract information. Please write when you can find a moment. I look forward to hearing from you.

With all my love to you and mother,

Podi Duwa (little daughter)

A week went by with the usual activities around the home and at school.

Then, one day, Sujith approached me during a tea break. He was brimming with cheerful smiles and offered me a large bag of freshly harvested potatoes. Potato farming had been well established in the area; I was not surprised by the contents of his offer, but the reasons of his bounty stirred my mind. He informed me that I was instrumental in keeping Don away from his home and his mother.

The bag of potatoes was an expression of his gratitude!

I was shocked. I had no intention of accepting such gratitude under a false pretence. I was direct, "I am sorry I cannot accept this gift, although I am grateful for your gesture because I have no alliance with Don in this capacity." Surprisingly, Sujith understood my sentiments and never spoke of it again.

Several days later, I received a letter from Father. It had a shocking revelation—a secretive plot seemed to be in the works.

20th October 19--

My dearest Podi Duwa,

Thank you for alerting me about your strange encounter with Da. I was surprised to receive a letter from him about two days after yours. He suggested a meeting with me in the near future about a personal matter related to one of his sons. I did not respond to his letter yet, since I needed to speak with you. Will it be possible for you to come home for a visit during the weekend? No need to write if you are planning to visit. We will be happy to see you.

With all our love,

Tha

I visited my parents that Friday, but unfortunately, I did not have any additional information on the subject to share with my family, and neither did Father. In his letter, for some reason, Da had kept the son's name a secret. I was oblivious to the name as much as Father was, until Da visited with Father, which happened during the following week.

It was Don.

Da had brought a proposal to Father on Don's behalf to ask for my hand in marriage. I was surprised and disappointed; I wondered why Don did not seek my consent on this very important aspect of my life before consulting anyone.

You think you know someone, and then they do something that makes you re-evaluate everything you thought was true. Don's secretive approach was unacceptable. He should have known that secrecy on this matter would mean this deal would go south faster than a flock of migrating Canada geese.

In Sri Lanka, match-making between two young adults for marriage had been considered a sacred event for centuries. In the ancient world, parents were responsible for finding a suitor for a daughter or a son, and in general, the couple never refused such a proposal out of respect of their parents. Based on this cultural practice, *marriage brokers* or *matchmakers* had been indispensable. But, they are now believed to be less prevalent because of other ways to find a match, such as notices published in newspapers.

Despite the modernity of our age, when I was of marriageable age, marriages arranged by the parents were still a large part of Sri Lankan culture. By tradition, it was customary for the young man's parents to visit those of the young woman to discuss a potential union. In modern times, this event was expected to occur with the consent or at least the awareness of both the young man and the woman.

Although my parents were inclined to follow traditions as much as possible in this regard, as a matchmaker had arranged their own marriage, Da's visit with my family, without my knowledge, was unusual and unacceptable to Father.

For me, it was unbelievable, as Da had made the proposal without any consideration for my feelings towards his son.

To avoid further misunderstandings, Father had directed a question to Da when they met: "If I were to agree to give my daughter's hand in marriage to your son, where would they live? Would you be able to build a new home for them?" Da refused to answer the question and had left without even having a cup of tea with my family.

I would come to know later that Da had transferred the message to his family upon returning home, but I was still kept in the dark. Eventually, Da had written a letter to Father refusing to part with his fortune, but had requested Father to reward his son with a handsome dowry in exchange for marrying me.

Dowry is a marital tradition dating back centuries. In Sri Lanka, most brides' parents believe the dowry was a voluntary act; in common parlance, it had been the price paid to have a son-in-law joining one's family. This tradition was not carved in stone and had been known to vary based on individual family wealth.

Perhaps Da was caught between the ancient and the modern practices, or he was simply thinking of feeding his fortune through his son. Indeed!

For me, regardless of whether a dowry had been a price to pay or not, the prerequisite of marriage should be the consent between the man and the woman. Missing this important aspect for a potential union was like throwing oneself into a deep end of an ice-cold pool in anticipation of leaving it without wrinkled skin.

Even after Da's visit with my parents, no one in the Thisera family had the courtesy to inform me of the back-door communications with my family. After hearing the details from Father, I held my tongue, hoping that Father's question to Da would close all doors to this ridiculous arrangement.

I was wrong. Don had become more determined to win me over as his life partner than before.

But Father's insight on this proposal was very clear and helpful: "Don does not have a bean to offer you."

I trusted Father's judgement.

A few weeks later, on one Sunday morning, I was comfortably seated under a garden umbrella reading *Sons and Lovers* by D.H. Lawrence. It was the *magical hour* when the whole world was yet to wake up to face the day, and nature still had its power over any human who would interfere with its softness. I felt the freshness in the mountain air, and with a wonderful book in front of me, I was enjoying the great outdoors.

Birds were enjoying the glorious morning at sunrise too. They sang as if they were intoxicated by the fragrance of the blooming flowers. Their songs swirled around me like an orchestra on wheels.

Then, my focus on the tranquility of the morning and my reading was completely disrupted. Don approached me and suggested that we talk. *Too little too late,* I thought. But, I was happy that he might have finally figured out the right forward path.

Out of respect, I did not dismiss his presence or his suggestion.

He wore a red velvet shirt and black pants and stood facing me while the rising sun warmed his tall body from behind. His smile was intoxicating, and his presence made me feel giddy. He looked very attractive.

Suddenly, he sat across from me and declared his love for me with teary eyes.

I looked at his face, and my soul felt a tinge of sadness. He sounded genuine. I sat still, like a wall without words. His eyes were planted on my face as if his gaze would encourage me to open my heart to his declaration. I was speechless, not because I did not wish to entertain his sentiments, but because his past activities flashed across my mind like a silent movie.

Those images made me shiver to the core of my being.

I smiled and offered him some comforting words. "I appreciate your friendship, but I need to take some time to give you an answer." He left without further attempts to persuade me. I had borrowed a little time to investigate my thoughts. I questioned myself on this decision.

My answer baffled my mind, as without a doubt, I had admired Don as a human being.

Since Don declared his love for me, he had kept my mind occupied like a relentless woodpecker pecking on a hollow bark to investigate the strength of the wood against its powerful beak. I agree that his gesture was thoughtful, and it was infused with buckets of affection, but I had to find the strength to follow the right track before his display of love for me could weaken my soul.

Don might have thought I had a blind spot on his past, and he could have a picnic in it, but I did not have this spot. For me, his past was like an open book. Based on that script, I could predict a future with this man and could sense an approaching disaster.

He had owned his personal playground and had played his cards on everyone he met and had enjoyed it very much. I saw his playground very differently; one with shattered lives, broken hearts, unfortunate financial dealings, lack of education, numerous affairs with unavailable women and men; the list went on.

Did I need a complicated life? The answer was clear, yet I was indecisive as I was attracted to his personality.

It was clear to me that charm oozed from every pore in Don's body. His aura was infused with pheromone fragrance for any female in heat. For some reason, a bubble around me had absorbed the pheromones before they reached my brain. My mind was clear. His kind and attentive nature, however, kept me looped in with his charm. Somehow, he knew very well what I liked and disliked.

I believed that he knew how to keep a woman engaged.

I acknowledged that his presence in my life had made it a little bit sweeter, and my tears had tasted a little less salty. He was the first man who reached my soul with a tender touch. I valued his offerings, but the risk would have been much higher than the benefits if I were to be his wife.

Based on this assessment, silently, I had rejected the idea of being part of the Thisera family. Yet, I needed the courage to reveal my sentiments to Don. It was very difficult to find the courage.

The time passed. I was still in two minds. I felt like my life was a hollow shell when I was around Don, roaring and clattering like the sound of the sea; the unsettling thoughts kept me bewildered.

I had to make a decision, and it had to be soon.

It was early November, and the cold air had started to linger longer. Distinct seasonal changes were not part of the weather in the hill country. However, the approaching cold weather was felt, and the farmers hurried to harvest their crops before frost could damage their livelihood.

At school, I accelerated the course work for the Grade 12 students as the end of the school year was approaching. The volume of questions from students had increased with time, which kept my evenings busy. With that schedule, personal issues were pushed to the back burner. However, in Don's mind, what my decision would be was front and center. He continued to speak with me as much as I had allowed it.

On the 15th of November, I received a letter from Peradeniya University with the final results of my degree program. The letter had been re-directed by Father, and he had included a personal note inviting me to come home to celebrate my success.

I had graduated from university with an honors degree in chemistry.

A second letter arrived the following day. I opened the white envelope that carried a letter of offer from the University of Peradeniya. It invited me to be part of the teaching staff of the Department of Chemistry. The image of me as part of the university faculty energized me, as it was considered one of the highest honors a student could receive. I was expected to start work on the 1st of December.

A twist in fate I presumed, as I was forced to meet new challenges and leave behind a volume of sweet memories, and my first offer of marriage.

I left the Thisera family the following week with a heavy heart. I felt a deep sadness because I had to leave a group of eager high school students without a chemistry teacher. They said goodbye to me with teary eyes, and I shed a few tears too.

The Thisera family genuinely expressed their distress and sadness for my unexpected departure. They gathered around me and offered me good wishes, but Da and Don were not among them. I presumed this was the end of Don's advances. I felt guilty that I did not reciprocate or negate his assertions. I hoped that the phrase *out of sight, out of mind,* would work for him.

I was wrong again.

It was wonderful to re-enter the familiar beautiful surroundings of Peradeniya University, this time as a member of the teaching staff in the Department of Chemistry.

I was also appointed as the sub-warden of Sanghamitha Residence Hall, which was situated on a hill on the campus grounds. In this all-female resident hall, a large room had been reserved for me. It had a great view of the Mahaweli River and the surrounding gardens with flowering trees and shrubs.

As a sub-warden, the food and lodging were free, and a stipend had been allocated for this position. I was very happy. The independent life, which I craved for years, had slowly approached and beckoned to me.

My parents had a small celebration to acknowledge my success, but Brother was absent yet again, which made me feel very sad. It was a great surprise that Mother did not have any hurtful remarks or regrettable attitude towards my achievements. She kept silent.

Father, on the other hand, openly expressed his joy and pride.

I started work as scheduled. I was excited to be among some of my old classmates, and I was happy to make new friends.

After a few weeks, the time I spent with the Thisera family and the associated memories had dissipated among the current activities buzzing around me that demanded my attention. The new scenery changed my mood and attitude towards life.

I was very happy and had the energy to live the life I always wanted.

The first semester of that year ended in April. Based on comments from my students, I was extremely satisfied with my performance as a university teacher. After conducting the final chemistry exam, I took a stroll down the corridor, passing the chemistry laboratories and staff rooms. I spoke to a few students who were heading home after ending their semester.

As usual, I checked the bulletin board on the wall for new messages. A poster attracted my attention: *A new university is being established in the southern province, and it will be named Ruhuna University. Applications are being called for various positions. Please apply before 30th May 19--.*

A new opportunity had been presented to qualify for a permanent position as a university teacher. It was exhilarating and uplifting as such opportunities were rare. The next day, I mailed my application to the registrar, and since then, I had been checking my mail every day. My hope was intense, and my expectations were high.

However, instead of receiving a letter from the registrar, one morning I received a letter from Don. I could not believe my eyes as I did not provide a mailing address to anyone in the Thisera family. The letter was bulky, and it was mailed a few months ago, almost the day after I left their home.

Don was not aware of the name of the department I had been affiliated with; he had printed the address as Peradeniya University with my name as the recipient. Based on that, the delay of its arrival was clear; the letter might have travelled through many departments before it came to me.

I postponed reading it until I returned to my residence.

The letter was filled with memories that Don had accumulated during my time with his family. The details were exhausting, as his language was not very clear. He confessed that he missed me and my loving presence. I thought it was natural, as he was still in the surroundings that I had occupied for a period of time.

Many things had happened during that short period, and his sentiments were just and acceptable, but I did not feel any emptiness in my new surroundings. I did not get an opportunity to miss him or anyone else I had met during that period.

I put the letter aside and thought at length on how I should respond. I could not come up with a reasonable plan. Then the holidays arrived, and the letter was forgotten until I received a second. After reading it, I was displeased with myself for not responding to the first.

He wrote with sadness and pleaded with me to respond to his mail. I could not make up my mind. The second letter also was neglected, because I already knew what I would write, and I did not wish to pen my thoughts as it would hurt Don.

At some level, I may have had feelings for him, but not enough to commit my life to him.

Time went by with no further communications from him, until one day, he walked into my residence, unannounced, dressed in a black suit with a red tie. He carried a briefcase, the contents that I did not wish to know. He looked professional.

He might have regretted his decision to visit me after seeing my nonplussed face, yet he spoke with great affection.

I cried with all sincerity when I suggested he look elsewhere. For the first time, I noticed the change in his cheerful disposition, a shadow of misery had replaced it.

Later, I tried to recollect my feelings at a cellular level at that moment of departure; I could not. The painful words he had spoken had left my mind too, but I could clearly recall that it was a rainy day, which had aggravated the misery of separation.

Don started to walk away.

With each step he took, I felt the silver threads of love and affections that had held my heart close to his were breaking one after another, and the soft tissues of my heart that housed the threads started to bleed ever so slowly. It was painful. By the time he reached the end of the road from Sanghamitha Hall, he was drenched, but he did not seem to care.

The blinding heavy rain took Don into oblivion.

I never saw or heard from Don again. Did I suffer because of my decision? Yes, I did. But I felt Don might have suffered more.

Mother had her own view and expressions on my decision. "Don was a good man, and I could not understand why you refused him. Are you expecting to meet a better man?"

Mother was wrong; besides, she had lost her rights in advising me on relationships or any other important matters in my life long ago.

Much later I wondered: Did mother express her true feelings about Don? Was she planning to give a dowry to him for marrying me? I would never know.

After my difficult decision, I realized that my mind was stronger than my heart.

Father did not speak of my decision as he had already advised me on this matter after meeting Da. He trusted that one day a suitable man would find his way to me.

Many moons later, he revealed that he knew Don would not be a part of my future, as it was not written in my stars. That was because Father believed in the mysteries releveled through my birth horoscope.

Several years later, Mother informed me that a few months after the brief encounter at Peradeniya, Don had left the country. According to her account, he was fortunate to find employment in Bahrain.

Perhaps she had kept tabs on Don, because she truly had liked him and wished him to be her son-in-law. Yet, she had not written a single word in her journal about Don or his alliance with me.

I was happy for Don, although at some level, I felt sad knowing that I might never meet him again.

That was the last time I communicated with anyone on this subject. No one in my family spoke of him again. Don vanished from my life, and I had very little space in my life to think of him or the time I had spent with his family.

I moved forward to meet the fate which had awaited me.

CHAPTER 11
The Meeting

Matara is the most southern coastal city of Sri Lanka; about 200 miles from our family home. The Indian Ocean, which boarded it, relentlessly lapped its coastline with powerful waves like a lively monstrous tongue. The coconut palm trees spread along the coast moved in response to the gusts created by the waves. The year was 19--, and this city had become my new place of residence.

With a new steady job in hand as an assistant lecturer at a brand new university, I felt like a winner.

I was happy to move away from Mother; perhaps her sentiments in this regard matched mine. From Matara, it would be too far to go home every weekend, so I decided to write to Father frequently to keep in touch.

In the past, Matara natives had experienced foreign influences from the Portuguese and Dutch who invaded the Island, contributing to their unique culture. Around this town, the remnants of colonial times weren't hard to find, and for a visitor, it was imperative to pay close attention to those speaking Sinhalese (the language spoken by the majority of Sri Lankans) to understand the words and expressions.

The most distinct change I had to endure, though, was the heat and humidity along the coast, in comparison to the cooler temperate weather in the mountains where I had grown up.

I felt as if I had landed in a new country.

I stood at a small window in my room that overlooked Vihara Lane. The late August northerly winds had cleared the skies, making the horizon crisp. I could hear the rustle of leaves from the soft sea-scented breeze, and I took a deep breath to feel the ocean around me.

The sea imparted a specific fishy-smell that I could not have experienced in the mountains.

Along the lane, a crowd dressed in white was heading to the Buddhist temple. It might have been a day of religious observances. Above the crowd, I could view the floating seagulls like shiny little airplanes landing in flocks, trying to grab scraps of food on the sandy shore. They would disappear just below the cactus bushes; only their screeching arguments could be heard.

The setting sun heated my body as if I had stood in front of a furnace. It was just as powerful in the evening as it was throughout the day. In Matara, unlike in Kandy, the sun stood unabated for twelve long hours. Without any mountains to hide the rays, an early dusk would be impossible.

At around 6:30 p.m., the sun descended slowly and disappeared below the western sky.

On that very first day, I felt like a child visiting a new theme park, and I looked forward to explore and discover the hidden treasures in it. Undoubtedly, Matara piqued my curiosity.

Over the next few months, this was where I met with an unexpected destiny. Then, Mother stepped in to implement her final plan to change my life for the worst.

A few days before, on the morning of the 15th of August, I travelled to start a new life in Matara. From Kandy, I hopped on to the train Udarata Menike, which connected me in Colombo, to the railway Ruhunu Kumari. This south-bound train dashed at a dizzying rate on the western coastline along the Indian Ocean, passing several coastal towns and fishing villages.

I was in an adventurous mood.

The sun rose with glorious hues, still hugging the wavy horizon. Through the rattling wooden cabin window, I witnessed fishermen paddling their wooden boats to catch their daily living. Above them, the brilliant blue sky flashed with only a few clouds slowly drifting, like feathery umbrellas, as if they were there to shade the scorching, hard-working fishermen.

It was my first encounter with the sandy coast of the Island. The salty breeze embraced my soul with a gentle and welcoming touch; I felt like I belonged there.

If I were asked what my favourite spot was on the Island, I couldn't choose. It would be like asking to choose a gem in a room full of sapphires, rubies, emeralds, and diamonds. Each time I travelled through Sri Lanka, I discovered yet another spot of breathtaking beauty.

For some unknown reason, the ocean won my heart over the rugged mountains in the central province.

In September, Ruhuna University was opened by the Sri Lankan government to accommodate the growing population and demands of youth for a university education. A building that once held a technical college had been designated to house incoming under-graduates and staff in anticipation of building the new university.

I had walked into the empty halls of this building a few weeks earlier with hopes and dreams of making a permanent home in Matara, with a steady income and the life of financial, emotional, and physical freedom.

Earlier, in June of that year, I was interviewed for the position of assistant lecturer at the newly established university. I received an offer letter from the University Grants Commission two weeks after, informing me that my duties were expected to commence in the first week of August.

On that victorious day, the question I wished someone would have asked me was, "Did you find the right job to fit your educational background?" I would have bear-hugged the person and answered, "Yes, I sure did."

Instead, Mother expressed her sentiments on my success with a negative comment. "You always had a big mouth. I am sure the professor who interviewed you would have felt great fear to say no to you."

"To tell the truth Mother, it was the opposite," I answered, "The professor was surprised how I was able to deliver a lecture on one topic, completely in Sinhalese, although I was educated in English during my university life. He said that my ability to talk clearly in front of an audience gave him the confidence to offer me the position."

My fearless words avoided further harassment.

I had won my battles with determination, and Mother was unsuccessful in taking away the bubbling joy in my heart and the blooming smile on my lips. Father was grateful that I had been born to speak well and that I had never shied away from any audience from my younger days. I had arrived at the pinnacle of my life, which was how I felt during this family discussion.

I rejoiced.

But who would have imagined that this height of my career would also lead me to great depravations.

Never mind the life I had known with a difficult mother, never mind the arduous task of following strict rules of the boarding school in Kandy.

Those were small inconveniences compared to what was about to be presented before me.

In Matara, yet again, I had to live amongst strangers. The new residence, owned by one Silva family, was within walking distance of the new university. They were proud to accommodate a university lecturer in their family home.

Comparable to the Thisera family, the Silva family had three daughters and two sons; two of the daughters were still in school, but the sons kept themselves busy by taking care of the family-owned businesses and properties.

It was a delight to meet the mother of this family. She was a tall lady with a distinct raspy voice as if she had accidentally swallowed a little whistle. She reminded me of a mother hen who would protect her chicks under any circumstances.

The father of this family lived in Point Pedro, in the Jaffna peninsula, which was at the northernmost tip of the Island. He owned a bakery and visited his family only once or twice a year.

On one of those rare visits, I met him and heard his reasons on why he lived that far away: "I prefer to live as far away as possible to avoid arguments with my wife." Ironically, he was separated from his family by the largest possible distance on this small Island.

The Silva family owned a few coconut estates and several businesses in and around town. They were wealthy and well-respected in the community as philanthropists. However, Father was skeptical about me staying with them based on my past experiences with the Thisera family. I assured him that I had learned much from the past and was ready to face my future. Father was satisfied with my assuring words.

Yet, I should not have assured him with such confidence because I was about to face new experiences with the Silva family.

At the onset of my life in Matara, my enthusiasm for a new, independent life was unparalleled. Naturally, I did not have a crystal ball to predict my future. Even if I had sensed any threat of dark clouds, thunder or lightning in the near future, I would have dismissed such thoughts, like a sailor who was unleashing his boat on calm waters, expecting to encounter sunshine and pleasant breezes. I did not have any concerns for what lay ahead.

That was because, during that exciting beginning, I was in a positive state of mind.

However, the next few months of my life accelerated at an unimaginable rate, and an unexpected moment would arrive in a flash.

It was September 5th. The staff of the Faculty of Science met with the Director, and the introductions were simple, and assignments were clear. Three assistant lecturers, including myself, would teach chemistry: Rajith from Peradeniya University and Himaly from Vidyodaya University in Colombo.

The new university came to life after the arrival of the pioneer batch of first-year students with hopeful eyes and unbounded enthusiasm.

Loads of new furniture had been installed in the lecture halls and the staff rooms, but the makeshift chemistry laboratories only had a few tables and glassware, without running water to conduct experiments. The students carried water in metal buckets to the lab to conduct their experiments without any visible complaints.

Rudimentary beginnings indeed, but it was exciting.

My life in Matara was uncommonly easy and enjoyable with the Silva family, whose lifestyles were extravagant. As such, I was fortunate to enjoy various culinary delights of freshly harvested seafood cooked according to a different recipe almost every day.

Buffalo curd (yogurt made of Buffalo milk) was served with honey as a dessert at each lunch.

I had my privacy as well as the good company offered by the family.

My professional life also was extremely rewarding. Teaching a group of enthusiastic young university students fulfilled all of my academic dreams, and my financial independence was invigorating.

Under such uplifting circumstances, who would anticipate any uncomfortable incidents? To my surprise, however, I began to encounter situations with the Silvas that had eerie similarities to the Thiseras.

On around September 15th, Gena, the second daughter, became my closest friend.

She loved to spend time with me, and to my surprise, I discovered we had similar personalities. With time, she won my trust like no other had in the past. After a few months into our friendship, I was delighted when she introduced me to her elder brother Sampath, but I did not anticipate that she would consider me to be more than a friend to her or to her brother.

Sampath was a tall man with a pleasant smile. He had a broad prominent forehead and a kind, constant stare. His genuine smile would put anyone at ease; no one would consider his personality threatening.

I had no intention of becoming his companion or friend; wanting to learn of his background in education, occupations, or any other interests in his life was not important to me. We existed in the same space, without many interactions, except for the occasional few words exchanged at dinner.

On Sunday, a week after Gena introduced me to Sampath, her mother invited me to join a dinner party at her eldest daughter's family home, situated a few miles away. I was delighted to have an opportunity to meet the extended family, and although I needed to prepare lecture notes for the coming Monday, I accepted her invitation.

I travelled with the Silvas, but Sampath did not join.

After dinner, mother Silva suggested I return to the residence to prepare for the coming Monday. I was thankful for her thoughtfulness. The driver took me back and dropped me at the gate.

To my surprise, Sampath opened the gate with a smile.

He spoke non-stop from the gate to the front door, as if he was either excited or restless about being alone with me. As soon as we entered the house, his endless chatter was followed by an eloquent but undesirable silence.

At that unexpected moment, I found myself standing utterly alone in the massive home, and Sampath stood next to me like a pillar in an abandoned kingdom. I walked hastily to my room. I could feel his gaze follow my every step, but I refused to look back. I sat on my bed and thought about how I should make my evening profitable.

The events that unfolded after that were unexpected.

Although I had decided to stay in my room, I soon realized I had no choice but to come out to prepare my lecture notes, as there was no table in my room. The lights were dimmed, and there was no sign of life around me. I wondered how I could get to the table in the adjacent room without making a noise to attract Sampath's attention.

I tiptoed through the doors and made a great effort to sit without dragging the chair on the cement floor. I was successful. I started to work on my notes.

A few minutes went by when Sampath surprised me as he dragged another chair to sit next to me. He must have anticipated my moves. At that moment, I remembered that the great theorists,

160

Darwin and Freud, repeatedly claimed that there is a survival instinct in humans.

My instincts kicked in.

"What are you doing here while all your family members are at a dinner party?" I questioned him, keeping my voice as normal as possible not to make him uncomfortable.

"I wanted to speak with you alone," he replied.

"About what, can we talk after your family returns from the party?" I asked.

"Well, it is very personal," he replied.

"I am not sure whether I am the person you should talk to about your personal matters." I tried to discourage him from being personal with me.

"Actually, the matter involves you," he insisted.

"Really, I hardly know you, and you just met me a few weeks ago." I raised my voice to express my surprise at his eagerness to speak to me.

"It is about considering a life together," he stammered.

"I am not sure what you are trying to say," I stressed with a perplexed look and tone.

"I am a wealthy man, and I own a business with one hundred buffalos. My company makes curd from buffalo milk, and we sell them across the Island. The business is great. I would be inheriting this beautiful home. Therefore, I assure you that we would have a good life."

After a pause, he started to say his intentions, but I interrupted him before he could finish his sentence.

"I would like to—"

"Please don't say anymore." I was firm in my tone.

I felt like I was forced to sit on a two-legged stool, unbalanced and fraught with imminent danger.

Two important factors rushed to my mind: (1) he had known me for less than three weeks, yet he was trying to propose to me, and (2) perhaps he expects me to have a conversation with him about buffalo if we would become a couple.

If so, I would be in trouble, as I had limited knowledge on this livestock and animal husbandry. All I knew was that a water buffalo was a large animal that enjoys eating grass and hay and loves to wallow in oozing mud.

I had to think on my feet, and so I did.

"I am sorry to interrupt, but I felt what was on your mind. You must be out of your mind; what do you know about me?" I asked.

"I know enough because I fell in love with you the minute I saw you," he responded.

"Did your mother know about your plans for this night?" I enquired.

He looked at me with surprised eyes, as if he had awakened from a bad dream. He stood up and walked away without responding to my question. I did not care to hear his reply, but I wondered whether his family had set him up for this unexpected encounter.

After that awkward meeting, Sampath courageously accompanied me to the university on several mornings, carrying my textbooks to help me. I decided not to make an enemy out of this pleasant man, but I kept my guard up to prevent further misunderstandings; I limited my conversations to subjects of the weather and teachings at the university, preventing discussions on any other topic.

Finally, he understood my sentiments about his proposal during our chance encounter. Sampath then had decided to leave his family home for a lengthy period.

According to Gena's account, he had left by train to visit a farmer in Anuradhapura, a city in another province over three hundred kilo meters away. He was expected to shepherd one hundred buffalos to Matara through jungles and fields. I was happy that he had found a way to relieve his stress and think about his life.

Several weeks later, Sampath returned. His appearance had changed to a skeletal existence. According to his mother's accounts he slept under trees and had not eaten a square meal for days.

With time, the undesired approach by Sampath was forgotten. Clearly, the universe had other plans for my future. My life had been interesting and pleasant again, until October.

In early October, my colleague Himaly introduced me to Prem, a fellow lecturer from the Math department. He had a dark com- plexion and beady eyes. His large teeth appeared through his thick lips when he beamed at me. They were as white as a marble statue. When he shook my hand, his grip was like a claw on a wet sponge that would squeeze liquid in a flash.

He invited Himaly and me for a cup of tea at the canteen. He bought pastries to accompany the tea, and he then invited us to join him for lunch the next day.

Unfortunately, Himaly excused herself from the lunch meeting, but I had to sit with this man and listen to his life story. That bored the life out of me, but I tolerated his lengthy expressions for that one lunch. I was determined not to accept further invitations.

Prem might have sensed my displeasure for his company, yet, he had become fixated on me after that single lunch.

A week after the lunch meeting, he had the audacity to visit my family home, which was about two hundred miles from Matara.

Mother had been at home alone. She must have been stunned by this uninvited and unannounced visit. It was clear that Mother did not appreciate his visit because, according to Prem's account, Mother had taken the opportunity to discourage this man from getting involved with me. In that effort, she had explained how she would not part with the family fortune as a dowry at my marriage.

I wondered why she had brought that aspect into their discussion.

In the coming years, I would learn the depth of Mother's intentions to bring dowry into her discussion with Prem.

Father was disgusted by Prem's behaviour, and he advised me to ignore what Prem had to say and carry on with my life. Unfortunately, that man had no scruples. He had already spread words to his friends about the way Mother had treated him. He never spoke to me again. It was crystal clear that Prem was looking for a woman who could enhance his fortune through a hefty dowry at marriage.

I should have thanked Mother for her efforts in discouraging Prem, even though she did not act amicably and her intentions were not honourable. After some years later, I realized that I should not have been too hasty to thank Mother in this regard, because I learned that her candor on a dowry was not to help me but to serve herself. How did I miss her objective? Perhaps, I had expected Mother to love her children without any conditions.

Evidently, Prem was not expected to be a part of my destiny.

The 16th of October started with a morning as bright as I could remember. I walked with Himaly to the canteen during our tea break. We had to pass in front of the main entrance to reach our destination. As usual, the guard at the door sat at the entrance and was busy signing in a visitor.

As soon as we turned the corner, a man spoke close behind us with a radio-perfect voice. We immediately turned to face the unfamiliar voice, and I recognized him as the visitor at the entrance.

"Where can I meet the head of the Chemistry department?" he inquired.

He had a powerful physical appearance that was as strong as his voice. There was nothing unusual about the way he dressed or the briefcase that he carried in his hand, but something about the way he carried himself exhibited self-confidence.

He did not speak to me directly, but he acknowledged my presence with a quick smile, which I thought was too quick to recognize me even as a woman. Himaly responded to his query with a hand gesture, directing him to the appropriate office.

We did not speak of him any further and that day moved on like any other. But I found myself thinking of this man more than once during my workweek. I was not sure why; perhaps he made an impression on me, unlike any other man I had met before.

A week after that, the same man arrived at the department dressed in professional attire. The head of the department introduced him to the Chemistry staff as a fellow lecturer.

He introduced himself as Richard.

The new addition had been assigned to deliver lectures on Analytical Chemistry, and a table facing mine had been allocated for him in the staff room. Richard later informed the staff that he missed the general interview for the post because he was out of the country during that period, but the head of the interview board selected him as his credentials qualified him. That explained the reasons for his sudden appearance, nearly two months after the official start date.

One month went by with a busy teaching schedule.

To relax between classes, I had a habit of reading at my desk in the staff room. One afternoon in mid-November, I sat down to read *Jamaica Inn* by Daphne du Maurier. I was deep in the story when I sensed Richard was watching me from his desk. He walked over and inquired about the name of the book and expressed his thoughts.

"Reading is a good habit. I could bring you books from the British Council Library (BCL) in Colombo, especially the chemistry texts that are not in our library," he said.

Finally, a man with a common interest—that was refreshing, I thought.

"Sure, that would be great," I responded.

Since then, although Richard did not express any other interest in my existence, he kept his promise and intermittently brought me books from the BCL. We did not mingle with the same crowds otherwise, and he remained a stranger to me, much like a man I would see only in a daily newspaper.

On December 5th, the first term of the academic year ended, and the holidays arrived. To start the holidays, staff members decided to take a day trip to the internationally renounced Yala National Park, about one hundred forty-five kilometres from Matara. A headcount had been established for seat reservations, and a ten-seater van was booked. Although I was expected at home for the December holidays, I decided to join the group to visit the wildlife sanctuary.

That decision would change my life.

The day arrived for the field trip. It was a fine morning. The sky was clear, remarkably clear. The laughter and chatter of the crowd energized the surroundings. I took a seat next to Himaly, behind the driver, while others sandwiched us from the front and back. Richard took the seat next to the driver.

When the group reached the national park just before lunchtime, the sun bristled down upon the land, making it difficult to gaze at the horizon without seeing a series of mirages spread across the flat surface. Large trees were rare, and the shrubs and bushes were scattered along the wetlands. It was nothing but another bare land in the middle of nowhere.

Eventually, wildlife arrived, mostly to have a drink of water at the nearby lake. Our group enjoyed the time together, taking a dip in the large lake to cool off while watching the animals.

From that moment, my life began to change.

Richard started paying undivided attention to me. The reason for his changed behaviour was a question, which I did not have an answer to.

I only noticed it as an incidental interest, but by the time we headed back to Matara at dusk, the whole group seemed to have captured the essence of his intentions.

When he casually said he would like to sit next to me in the van, I accepted his invitation as if I was in a sedated state with no power to change my mind. As we sat together, I did not see any wild animals, I did not care that a group of people surrounded us, and I did not feel fatigued. I felt ease and joy.

I distinctly remember losing my sense of time and place.

At the end of that long day, I was surprisingly not exhausted. Night had fallen, and there was no rustling of the tree leaves in the sea breeze. The whole world had gone to sleep, but I was wide awake, like a hamster on a wheel, reminiscing over and over on the adventurous travel and looking for answers to millions of questions about the future.

As far as I could remember, Richard was the first man who had kept me awake at night.

The day succeeding this remarkably restless night proved to be an uncommon day. The sun rose with a dreamy face, which was decked with beauty. My new reality changed my vision of the world. The sun that rose every day over the seashore did not seem to have an intolerable heat, but rather had the capacity to warm my skin with tenderness.

My environment had been altered to fit my new frame of mind. I was certain that no one around me would have remembered these pleasant facts. I did not want to share such feelings with anyone anyway. My new mindset would only belong to Richard and me.

Over the next several days, we travelled on clouds, exchanging messages mostly through our eyes. We understood each other well.

In this new reality, my heart chakra had been opened wide; I felt energized. An unknown source of happiness had enveloped me. I was certain that life had started all over again, but in a new direction after reaching an unexpected point-of-no-return. I wished to hear songs of happy birds and follow a yellow brick road to the wonderful *Land of Oz*. All in all, I anticipated a miracle in my future.

"This must be love," I concluded.

Love is a powerful emotion, which could manipulate one to take actions that one could regret later. Shakespeare evaluated this emotion in *Romeo and Juliet* explicitly.

Although I could not compare our emotions to those that were detailed in this play, there was a connection between us that could be described as Shakespeare did: "Love is madness with discretion."

It was a beginning to an end of the life I had known.

I wondered if that was a call from the universe: had it planned to play a nasty trick on me, nudging me to support the theory of evolution, or was it a true calling of the hearts? I thought at length and made a decision. I had no power to question the universe or negate a call sprouted from my soul.

I followed my heart.

Since then, I dreamed. Would there be an adventurous future ahead of us? Would we hold hands to climb hills to view wondrous lands across the globe and pass through meadows with natural beauty where the animals roam free? Would we climb mountains through thorny bushes and enjoy a unified life filled with a million little surprises?

I dreamed on, and I wondered whether Richard's dreams were comparable or whether he dreamed as much as I did.

An unexpected future had arrived, and an unusual story about the two of us started to unfold. Ironically, our story mirrored the story of *Romeo and Juliet* in more than one way.

Although my dreams were rosy, the path laid ahead of us was daunting and rocky. It would be blasted with discordant bell chimes from conflicting religions, but most of all, the route would be overcrowded with unimaginable parent-child attachments to our individual families.

However, unlike the star-crossed lovers in *Romeo and Juliet*, we survived—barely.

I had met my destiny; Mother then stepped in to create chaos, with the hopes of changing it.

CHAPTER 12

A Very Short Courtship

From the moment of birth, we search for love to build relationships; first, among our kith and kin, then with those we think we could emotionally connect to. Later, we might discover that relationships are the root cause of many of our life's problems, but a strong emotional connection with another human would be intimate love, if it brings romance and excitement and provides drama in life.

Such was the case with the relationship that I had developed with Richard.

Soon after the trip to the Yala National Park, we had to head home for year-end holidays. This separation came at an inopportune time, as we needed close communications to find our way within our newfound emotional and physical attraction.

Back in those days, we had no internet or cellphones, and I had to keep our emotional connection alive by dreaming of him and reliving the events that had unfolded during the trip to Yala.

The waves of affection for Richard had encased my soul and kept me warm and fuzzy through our temporary spatial separation.

Then the university reopened for the new academic year on Monday, January 8th, 19--. After travelling to Matara the previous day, the next morning, I anxiously waited to meet Richard while pretending to read my lecture notes in the staff room. Many thoughts raced through my mind. The wait was pure agony without knowing whether Richard would return to work on time.

Finally, I heard approaching footsteps close to the only entrance of the staff room through the Chemistry Laboratory. My heart skipped a beat. But I was disappointed to see Himaly. She inquired about my holidays, but her expressions suddenly changed.

"Are you alright? You seemed different today," she commented.

"I might be tired after travelling last night. I had to stand on the train for a long time because of the crowds returning to the university," I responded.

She was satisfied and left for the cafeteria. A few minutes went by. Then Richard entered the room nonchalantly until he realized we were alone. He seemed nervous.

"I missed you," he quietly said while sitting in front of me. He looked at me with a loving gaze that warmed my heart. The holiday separation had created a deep longing to see one another. Genuine happiness filled my heart with anticipation for the future with this new attention from Richard.

At that moment, an electrifying spark passed between us, priming us for a sparkling courtship.

When I was growing up, I had not received deliberate instructions on romance. To initiate a romantic relationship, I had no choice but to listen to my heart and wing it by using any bits and pieces of clues and cues I had picked up from my parents or other acquaintances.

I yearned to know "the ropes" because this attempt would be in pursuit of finding a lifelong mate.

Unlike the current generation, I did not have novels such as *Fifty Shades of Grey* or articles that I could refer to for help. It was obvious that we needed to find a unique approach to our courtship.

The discipline, religious beliefs, and family influences I had encountered in my younger days had an enormous impact on my approach to have an intimate relationship. I imagined that Richard might have had similar encounters in his past, although I had no knowledge of the extent of his experiences.

Finding the right rituals for our budding relationship was hard-work, and the route to intimacy was even harder.

In the coming days it was proven to us that finding intimacy would be daunting and unbelievably torturous, because we would encounter sharp objects and rising flames along the sacred path to it due to other individuals' life insecurities.

With such hindrances our efforts to achieve intimacy mimicked Menelaus' quest to return his queen to Sparta, which led to the Trojan War.

The new academic year started soon after I met Richard in the staff room on that January day. No one had any inkling of our thoughts or of a brewing relationship between us. We were not ready to reveal our closely guarded secrets to anyone. Our regular activities commenced and progressed.

A week went by, and we both realized that unless we could cleverly plan excursions, we would not be able to express our feelings to each other during our busy work schedule, because we were constantly surrounded by students and staff. Our affections were expressed only with smiles and messages through the eyes, but the tension of not being able to express our feelings verbally was unbearable.

Then, Richard surprised me with a plan.

"I am willing to break my routine of leaving the campus around 4:00 p.m.; could we hang out together after hours?" he whispered while we were passing each other in the hallway.

I thought for a moment and considered his offer as a measure of his affections towards me. But I needed to take time to make my decision.

I contemplated his proposal within many aspects of an after-hours meeting: how the premises would look after a work day, whether it would be very dark to walk back to my residence, and how the Silva family would react to my late arrival for dinner.

In Matara, dusk sets around 6:00 p.m. every day; therefore, the timeline set for this meeting was acceptable. Although my heart knew that I could fully trust Richard, I was hesitant to meet him alone in an empty building at dusk. I decided to delay my response to his plan, yet temptation surpassed my discipline.

Within a few days, I concurred with his suggestion.

I informed Mrs. Silva that I would be returning late in the evenings from now on, as I had decided to spend some time with friends after working hours. I promised her that I would join them at dinner, which was usually around 8:00 p.m. She was satisfied; I respectfully believed that she did not have the authority to stop my plans anyhow, but I did not wish to jeopardize the cordial relationship I had with her.

The next day, a plan was set in motion as we both agreed for a short meeting after work hours. For me, the uncharted territory was in some ways thrilling, though it was still mind-altering. During the first week, we met at 5:00 p.m. each day in the staff room. We had long chats until about 6:00 p.m.

During such conversations, Richard mentioned that he has three siblings: eldest sister Ramona, his brother Ben and Bridget, another older sister who now lives in Oman with her family. He also informed me that he was brought up in Catholic faith and that his father is of Portuguese descent.

For some unknown reason, such details had not been of interest to me. I only had an interest in Richard and his pursuits in life. At the early stages of our relationship, it was obvious that the commonality between us was limited to the knowledge in chemistry, but I was fully satisfied with that.

Many years later I would realize that the true 'chemistry' between the couple is far critical to make a marriage to last, more than the knowledge of the subject chemistry.

We were exhilarated to find the freedom to discuss our lives without having to watch over our shoulders. Yet, after having enough discussions of our families, our personal belief in spirituality, and other common and different interests, much like "Laon and Cynthia" in Percy Bysshe Shelley's epic poem , the urge to feel each other was mounting.

Our instincts nudged us to take a step closer to becoming a committed couple.

In today's cultural milieu, even in conservative societies, young adults have no qualms of physically expressing their feelings to another. But, society's expectations in the 20th century had been in line with the *Last Judgment,* especially for unmarried women. More importantly, we had to be careful of our reputation, as our meeting was within our professional environment where we were expected to be exemplary to those around us. We also had to consider our family upbringing; each step in our relationship had to be measured.

Yet, for the first time, we decided to meet in the staff room and remain there beyond 6:00 p.m.

It was a Friday. Naturally, the staff and students had left the premises earlier than usual. But, the warm, humid air had not left the staff room, although the sun was setting in a crimson red horizon. The slanted rays illuminated the room.

The clock in the hallway struck 6:00 p.m., and I felt like *Jane Eyre,* who had received an invitation from Mr. Rochester to have tea with him in the drawing-room. Indeed, I had not changed my frock as Jane did, but I was ready for intimacy with Richard for the first time.

I sat at my desk and waited for Richard to arrive. I felt a stir in the pit of my stomach; the longing to be with him fluttered my heart with unusual vigour. I was expecting an experience that would last a lifetime.

As D.H. Lawrence detailed in *Lady Chatterley's Lover*, "Life is bearable only when the body and mind are in harmony . . . and each has a natural respect for the other." I felt that the time was upon us to feel the harmony of two bodies and the two minds.

In the dimly lit staff room, we faced each other for the first time without a soul around us.

Neither of us moved. Richard's eyes came on me as if they had just awoken. He did not say a single word, and for a moment I thought that he did not recognize me. His muscles seemed frozen. I might have thought this to be an easy task and would know what to say, but everything that appeared in my mind seemed inappropriate.

I decided to let nature take its course.

Without uttering a single word, we came together. He put his arms around me, drawing me closer to his warm body. I shivered in his warm embrace. We held each other as if we did not wish to let go. We felt our energy mix dramatically within the united souls. Time flew by, and we did not care while one body supported the other to stay in the same position.

Many minutes later, I pulled myself back to peer into his face; the light in the room had changed, and his face was unclear, but the expression in his eyes had a captivating draw, which would remain in my mind forever. His eyes told me a story, and the script was delightful and filled with desire and warmth.

I had come home.

The staff room was in complete darkness. Neither of us wished to have any light; the light that imparted from our minds and our bodies was bright and warm and delighted the world around us. The smell of chemicals that had swooped into the room from the adjoining laboratory did not bother us. The ground that we had occupied belonged to a garden full of aromatic flowers and singing birds.

It felt like paradise.

Suddenly, the spell that bound us broke from an unusual sound outside the door. A shadowy figure moved across the glass panel. Someone was there. Richard ran to the door, but it was too late. Whoever was peeping had vanished. His eyes were brimmed with tears. We both knew the consequences of this unexpected interference, and we were both right.

The weeks following that evening were stormy and filled with nightmares.

I had inadvertently inherited solitude and the associated loneliness by spending a good chunk of my childhood in the girls' hostel and the rest with a Mother who did not wish to develop a relationship with anyone but herself and Father.

Although I did not perceive loneliness as a catastrophe while growing up, it was obvious that I approached life differently from those I had met at Peradeniya University and then at the Ruhuna University.

Although I had accomplished much professionally, I realized that I lacked companionship and meaningful relationships. I could not deny my loneliness, which would be like denying hunger or thirst. I realized the cognitive feeling of social separation. I had no lever to pull to feel connected to my co-workers.

I had been locked into a pattern of thinking in isolation. Other than Richard, I was only able to develop one friendship, which was with Himaly.

Himaly became my closest ally from day one. Since Matara was her hometown, she helped me a great deal with understanding the southern culture of the Island and the nitty-gritty of the ups and downs of being in this coastal community. Her description of people being too nosey and having a penchant for following people around to interfere in personal lives was shocking.

Being a southerner, she already knew who her friends and enemies were. I had limited practice in understanding others' behaviour but based on Himaly's guidance, I decided to keep my eyes peeled and ears cleared to safeguard my privacy. Thanks to her, I monitored and recognized the differences between people from Matara and those from out of town.

Yet, I was no match for those busybodies of the sea-scented, hot and humid Matara.

I had learned early on in my career that higher education must lead back to the fundamentals of human relationships. While this statement might be true for some, the university staff at Ruhuna had no scruples; perhaps the warm sea breeze must have twisted their moral compasses. Eventually, I found out that Himaly was not different from any other Southerner.

Since the winds of my relationship with Richard swirled around the campus, Himaly became the first culprit.

Every Thursday afternoon, I was scheduled to conduct an Organic Chemistry laboratory for the undergraduate students. I walked into the laboratory ahead of time to ensure the ice cubes I had stored in the refrigerator were sufficient for the experiment. I opened the door, and there were none.

Himaly had thrown the bags of ice into the trash.

The explanation for her action was unbelievable as she knew the laboratory schedule and the need for the ice cubes: "I could not find enough room to keep my lunch, so I threw away ice because, I could understand why ice needs refrigeration." Later I would learn that she had purposely ruined my laboratory session as she got a wind of Richard's affections towards me.

It was obvious that she had secretly desired Richard, as he was a good friend to her. She had failed to grasp Richard's friendly approach to all women.

I felt betrayed by my closest ally.

Unexpectedly, serious attention from acquaintances heightened after our relationship became common knowledge. Some unknown person had spread rumours about our after-hours meetings. Some staff members had direct questions, which were easily answerable, but some had decided to find their answers by forcing a laboratory assistant to follow us around daily. Our effort to catch the Black Hander, who surprised us behind the closed door during our after-hour meeting, was fruitless. That was infuriating and disturbing.

Strangely, no one had realized the efforts they had taken to interfere in our affairs were counterproductive.

Naturally, our relationship grew stronger with the opposition and inquisitive eyes that followed us. After a while, most people started to ignore us after realizing that their efforts were unsuccessful, except for one man, 'Mr. Ruthless'. He relentlessly continued his efforts to ruin our happiness. He was an assistant lecturer from another department who was introduced to me by Himaly during our very first meeting in September.

His misogyny was quite clear and the reason for his undesirable behaviour towards us was revealed much later.

The calamity surrounded us through evil eyes, and snippy remarks continued and made us miserable. Then, in February of 19--, Richard was called to a meeting in Thailand. He had been representing Sri Lanka in a Student Christian Movement to help gather funding for the national organization.

His sudden departure made me feel like a vulnerable deer stood among a pack of wolves.

During Richard's absence, the most difficult thing to digest was the ruthless words of the female staff members who indirectly suggested I had stolen their most eligible bachelor. Seemingly, every one of them had an interest in Richard.

The vulgar remarks from male staff members surprised me to my core, suggesting they had developed jealousy over my attention to Richard. The world around me had expressed its true colours. I had nothing to offer to soothe their hurt feelings; I had no responsibility to curb their inappropriate thoughts.

A few days later, I received a letter from Richard, mailed just before boarding the flight to Thailand from the airport in Colombo. After reading it, I felt his arms around me, although he was thousands of miles away. That feeling helped me forgive all those who had hurt my feelings.

Rumi's words in [4]"You and I" vibrated within my soul:

You and I unselfed, will be together, indifferent to idle speculations, you and I.

The parrots of heaven will be cracking sugar; as we laugh together with you and I.

In my mind, time stood still while Richard was away. Though it was only for one week, our separation had created a vortex of emotions when he returned. My urge to meet and feel him was like a fish waiting to be returned to water; the agony was natural.

On his first day back from Thailand, our meeting at dusk in the staff room was exciting and energizing.

---

4 **Kabir Helmiski**; *The Pocket Rumi; GHAZELS*; (pp 51, Shambhla Publications Inc., 2001)

The clock on the hallway struck 6:00 p.m. There was a smile on his lips, and his eyes sparkled, perhaps with anticipation to be with me. I felt like a cat waiting to be fondled and comforted after being chased by an angry dog. The room was in darkness, and the silence around us was thick and welcoming.

Richard put his arms around me and lifted me against him. We began to kiss like lovers who met after a long separation across an expansive and rough ocean.

"I offer you my hand and my heart," he murmured while holding me close to him. Tears streamed down my face, soaking my cheeks and choking my breath. Richard gently wiped my tears with his thumb while caressing me with his warm body. We stood in silence; the whole world disappeared around us.

We set sail to an island that would protect us from all negativity.

The mid-year holidays for the university had approached sooner than we anticipated. It would keep us apart again when we needed to be with each other.

The sounds and aromas of the upcoming Sri Lankan New Year were very clear. The trees were adorned with beautiful tropical flowers. The birds had migrated from all parts of the world to enjoy the warm weather; they appeared in rainbow colours, and their joyful music vibrated in the air, energizing the human mind.

On the last Saturday before our holidays, Richard invited me to take a day trip to a local botanical garden. We spent the day walking hand in hand and chatting for hours under a large tree while watching the ducks roamed on a nearby lake. The birds enjoyed little bits of food we offered them after our outdoor picnic. We had arrived at our heaven on earth.

"Would you like to travel with me to Colombo on your way home for the holidays?" Richard asked.

"I would like that very much. Perhaps we could start early, so I could catch the train or bus to reach home before dark," I responded.

As planned, on the last Friday before the holidays, I brought my packed bag to the staff room for an early departure from Matara. Himaly and other staff members were inquisitive. They needed to know why I had brought my bag to the university. Although I was preparing to go on holiday as all others were, I explained that I planned to take an early train to Colombo. They looked at one another.

I had no inkling of what was about to unfold.

The afternoon sun had streamed down, and the hot air felt like it was blasting out of an erupting volcano. I looked at the time and noted that it was 2:00 p.m. Then I looked over at Richard's desk and noted that he also was getting ready to leave.

Carrying our packed bags, we walked down the hall together. As soon we turned from the hallway to the main entrance, we noticed a large number of people had gathered blocking our exit.

Himaly was leading the group with 'Mr. Ruthless'. All other teaching and technical staff stood behind them. Richard and I looked at the group, trying to understand what was upon us.

"Could you please step aside for us to leave?" Richard politely suggested. No one moved.

"We want to know where you are taking her and why," 'Mr. Ruthless' directed the question to Richard while stepping forward.

"I am not sure why that would be any of your concerns," Richard replied calmly.

"Well, she is one of us, and we need to make sure that she is safe," 'Mr. Ruthless' responded.

"I am not forcing her to leave with me. We agreed to travel together, and there should not be any concern for her safety," Richard bravely explained.

"I cannot let that happen, because I have the right to protect her from you. I believe that she wanted me to be her partner before you even stepped into this building. You ruined that chance for me. So, I am not letting you pass through this entrance!" 'Mr. Ruthless' shouted in anger.

Suddenly an ugly, despicable scene unfolded.

'Mr. Ruthless' stepped forward to grab Richard's arm, and Richard reacted by pushing the attacker aside. They went back and forth. I stepped aside, not knowing what I could do to prevent any damages. Richard had the upper hand based on his greater physical strength. 'Mr. Ruthless' fell on the floor and stood up immediately to continue his attack. Suddenly, the security personal arrived to separate the two men.

"There is nothing that you could do to prevent her from coming with me. We love each other, and you need to deal with the situation!" Richard bellowed.

'Mr. Ruthless' finally faced a new reality. His eyes popped, and his mouth opened as if he had something to say, but he closed his mouth and walked away. The crowd stood still as if they heard unpleasantly surprising words. Much later, I would learn that all of the women were shocked that Richard used the word 'love' in his final sentence.

Richard had declared his love in public.

While my eyes were watering with tears of joy, I held his hand in public for the first time. We walked through the main entrance without a care in the world. My mind had opened widely to view a future with this man without any fear and with much love.

We felt happy, as we were able to divert a disastrous intervention.

Yet, in the coming days, another enemy emerged to destroy our happiness as a couple; Mother would unleash a devious plan. Her vengeful jealousy and hateful interferences would surpass those of the strangers we met in Matara.

Would we survive *that* intervention?

CHAPTER 13

ℰTERNAL 𝒟USK

Hitting rock bottom is often applied to reaching a state of mind with an overwhelming feeling of hopelessness. The events that unfolded from the beginning of our married life were unexpected; they made me feel like as if I had hit the rock bottom, and I almost gave up.

After having a close relationship only for nine months, we thought our path was clear to reach the ultimate goal: marriage. However, there were numerous obstacles in our path before we had reached the altar: emotional spears, economic slings and arrows, and familial landmines, to name a few.

But our hearts were filled with love and we felt that we belonged together, as if we had etched the image of each other on our souls.

While looking forward with excitement to progress together, with great faith and much love in our hearts, we made our plans to become husband and wife in May of 19--.

Then, like the sparrows in the wild, in July of that year, we got married.

Unfortunately, soon after that, Mother was there with her weaponry; she would unleash a pre-meditated plan to inflict pain and suffering, and ensure that we would start our married life in poverty. The lack of support from our families was unbearable.

With that, I felt hopeless.

Hopelessness had not been on the list of my expectations for a future with Richard, as I had the opportunity to marry the man that I loved. However, unexpected challenges began to loom. For our marriage to survive, it was essential for me to see the bright side of all events, which was harder than I had imagined.

Instead of finding a dawn of an exciting life we had dreamt of, we faced eternal dusk. Then an unexpected light would shine through the dark clouds that hung over our lives.

We were given a second chance for happiness; seemingly, the universe had a plan.

A glamorous wedding ceremony was held in Colombo to unite us for life. Father's financial support for the event was generous. He took his responsibilities with grace and wit for his only daughter. The marriage was witnessed by over one hundred invited guests and family members.

Father looked remarkably debonair, yet official in his newly tailored suit and tie. His sudden beams of pleasure, the flashes of physical and vocal gestures of his happiness, and his mischievous dolphin smile that spread and flited away were all before me. His genuine joy was evident to both of us and to everyone around him.

Mother was fashionably dressed for the occasion but kept a low profile throughout the event. As in the past, I did not expect expressions of happiness from her, and I was thankful that she remained in her world without disrupting mine. She played a role of a loving mother, but I was not fooled by her act, even for a minute.

After keeping out of family activities for several years, Brother's presence in the wedding party as the groomsman was the most significant and memorable. It was a delightful surprise. He looked handsome and polished as a young man. His participation in my life-changing event encouraged me to face a future with a man I had only known for less than one year as a potential life partner.

The glamour and the expressions of wealth during the celebrations of our marriage might have impressed the spectators, but they were not helpful for us in starting our new life.

When the wedding had ended, reality beckoned us with unexpected harshness.

Our honeymoon was brief, one week to be exact, at a hotel in the heart of Colombo. It almost felt like a dream on a midsummer night. Soon after, we had to return to Matara to fulfill our duties at the university.

Since we did not own any property, we had to reach out to a family friend for accommodations. They offered us space to bunk for two weeks until we could secure a place of our own. Finally, we had negotiated with a wealthy landowner to occupy a small one-room annex in his home, which was within walking distance of the university.

Our 'new' residence barely had the strength to stand on its own. It was an old, rickety building situated in the back of the owner's main house. It had been uninhabited and neglected for years; it might have been built during the reign of the last monarch of Sri Lanka, King Sri Wickrama Rajasinghe, in Kandy a century ago.

It would have been rejected by anyone with common sense as an unlivable abode because it was ancient. But as a young married couple who did not have a solid-state of financial independence, we were willing to give it a try.

We took residence with our limited belongings: one bed and a clothes horse offered by Richard's parents and one cupboard by mine. The landlord provided a small wooden table with some cutlery and crockery. We were pleased with any small help, as we did not own anything other than the clothes on our backs.

Among the gifts received from our families and friends at the wedding, the most significant was the one from Mother: *a used kitchen knife.*

Gifting a knife to newlyweds was considered as a bad omen; an intention to sever the union. I was unaware of this omen until a friend at the university spelled out the meaning, but by that time, it was too late as I had already used it.

With all the unacceptable motives expressed by Mother in the past, I considered this one as the most damning. I could not believe that Mother would secretly desire to break off our marriage.

With that intentional cruel action, the 'step-motherly behaviour' in Mother had been confirmed.

Should I be surprised or discouraged? Not at all; since then I was more determined to make our marriage a success. Later, I would understand that this was a small drop in the bucket compared to what lay in store for me. Mother's many stabs to destroy our happiness continued, like the numerous attempts of a hovering hawk, waiting to catch its prey.

With our limited belongings and moderate salaries, our married life started with a whimper.

Once we had settled down, cooking our meals was one of the most important aspects of our survival. But neither of us knew how to cook. I thought back to when I wished to learn the culinary craft. I felt miserable remembering how Mother had prevented my efforts to learn it. It seemed that Mother planned for my life to be difficult ahead of time, knowing that the ability to cook would be essential not only for survival but to keep a husband happy.

In Haudenosaunee's philosophy, there is a principle of seven generations: the awareness that the consequences of your decisions will ripple through seven future generations. This philosophy was no longer abstract based on Mother's past behaviour; it was real to me. While I refused to blame Mother's ancestors for her unpardonable behaviour, it built fear in me because Mother's decisions had the potential to perpetuate in a potential family of our own.

How we could survive without home cooked meals was a mystery to us, but I was determined to give it a try. Fortunately, Richard knew how to boil water for tea and how to prepare a hard-boiled egg. After burning a pot of rice that almost burnt down our home, I gave up. Fortunately, the city's Rest House offered delicious meals for a hefty price. Although such a practice would not be sustainable, the meals from the Rest House had saved us for the foreseeable future.

Though our future looked dim and overcast, one comforting thought prevailed: no matter where we lived, we were together. We had the courage and confidence that we would make it. Unfortunately, we needed more than those qualities to meet the obstacles placed on our path in the upcoming days.

I woke up the very first morning in our "new" home to a crackling sound of a radio; a neighbour's frantic attempts to tune into *Sarasavi Sewaya* for their early morning segment on patriotic songs. The tranquillity of the early hours was further disrupted by the unpleasant sounds of several crows looking for breakfast.

Our bedroom was dark, and the air smelled damp and musty. The first coherent thought I had was, "I wish I was not living." But I was very much alive, gradually waking up to face a day of misery.

Numerous thoughts flooded my mind after I realized where I was.

How could this be my destiny? I was an energetic young woman who had overcome numerous obstacles to accomplish greatness in life. This had to be a temporary setback. I was confused and felt lethargic about making future plans. While keeping my eyes closed, I remembered how the past had unfolded to reach this unimaginable present.

Six months before, in December, Richard had expressed his feelings for me. He confessed that he felt a deep connection to me, and I mirrored his sentiments. We both agreed, however, that without the blessings of our parents, we should not take further steps towards an intimate relationship.

Four months into our relationship, he had decided to meet my family.

Early in May, on a full-moon day, Richard arrived to meet my parents, asking for my hand in marriage. Father greeted him with a smile while Mother looked on. The conversations between Richard and my parents were casual, but Father posed important questions about the future.

Surprisingly, he was satisfied with all of Richard's responses.

After comparing my horoscope to Richard's—a standard process used for matchmaking in Sri Lanka—Father assured me that my life with Richard would be satisfactory for up to seventy-five percent of what was expected as a married couple.

Yet, he sincerely expressed his concerns about the future of our children, if we would be successful in having a family of our own.

His concerns were based on our religious differences; Richard's faith in Jesus Christ and my adherence to Buddhism. We believed that we could get through life without having to face difficulties based on this single difference. Unfortunately, years later, we had several experiences that revealed this difference could adversely affect our relationship. Then it was too late; we decided to deal with any emerging situation due to this difference in our own way.

Richard had informed his parents of his intentions of marrying me, and they had agreed to meet my parents. According to the cultural practices of Sri Lanka, the bride-to-be is expected to meet the respective in-laws accompanied by her parents.

On a bright sunny day in late May, I travelled with my parents to meet Richard's family. The family lived in a semi-detached home that was situated off the main bus road. A large black lab barked when we approached the house, but he greeted us with a friendly wag. It was a sign of friendship indeed. Richard's parents greeted us at the door with a welcoming smile.

Richard's father was a quiet man with a gentle smile. He approached me with a gesture of friendship and goodwill but did not utter a single word.

Communication had been my approach to a relationship, and I wondered what I would need to do to garner his attention. As expected, I was bewildered about whom to be for him. He was a man who gave his trust slowly and with the greatest care. I thought that he would also take it back without a blink of an eye.

As time went on, I learned more about him; silence does not equate to discipline.

Richard's mother had draped a saree for the occasion and had pleasant words, encouraging us to enter their home. I looked into the eyes of his mother, the woman who had brought up Richard, and I felt a most unusual sensation that I had never experienced before. I knew this woman had the power to make or break our union if we were to share a common space. I should have felt uncomfortable, but I did not.

Instead, I saw and felt empathy in her eyes.

Empathy opens up one's mind to other people and naturally draws one closer to them, but this could be challenging. I had struggled to find empathy in Mother, which was like attempting to break the glass bubble around her.

Based on my relationship with Mother, my instincts had developed defensiveness not to get close to other humans. Richard broke that barrier in my mind, and to my amazement, Richard's Mother projected a similar level of comfort that enabled me to feel at home around her. When we first meet someone, we can make mistakes in our judgement because we are human.

With Richard's Mother, that would be my experience in the years to come.

I would later learn that she was authoritative yet owned a kind heart for those who would abide by her rules.

I stepped into Richard's family home with encouraging thoughts because of the empathy I felt through his mother. I expected a familiar and soothing home environment, which would match the warm, welcoming words.

Apparently, my expectations were unreal.

As I entered their home, I witnessed an unusual scene: facing the main entrance, in the living room, was a homemade shrine. It attracted my attention like the sudden appearance of a beacon during a cave exploration, which would unbalance one's step in the darkness, while illuminating the immediate environment.

In the far corner of the room, on a tall wooden altar, a colourful statue of Christ and Mother Mary stood, with several rosaries hanging from the wooden frame. A flickering flame of an eternal lamp spread a glimmer of light around the statues.

A moment of truth flashed in my mind: my life would never be the same again if I married Richard.

As an undergraduate, I had attended a Catholic Church service held in memory of a student who had committed suicide by jumping into Mahaweli River. Someone in the congregation told me that the student had a difficult time living away from his family and had felt lost and isolated. The shrine in Richard's living room had triggered a similar sensation in me. I wondered why. Later I would understand the reason: I felt lost and isolated while attending a mass with Richard's family.

I felt much like a duck out of water.

But during this very first meeting with his family, I was in love. This forceful emotion of bewilderment at the first encounter with their religious practices had no power to change my mind or hinder the progress of our relationship.

I had been blinded by my strong affection and attraction towards Richard. I was the embodiment of the phrase: *Love is blind, and marriage is an eye-opener.*

Regardless of the unusual home environment, my parents blended well with Richard's, and the communications were smooth as one could expect during the first visit with future in-laws. My parents either ignored the shrine in the living room or were oblivious to the contrasts between our two family's lifestyles.

No one mentioned this major difference during their discussion.

They only spoke of the commonalities between the two families. They did not discuss the two of us being a couple at all. Surprisingly, the most important item on my parent's mind was that Richard's mother was Sinhalese, similar to their heritage. Unfortunately, the elephant in the room—Richard's father's Portuguese heritage—did not surface in the conversation at all, although I had already related the details of his heritage to my parents earlier.

The meeting ended after a meal, and the families parted with the understanding that an agreement had been reached to make arrangements for a wedding.

I was very happy, and so was Richard.

How could we know their inner thoughts or anticipate any disagreements within the two families after the marriage? At their first meeting, they exhibited only love and harmony. Seemingly,

Richard's father's Portuguese heritage and religious differences within the two families had not been an issue.

Both families were excited to receive us as a married couple.

To satisfy both parties—Catholics and Buddhists—we decided to have two marriage ceremonies on the same day to conform to each religion: a morning ceremony at the Catholic Church, followed by a *Poruwa* ceremony, respecting the Buddhist practises of a Sri Lankan marriage.

It was a spectacular event for the on-lookers, but it was the longest day of my life.

After all our efforts to make everyone happy, there was no doubt in our minds that both families agreed to our union, and we had no reason to suspect future calamities. We trusted that our parents were delighted with our decision to be married.

We were young and naïve and our implicit trust would turn out to be unfounded.

Ironically, from the moment we said, "I Do," the monumental difference based on our different religious faiths sprang out like a Jack-in-a-Box to haunt us. Eventually, important decisions about how our two families should interact would be based on this single difference.

This reality was hurtful, and their decisions to argue about this difference brought disharmony and sadness to our marriage.

According to Sri Lankan culture, some financial support for the newlyweds was expected from the bride's parents. Although I had not expected such provisions from my parents, I had hoped they would come forward to support our married life, as neither of us had any sources of wealth other than our limited income as entry-level university teachers.

Instead, soon after the ceremony was over, the most alarming news was delivered to us. According to Father's account, as a punishment for not obeying my parents' instructions on who their son-in-law should be, Mother would not release any family wealth to support us as a couple.

What instructions did I not follow? Did we not receive blessings from both families? According to Father, Mother's explanation was that I had married a man who had faith in an invisible God, unlike the majority of Buddhists who did not.

In my mind, it was clear that she had found a loophole because she had no intention of parting with the family fortune, whether I married as they saw fit or not.

Mother had conspired to disown me financially after the marriage.

I firmly believe that Mother's decision had been premediated, and that decision broke my heart and made me immediately withdraw from my family. Mother held the hammer and secured the final nail on the coffin to our relationship at the most important time of my life.

Henceforth, I decided that this woman, who had given me life, could not be trusted anymore.

It was incomprehensible how either party could fail to see our strong compatibility in non-religious components such as education, common interests, and most of all, the pure physical and emotional attraction necessary for a sustainable married life. This remains a mystery to me to this day.

When I asked my parents why they agreed to our union, Mother's answer was disturbing. "We did not agree to the marriage, but since you were adamant about marrying Richard, we could not stop you." Father did not present his views, but raised concerns about our future as a family. Perhaps his hands had been tied by Mother.

Regardless of who was at fault, our marriage started with poverty and despair; we both saw an impending struggle we should expect to face in the future.

Being the youngest among four children in his family, Richard might have expected to have some support from his parents too, but his family was displeased with him as well, as he married a woman who did not have faith in God. This baffled my mind, as no one in his family had brought this subject up for discussion during our first family meeting.

They eventually offered a financial gift, although their wealth was limited. Unfortunately, that gift was not sufficient to move the needle in our financial meter, but both Richard and I were grateful for their gesture, as that was the only seed money we had to start our lives.

I thought my family was selfish and uncaring. I had feelings of abandonment that stayed with me and they were tender as an open wound for many years henceforth.

Richard and I held each other's hands and walked together to find our own wealth. But, it would take many years before we could find any. By that time, we were exhausted and remained distressed over the losses encountered along the way.

That would change my personality for good; I silently feared to hope for happiness in our marriage.

I acknowledged that I had drifted to the past while waking up to the realities in my new married life.

I slowly came to my senses while keeping my head on my small pillow, and I knew that I needed to move forward by leaving the dreadful past behind. I turned to look at Richard, and my thoughts changed when I saw how his head was buried in his pillow next to mine, and his body rested under an old cover given by his parents.

"We will make it through this difficult period, and then we will thrive," I thought. Then my mind changed again after realizing that there was no one to help us except our faith and love for each other.

I felt lost and desperate.

I sat on the bed and found that my body was covered in soot-like dirt, shredding from the roof with no ceiling to protect anyone or anything below it. Richard had the same fate. I feared that the roof might fall on us one day, crushing us beneath it.

The walls of this building were as old as the roof. Their discoloured paint was peeling like birch bark, exposing the aged brittle bricks plastered with dirt. The cracked cement floor had been neglected for many years and could not be cleaned if one would accidentally drop anything on it. It was rough and seemingly disintegrated as we watched.

A drop of rain from the old roof landed on my face.

The Monsoon season had arrived from the Bay of Bengal with relentless stormy weather. When it rained in Matara, it poured. The pounding sound of the torrential rain on the roof was daunting, as there was no ceiling to dull the sounds of the outdoors.

I felt that we would be drenched at any moment.

I had to get out of the bed to find something to protect our bed from the leaking roof. As the wind would move the old roof tiles in various directions, it was hard to predict where the leaks would come from. I found an old metal bowl in the kitchen for the current leak, but by the time I returned to the bedroom, the leak had changed from a drip to a stream. It sounded like an opened tap, hitting the metal bowl and splashing water onto everything in its vicinity.

I frantically looked for a bigger vessel, and I suddenly realized that a long, black creature was moving along the bedroom wall. I screamed when I found myself staring at a large centipede, followed by a few others. They were creepy and looked dangerous.

The heavy rain had brought the unsuspecting creatures to a shelter, which was our home.

How could these critters know that? They were as helpless as we were.

My scream woke Richard. He sat on the bed and smiled. I felt joy and comfort. He took me in his arms and warmed my chilled body. Though I knew we were poor, when Richard's arms were around me, I felt all would be well, and I wanted to believe that one day we would leave this phase of despair and emerge victoriously.

It was wishful thinking; that's all it was.

I returned to continue my efforts in protecting our bed, and now the clothes horse from the leaking roof using a variety of cups, mugs, and basins. I ran out of options after the seventh leak.

I was hungry. I walked into the kitchen and found that Richard had prepared two boiled eggs and sliced some bread. The butter dish had been kept open with a small knife next to it. A small butter puddle had covered the bottom of the dish; refrigeration was beyond our reach.

I sat at the only table we had, which served us in many different ways: the study desk to prepare undergraduate lecture notes, a kitchen table to cut or slice vegetables for steaming, and as the dining table.

We sat facing each other and started our breakfast with happy thoughts. We felt at home and happy to be in our own place, no matter how rustic, old, and frowzy it was. When we finished breakfast, we felt that we were in a luxury hotel at a beach resort because we were content and filled with joy.

Yet, in the next few seconds, this situation dramatically changed.

I sensed that some creature had climbed on my foot, and I felt tingles. Richard quickly investigated and found a large scorpion.

Based on its enormity, it was sitting on both our feet, which we had kept in close proximity to one another.

I was dizzy with fear as scorpions are known to be venomous. The rain continued to hammer the weak roof, delivering a message of danger from above in addition to what lay on our feet. We knew that our voices would be drowned by the rain and help from our neighbour would not be possible.

We decided to give the power to the arachnid: we sat calmly and motionless until it would decide to move. Any movement could have triggered fear in the creature, which would have instigated an attack on us for its defence.

Unfortunately, the scorpion had a nap on our warm feet and only decided to move when the rain ceased.

Sitting in the same position for a lengthy period of time made our muscles stiff, but it was better than being stung by the venomous arachnid. After the scorpion left, we held each other for comfort, not knowing what the next challenge would be.

We did not have to wait too long for the answer.

In September, with the hopes of cultivating a good relationship with Richard's family, we decided to visit them to celebrate my birthday. We arrived on a Friday night and had a pleasant dinner while sharing news of our new life together. After dinner, Richard's mother wished me a happy birthday and presented me with a small, boxed gift. With Richard's assurance, I opened it immediately.

It was a pink rosary, which held a beautiful cross.

I looked at it with amazement as I had no idea what it was or what was expected of me. After accepting her gift, I looked at Richard, whose face was flushed. His father kept silent. Richard tried to explain what it was, and his mother interrupted his efforts.

"This is presented to you as a gift from above, for you to hold when you pray to God every evening," she said.

I looked at Richard with surprised eyes, and he was silent as the grave.

"Thank you for your thoughtful gift, but I am not a Catholic, and I do not believe that I should be converted to your religion just to fulfil your expectation. As you already knew, I was brought up as a Buddhist, and that will be my faith for the rest of my life." I responded to clarify my thoughts.

"Now that you are married to Richard, it may be better if you would become a Catholic," she was relentless in her assertions.

Richard responded. "Perhaps we should give her some space to make up her own mind. That way, it will be her decision. After all, religion is a personal matter, and no one should enforce that on another."

That conversation had a lasting adverse effect on my relationship with Richard's mother.

She spoke to me the next day and asked me why I had never thought of reading the Bible. I felt extremely uncomfortable. Unfortunately, at that moment, I lost any respect I had for her.

It was incomprehensible why she did not understand that her gesture was like handing a book written by Pushkin in Russian to a prisoner who was only literate in English. A teacher in an incomprehensible form!

That would be counterproductive, would it not?

By the time we returned to Matara, I had raised many questions about how the differences in our religious practices could affect the future of our marriage. Richard, however, consoled me, stating that he had no expectations for me to change my views and that he felt confident I would adopt a similar approach towards his faith. I could only speculate how well this agreement would work if we were fortunate to have a family of our own.

Then an unexpected moment arrived with a glimmer of hope for our future.

In October, I had conceived our first child. Richard praised and thanked the Lord for his gift to us while I hoped that the child would be healthy.

We were united forever.

We felt fortunate and optimistic and started planning for our future as a family. Our outlook changed: we began anticipating rainbows and pretty flowers after enduring only harsh realities since our wedding. We envisioned the dawn of a better future.

Yet, we could not envision what was looming on the horizon; Mother had been waiting to cross our paths with vengeance. Our lives were about to change forever.

I felt it as a nod from fate.

CHAPTER 14

A *M*IRACLE

There was nothing unusual about the morning of the 8th of July of 19.., except the excruciating pain I felt in my belly and how fruitless my efforts had been to relieve it. Since the previous evening, I had been in and out of pain, and felt like I was on a physical and an emotional rollercoaster ride.

Yet, as a first-time mother-to-be, that day I had witnessed a miracle. But, Mother had dismissed my precious moment in life; she had not written anything about it in her journal.

After spending twenty-some years on Earth, I could not recall having been disconnected from living until that day. I felt dismayed because I had no control over the movements of my own body.

I wished that I could be fearless of losing control, and that some other power had taken over me but I had one option: renunciation. Resisting what was upon me was not a choice, and a nudge from the universe signalled my purpose of being a woman and my responsibility for humanity: bring a new life to the world.

I had reached a moment of knowing and reckoning.

A few days before, we had arrived from Matara to Colombo, as Richard's family had selected a hospital close to home—St. Michael's nursing home—for the birth of our first child with the due date of July 10th. By the time we reached Colombo, I had progressed well, reaching the full-term, and had grown into a large ball, which severely restricted the movements of my body.

Three days before the due date, Richard took me for a walk along the popular Galle-Face beach promenade to help me to relax and exercise. After a long stroll, I remember experiencing a bumpy ride on a bus. Having only a few passengers made the bus rock-and-roll on poorly paved roads.

The high humidity in the air made my body convulse, and the rough bus ride changed all of our birthing plans on the expected date.

After alighting from the bus, we walked along the grassy path to Richard's parent's home. I dragged myself, hoping to reach home quickly. That was not easy.

I could not see my toes, as the belly had grown large. Finally, I was happy to see the dim light on the veranda. Richard's parent's dog Flash looked at us from the parapet wall where he had been perched. He briskly got up to greet us. He had the habit of meeting us with excitement every time we approached, as if it was his undying duty.

It was a delightful distraction.

By the time we had reached the entrance to the home, I was wrung out and exhausted. My breasts were painful, and my large belly prevented me from lifting my legs far enough to climb the few steps to the house.

Suddenly, an unusual pain in my stomach made me scream.

Richard led me to the bed. He assured me that it was nothing I should worry about, but he was wrong. I had much to worry about. Seemingly, I was going into labour two days before my due date.

Later, I surmised that the bumpy ride in the bus might have signalled my baby to emerge sooner to avoid internal turbulence that could harm its restful living environment. I concluded that my baby must have had their instincts sharpened while cuddled in my womb.

Misunderstanding the periodic stomach pain, I was in and out of the toilet all through the night. The sleepless night made me groggy and weak at dawn, and by that time, it was obvious that I needed medical attention.

I realized that the reservation at the nursing home was only for two days later—I had nowhere to go. I knew that it was time to panic, as I was uncertain whether another vacancy would be available for the delivery. Because of the commotion around me to take me to a doctor, I did not want to alert Richard.

His elder brother Ben, who lived at home with his parents, appeared at the scene and was bewildered by the unusual activities. Ben had a healthy build and a kind disposition. Although he was the best man at our wedding, who presented me with my bouquet just before walking down the aisle, he hadn't spoken a single word to me since that day.

Seemingly, silence runs among the men in this family.

With time, I learned that Ben had an accident as a young boy and had suffered from a serious concussion, and as a result, he had difficulty maintaining balance in his thoughts. To me though, he was the most sensible person in that family. He had accepted me for who I was, and his approach towards me had been decent and caring. Ben had been a loyal and helpful man to his only brother and me until his premature death.

After I went into labour that July morning, recognizing the time of need, Ben had boldly come forward to help. I had the most difficult time walking during my labour pains, and when he suggested that he would carry me to the car, I showed no resistance.

I remember how Ben picked me up with his arms, much like cradling a fragile doll, and laid me on the backseat of a car with great care. That was all I could remember. I had passed out. I woke up a few minutes later, overhearing a loud discussion between Richard and the receptionist at the St. Michael's Nursing Home.

In Sri Lanka, public healthcare was free, but maternity wards were extremely crowded; expecting privacy would be unwise. Based on that understanding, Richard's family had chosen the reasonably priced, privately run St. Michael's Nursing Home for the delivery.

"I am sorry, sir, we do not have a reservation until Thursday, July 10th; you will have to find another maternity hospital," the receptionist had informed Richard. I could only imagine his panic at that moment. But Richard kept himself calm and had persuaded the receptionist to find another local nursing home with a vacancy.

We had no choice but to head out to the nursing home that was willing to take me in. The car moved ever so slowly out of St. Michael's.

The early morning air was sharp as always. I profusely perspired while Richard held my hand, a small comfort to endure the gut-wrenching pain in my belly.

I felt tightness in my chest and sadness, bringing a flow of blurry tears because of the trouble Richard had to undergo at this eleventh hour, but I tried to keep my mind at ease. The sun was streaming down through the car windows and heating every conceivable item in it, making my current surroundings unbearably hot and humid.

At that moment, for some unknown reason, I observed my pain clearly and saw it as being connected to living and loving. That idea was new.

I realized that I would no longer be alone on this earth.

A new life would walk with me. The pain then turned to joy, as I felt the tightness being lifted, and my heart opened wide, filling my chest with golden warmth. That fleeting moment was magical, and it gave me clarity and maturity, reminding me of the deep significance of life.

It was enlightening!

We arrived after a stressful ride through the busy streets of Colombo. The first view of the Cinnamon Gardens Maternity Hospital was unforgettable. Although I was about to deliver a baby and my body was changing by the minute in preparation, I felt like I was about to meet the queen in her castle.

It was a mansion compared to all the houses I had been to; it looked like a beautiful model home. The steps to the entrance shone like silver, and the borders of the garden bloomed like garlands. The front door was adorned with climbing vines of pink and purple bougainvillea flowers. The windows looked clean and bright like diamonds. The magnificent view was breathtaking.

I wondered which wealthy Sri Lankan family owned this home.

I came to know later that this nursing home was the most prestigious one in town. Only the wealthy in Sri Lanka had the privilege to deliver a child at this home. We had been fortunate to find a vacancy here, though no one could see what was to come after delivering a baby at this high-end private hospital.

It would be the first of many disappointments in my married life thus far.

After recovering from another crushing pain, a sudden revelation flashed in my mind! The baby I was about to deliver might be someone who had the predisposition to embrace wealth, because this was not the first time we had encountered a sudden good fortune after I had become pregnant.

In October, we were going through a difficult time with our home in Matara.

Pregnancy had made it more difficult to bear the discomfort of that house, being surrounded by dirt and undesirable critters visiting the premises more frequently than before. When I had developed morning-sickness, Richard had been frantically looking for a cleaner place to live, but nothing had surfaced.

Almost every day, my life had changed rapidly along with my body: the seven-minute walk to the university now felt arduously long. Eating corn sprouted stomach cramps. During sleep, my large belly—without my knowledge—had to be positioned to avoid crushing the baby, leading to morning neck stains and uncomfortable bowel movements.

The visiting creatures needed to be eliminated from the premises using awful, strong-smelling chemicals, which made me anxious about my baby's health and prevented me from relaxing when at home.

Most of all, I felt like a victim of a wrongful conviction who needed answers to why I had to pass through this difficult life. Although the suffering was great, I was willing to endure anything for the sake of our child, and I was determined to carry my baby to full-term.

Then, to our greatest surprise, when November arrived with cooler air and a different set of critters to invade our home, Mother informed us that she would find a woman to take care of our cooking and cleaning. Indeed, we were ever so grateful for her suggestion.

Unfortunately, when the woman arrived later that month, it was a great disappointment to both of us, as she was nearly seventy-five years old and could not do much physical work around the house. Mother's thinking process was a puzzle; but then again, Mother's thought processes never made sense to me.

Our home did not have water on tap, only a very deep backyard well. Everyone had to draw water in a bucket attached to a rope for personal use. There was no pulley system to support the draw. By that time, I was nowhere in a position to pull up the water; I had to depend on the woman to help me. After watching her try hard to complete this task, I had to wonder whether we might find her at the bottom of the well one day.

She tried her best, and that was sufficient.

Her cooking enabled us to have a meal at the end of every workday, which was wonderful. She was a loving woman and a Grandmother, and her empathy towards us was memorable. We called her Ammé, as she was like a mother to both of us.

Ammé had several admirable qualities. She was a deep scrubber and a corner cleaner, yet the home she constantly cleaned did not respond well to her efforts. It was too old, and I believed it had been occupied by the spirits of a long list of humans who had lived and perhaps had died in the premises since its inception a century ago.

At times, I felt that the whole house was alive and had eyes everywhere. I also felt that there were people behind the only door inside the house, which separated the room from the kitchen, just ready to come out if we would look away.

That spooky feeling made my skin crawl.

One day, I heard two crackling blasts right next to our bed while I was taking an afternoon nap. Ammé had been in the kitchen. She ran to me when she heard my scream, but she would not come close to the bed after I explained the reason for my fear.

She stressed that she did not have the strength to fight off a ghost, but she would crush a snake with her bare hands if that threatened either one of us. She was frightened, she was cold, non-comical, and was white as a sheet.

Only a whisper came out of her mouth.

"Let's go to the kitchen; I could make some hot tea for you," she said. Since then, she refused to enter the room, even to clean it. I had no choice but to take up the cleaning job for her.

It had been a difficult period in our lives, and we both had wished for a change.

Then, soon after the end of my first trimester, the universe saw the need for my baby to live in a safer environment. One Sunday morning, the parish priest of the local Catholic Church contacted Richard to inform him that the church house facing the beach could be ours rent-free. In lieu, the church suggested any donations for the occupancy—what a stroke of luck!

In December, we moved to the new location with our limited belongings and Ammé.

After passing through a difficult life at the old annex, it was like living in a luxury home on the beach: it had water on tap, a water tank for bathing and washing, and most of all it was completely free of unwanted critters.

Perhaps the universe had presented us with a fortunate child who would bring glory days to our little family; much later in the future, my sentiments on this matter would be proven right.

We were grateful.

The voice of a very gentle man, Doctor Nanayakkara, my gynecologist, brought me back to reality. He had arrived on time for the delivery. Richard assured me that I was in good hands.

I was gently placed on a stretcher, and someone carefully rolled it along a corridor. Though I had periodic episodes of insanity due to intense labour pains, I was able to get my bearings.

It was fascinating to view the interior of this prestigious nursing home. All manner of furniture adorned the hallway. Pictures of tall ships, beautiful women, and dreamy landscapes of lakes and oceans were hung upon the walls in golden frames. It created a calm, peaceful, and joyful environment. *What a great camouflage,* I thought.

What I was about to face might need a soothing precursor to leave my mind at peace. I was right. The pain returned with a vengeance to eclipse all that was pretty. I had lost my sanity again in the wonderful surroundings.

I had come to my senses when the pain had subsided. I had been taken to the delivery room, where I woke up facing a large group of strangers. As a general rule in Sri Lanka, only medical staff would be allowed in the delivery room.

I had felt fear, and I needed Mother, but she was nowhere to be found.

Mother had refused to come to Colombo until the delivery, stating that the baby would not come before the due date. She always found ways to make her life comfortable. I wondered whether she would come to visit me. I felt abandoned.

Yet, the universe kept sending me messages: this is your responsibility. You have all the tools you need, and you do not need an uncaring mother. I concurred.

I was in a blur, and my mind could not think due to the pain.

For support, I had held onto the hand of a near-by nurse. Later I learned that I crushed the fingers of that nurse during each episode of intense pain. I was embarrassed, although I had intended to hold on to something to bear the pain. I heard that she had to be medicated to relieve the pain in her swollen fingers.

I heard voices around me, and someone questioned, "Would she need an epidural?"

Who are these people? I questioned myself. A gloved hand touched mine. I opened my eyes, hoping to recognize the person, but a mask had covered their face. I gave up.

"Would you like to take the epidural?" The question had been directed to me this time. Before I could understand the question—as I did not know what an epidural was—I blacked out.

The pain had engulfed my body and my mind, and I had floated and landed in another place.

"Mother, is that you?" I called out.

I was seated on a mat, hands folded, and sweat dripped from my forehead. I wondered whether I could lean far over and whisper to the woman that I saw at a distance, but then, what I would whisper was a question.

"Mother, why are you not sitting next to me?"

"You were a wanted child," a voice responded. *What does that mean?* I wondered.

I peeled my eyes towards the voice, but I could not clearly see the floating figure. The hazy air swirled around me and air smelled of spices, much like those that Grandmother used in her sweetmeats. A warm hand nudged me.

"There is no time for the epidural because the baby would have a natural birth. Don't worry. All will go well." It was the same soothing voice of the male I had heard before. I had come back to Earth. I had my duties listed out. It was time, I was informed.

"Breathe, breathe, push, push," someone chanted. I obeyed. Someone had wiped my forehead with a damp cloth. I had lost my mind again and the routine continued, for how long, I did not know.

A gentle and soothing cry of a baby brought me back to reality.

"Professor, you have a baby boy," the same male spoke again, "it is very good news, he has all the fingers and toes, and he is very healthy." Throughout our visits, Dr. Nanayakkara had called me professor because of my occupation.

The universe had given me the greatest gift of all: motherhood.

I had woken up to face a new world; I had cried tears of joy. A new healthy life had joined us. I had fulfilled my duties as a woman. Soon after, I had passed out, this time as if I would never wake up. It was a deep sleep without any interruptions, and I did not have any dreams; it was the ultimate peace.

I had woken up on a comfortable bed in a quiet room and had waited for a second to see whether my belly pain would return. It did not. The crowd of people had left, and I had no more pushing to do. Gentle light streamed through the curtained windows; a small vase with beautiful, tropical flowers sat next to the bed on a wooden table.

I must have died and gone to heaven, I thought.

Then, I felt extremely uncomfortable because my body had been injured. Seemingly, some damage had happened during childbirth. I was stiff and aching, and I could not move without a groan. I was groggy because of the pain medications; I decided to keep my eyes closed. My body needed healing and recuperation.

I desperately needed to express my feelings to Mother.

Perhaps I felt grateful for the efforts that she might have had endured to bring me to life, but she was not there. Tears rolled down my face with extreme sadness.

Suddenly, the door opened, and a nurse entered the room. She carried a small bundle cradled in her arms. A small head with a visible crop of jet-black hair peeked out of the bundle.

"Your son is ready for feeding," she said with a wide smile.

I smiled with enthusiasm. I had forgotten my pains and my sorrows. I had much to celebrate. Who would care about any damages done to the body? Never mind the difficult life that awaited me. I needed to forget about my missing mother, because the universe had entrusted me to take care of a new life, acknowledging my abilities as a mother.

The nurse had kept the warm bundle close to my body. I looked at the little face of our baby for the first time. It was pure joy. He kept his eyes closed and was fast asleep. I was not surprised, he might have felt tremendous exhaustion after entering this world, as much as the great efforts I had taken to perform my universal duties.

Gautama Buddha had described childbirth as "an elephant pushing itself through a wedding ring on a finger." I agreed.

Indeed, the life-long suffering would start for a newborn with this unavoidable pain at birth. I looked at his little face and believed there would be much more suffering that we would endure together.

The sight and the warmth of our son filled me with pride and nourished my weary-burdened body, which enabled me to stay in the moment and embrace the miracle of birth.

Then the moment of realization arrived: no other human should usurp my maternal responsibilities entrusted by the universe. This child is my responsibility, and I had the right to defend myself if anyone tried to take my baby away from me.

The universe would protect our rights.

Unfortunately, such trust placed in the universe was misplaced. Even before I could fulfill my duties as a young mother, others within my extended family interfered with the natural progression of bonding between my child and me.

The universe had teased me with the cruellest sentiments.

Suddenly, the baby awoke with unbelievable expressions. Although his eyes were closed, his face started to explore for a possible food source: Mother's milk. His instincts were remarkable. His little face had pressed deeply into my tender breasts; the quick movements of his face landed his little mouth on my nipple. It was unbelievable how my body reacted to his needs, like a fountain of water springing into the air on a warm summer day to cool its surroundings.

I had been waiting for this naturally dutiful and pleasant experience.

My body had all that was needed to nourish his little body, and it was all that I had wanted; his life needing mine. From the moment his warm lips touched my body for nourishment, he had roped me in to keep the umbilical cord virtually wrapped around my little finger for the rest of his life.

We were one life, in two different bodies.

Richard had entered the room with hopeful eyes to embrace our son. He had washed his hands several times to ensure that our baby would be protected from any germs. He had bent over and carried our son with tenderness.

"We need to name him. Any thoughts of a suitable one?" he inquired.

"When I saw his face for the first time, the name that came to my mind was Sumudu. He had a very pleasant face; perhaps that was the reason," I responded.

"I will also give him a Christian name, James," Richard suggested.

We hoped that he would like both names we had given him. Both were registered on his birth certificate.

Our family members had started to emerge soon after: his paternal grandparents, his great uncle Philip, his aunty Ramona, followed by my parents. I did not see Brother or Ben in the room, which had saddened me very much.

Without a doubt, Mother's visit had been the most memorable and alarming.

This was the first time I had seen Mother after she had fiscally disowned me. She walked in with Father as if she had been around the world and back. Then, she flopped on the nearest chair and did not want to stand up to visit my baby or me. Instead, she started complaining, pointing out to those who were present that she had a difficult ride to arrive at Colombo, and needed rest. No one spoke. Everyone looked at me with wide eyes.

I looked at Father, and as usual, he had to defend Mother's behaviour.

Who could imagine a grandmother would be so selfish that she did not wish to embrace her first grandchild? Only Mother could be that uncaring and selfish. To me, Mother's neglect felt like a kick on my child's gut. However, as a new mother the universe had accepted me to take care of her child; that was significant to me.

I accepted Mother's behaviour with sympathy towards her loss.

Father, on the other hand, had reached my bedside slowly and had peeked into his little face while making his own loving remarks. After that, he had been rather concerned about my physical condition and how I could care for the baby.

It had been recorded many times in many ways that no other love in the world is greater than a father's love for his little girl. That day, Father had been successful in proving all related famous quotes. His genuine love for our well-being had been like a cleansing balm to an open wound.

Five days had gone by. I had rested as much as I could at the nursing home to prepare myself to look after my newborn. I had known that it would be a great responsibility.

Mother had been forced to live with me during those few days, although she complained and grumbled throughout the whole time. *I am tired. I need a break, is there anyone else who could take a turn?* I had ignored all that, but I felt I would have been better off without her as my caretaker.

It must have been hard for Mother as she never had motherly instincts towards me as a child. How could I anticipate her to grow such instincts for her first grandson?

The time had arrived to leave the hospital. Richard had come early to take care of the transfer. Soon after came the most embarrassing moment of my life.

A large hospital bill had been presented to Richard for immediate payment.

The change of the delivery date, which led to choosing this high-end nursing home at the eleventh hour, had led us to this unexpected burden. Who should we blame? Our baby was destined to be born at this prestigious hospital. We had no control over his destiny but to bear the burden of his predisposition for greater comfort and prestige.

We looked at each other, wondering how we could pay, because we knew we did not have enough money to cover the total cost. I had choked on my sadness while holding my son close to me; I burst into tears. I never imagined that after the universe had presented me with this great gift, it could bring me to my knees with desperation.

Richard stepped aside to review the bill more closely; he found that it was much more than what was anticipated based on the estimate provided by St. Michael's Nursing Home.

Like a stone statue, Mother had looked over the events that were unfolding.

She showed no emotions. Mother's journal revealed an alarming fact, which later clarified her strange behaviour: *My anger towards my daughter was born out of my sense of loss of control over my own life.* Seemingly, she always had reasons to disregard me as her daughter.

The revelation of this strange statement about her life had been scribed in the last few pages of her journal, as would be the case in this narrative. This stated loss that she endured might have created a woman with no emotions towards anyone.

The hospital staff stood around with puzzled looks. One nurse had come forward to comfort me. I had cried with self-pity. Richard could not find any words to explain our inability to pay the total bill.

Then, to our greatest comfort, Father came forward with his generosity. His gesture had angered Mother greatly, but because the hospital-staff was sympathizing with us, she might have held her tongue. I could see her wheels turning to develop a devious plan to attack Father at the very first moment she would be alone with him.

"Thank you for your help, but we will pay back all of it as soon as we can," Richard interjected. Father refused Richard's offer.

Finally, as we were saying goodbye, one nurse approached and whispered in my ear, "Usually, the new family would treat the staff, offering them a grand lunch, but I could understand that you do not have the means for that."

Was it necessary for this nurse to insult me? My tears poured down my face, wetting the tiny face of our son. He still did not open his eyes; he kept sleeping in my arms. I was happy, because our son deserved respect and dignity. I kept this incident a secret well into the future.

Nobody, especially not my immediate family, deserved such a burden.

We had left the nursing home with heavy hearts, a hefty debt, and a bundle of joy. The irony would have viewed us with shameful glamour.

That was the beginning of a stream of insults and episodes of fiscal and emotional starvation. When all was said and done, I would lose everything and everyone I cared to have in my life. Our world would turn upside-down.

Mother had been the front and center in all that had unfolded. She enjoyed her life with a vengeance, and the hate she meted out was enormous.

Mother had not scribed a single word in her journal about the birth of our son, her first grandchild; it made me very sad. Only after reading the last pages of her journal, I was able to fathom her emotionless behaviour on that important day.

In the coming days, Mother would make many cruel decisions to make my life miserable. But she had no inkling of what *she* would lose in the future because of her selfish decisions.

CHAPTER 15

$\mathscr{T}$HE $\mathscr{B}$EGINNING OF THE $\mathscr{E}$ND

When Richard and I left the hospital with our newborn baby, I had no idea that a devious plan to destroy my happiness as a new mother was in progress. Seemingly, Mother had planted the seeds for that plan even before I had become a wife.

In the coming days, those seeds would sprout rapidly and grow into a thick forest that obstructed my life in the most unimaginable way.

Naturally, as a new mother, I had started to dream of our wonderful future as a family, but Mother ensured it would be a hollow dream.

The wrath of Mother's wicked mind would be felt deeply.

During the period Richard and I had been in Colombo for the birth of our son, Ammé willingly took care of our home in Matara. Yet, because of the uncertainty of a return day, we suggested that Ammé should reunite with her family in Kaduwela. In a letter written by her daughter, Ammé had expressed her distress experienced after departing.

I never had the opportunity to meet her again; she had passed away within a few months after leaving us.

Based on the events that would unfold since the childbirth, we could not return to our home in Martara. Eventually, our personal items were removed from the premises. To thank the Parrish Priest for his kindness, our charitable donation was sent by mail.

Seemingly, the universe had a mysterious plan for our future.

While carrying my baby in my arms, we arrived at Richard's parents' home on a hot and humid day. Richard held the door to a room that had been assigned for our family. It had been filled with items that belonged to the rest of his family, but it was large enough to hold a bed for all three of us, a clothes horse, and a small cupboard to store our clean clothes.

A new life as a mother had arrived.

As one would anticipate, it was daunting to begin with to have the responsibility to take care of another life. The exhaustion after giving birth was unimaginable and the lack of rest because of humidity and heat in Colombo had added stress to my weakened body. The only consolation was that the baby was very healthy and he slept through most nights giving me a chance to rest.

I had decided to take one day at a time to get accustomed to this new life.

Yet, since then, unexpected events would unfold, resulting in dramatic changes to the circumstances surrounding our lives; my life would never be the same.

The morning after I had returned from the hospital, I woke up drenched in sweat while listening to the sound of a buzzing old table fan that struggled to keep the air cool. Seemingly, the fan blades had become caked with dust mixed in with the humid air. The heavy blades could have fallen off the base at any given moment; they needed to be cleaned, but I was too tired to try.

I slowly blew on the little head of my infant son, who slept next to me on my pillow. Regardless of the heat and humidity, my baby slept with ease.

Apparently, Richard had left home early that morning to start his work back at the university. He had decided to commute each day from Colombo. He did not say goodbye to us; perhaps he did not wish to wake me after the difficulties I had faced during childbirth.

I was left alone to take care of the baby.

I realized that I needed to feed the baby, but I needed to feed myself first. I hoped that someone would bring me food, and I waited for a long time. Suddenly, carrying a small tray, Richard's mother Milly entered the room. My smile would have indicated how grateful I was to see her bringing my breakfast.

Milly was a woman who had been responsible for the family home and its occupants. She ensured that her family was safe and they would be fed on time. Every day she lit a lamp at alter in her sitting room and one at the back of the home in an alcove made into the rocky wall, that bordered the property line. With that, she would have hoped to bring fortune, good health, and peace to her family.

She regularly cooked meals and cleaned the home from top to bottom.

One night, I found her in the bathroom scrubbing the toilet at midnight when all the others were fast asleep. Unfortunately, she had expected me to help her with her duties, and she was undoubtedly disappointed when I would not comply with her rules. I wanted to help her, but because I had never been trained to do household work, I was not confident to take over her duties.

She had been a gentle soul who was kind with loving expressions to all, including me. One time, during my pregnancy, she had decided to comb my long hair, which fell below my calf muscles. While doing that, she blessed me and her expected grandchild a million times. I let her practice her religion as she pleased because I did not see any harm with her good thoughts.

But that morning, the food she brought for me had expressed her true feelings about me with crystal clarity.

She left the tray on the bed and sat on a chair next to it. She then peeked into my baby's face and made cooing sounds although he was fast asleep. She looked at me through her thick eyeglasses and smiled. I was happy that she was in a good mood.

But I eagerly waited for her to settle down because I was famished.

Finally, I looked at the food on the tray; the sight of those items made me cry: a dried, unbuttered piece of bread; a small overripe banana; a cup of plain tea, and a bottle of Marmite with a knife left inside the bottle. I looked into the bottle, and it was empty. Could this be a suitable breakfast for a breastfeeding mother? My heart sank with sorrow, but I had no one to ask for anything more. I burst into tears.

She ignored my reaction to her offerings and left the room.

I tried to understand why she had decided to present me an unsuitable breakfast on that first morning in their home.

According to Buddhist teachings, feeding the hungry is considered a meritorious act. I wondered what Christ had taught his followers in this regard. Why she would not follow her instincts to feed a hungry new mother was unclear to me.

I would later learn the truth about Milly's unpardonable behaviour. It was because Mother had disregarded the traditional practices in Sri Lanka to either gift money or useful items to her only daughter in her marriage.

With that intentional neglect by Mother, cascading events had started to unfold, and none would bring positivity to anyone's life.

According to Richard's account, his parents had high hopes for him to get educated and marry a woman of the Catholic faith. His decision to marry me had shattered those family dreams, yet, they all agreed to our union.

It was not my fault that I was not their "dream bride." Their blame towards me was misplaced.

Since I hardly had time to learn about Richard's heritage before marriage, I needed to refresh my knowledge on this subject to understand the behaviour of his family towards me. To my disadvantage, such knowledge came to light only after I had endured many painful episodes of distressful encounters with his parents.

Several years later, I had a lengthy discussion with Richard about this time in our lives, and the details he revealed were enlightening, though that was too little and too late.

Richard's father was of Portuguese descent; this was not a secret to anyone in my family. Yet, after our marriage, his decent had been taken into account by Mother in a most bizarre manner; she had used these known facts to her advantage.

Accordingly to the history of the Island, Portuguese travellers had landed in Sri Lanka in 1505, with the hopes of capturing the Island to teach the Catholic faith to the Buddhist natives. Naturally, the ruling king had resisted their assertions. Since then, the Portuguese had been viewed as invaders. As they had been unsuccessful in capturing the Island, they had been aggressive and cruel to the natives.

While the Portuguese rulers were ruthless and used force to convert the locals to Catholics, the descendants in the 20th century had no lineage to them. Regardless, they were despised by the Sinhala majority for the transgressions of the original invaders since 1505. Based on these unpleasant experiences, the Sinhalese on the Island had rejected any alliance to the decedents of the Portuguese.

For over centuries, the past continued to haunt the Portuguese living in Sri Lanka. Even today, the disadvantage of being of foreign descendant, or being married to one, is apparent in the country. Learning about Richard's father's heritage and its impact had brought clarity to some of the unexpected reactions I received from his parents.

During his younger days, Richard's father and mother constantly found ways to shield their children from racial bias. For example, Richard's father had been adamant that all his children study in Sinhala, which was the country's only official language during that time. His parents' efforts had helped Richard, and his siblings overcome hindrances from the Sinhalese and dodge the disadvantages.

Unfortunately, being Portuguese, his father faced many forms of discrimination and deep-seated bias that adversely affected his life. Yet, he arose from it all to retire as a high school principal at the leading Catholic Boys' School in Sri Lanka.

I hadn't the slightest idea that marrying Richard would attract negativity towards me simply because of his heritage, and rightfully his family name. Yet, there it was. Seemingly, since my marriage, I was also viewed as a traitor among Sinhalese Buddhists.

By understanding Richard's heritage, I could sympathize with his family. Yet, I could not justify Mother's actions towards me based on this knowledge, as both families were aware of the status of each other when we tied the knot.

We did not blindside them.

From the moment I entered Richard's parent's home as a new bride, there were millions of little hints thrown at me, mostly by Milly, to let me know that I had arrived with empty hands after 'capturing' Richard. From their point of view, I had planned to secure a better and privileged life through marriage. That notion was far from the truth because I had the same level of education and was in the profession as Richard.

I firmly believed that my education would have allowed me to earn enough money to survive without any support from an external source. Yet, I had no evidence to prove that I was not a pauper who had been looking for someone else's fortune.

There were several incidents where Milly boldly questioned why my parents did not help us by providing useful items such as bed linens and towels. She once asked about the furniture my parents would deliver to our new home, if we were to secure a place in Matara. During those question periods, she did not hesitate to point out that she had provided us with bedroom furniture. What could I say to her? It should have been obvious that I had no control over my parent's decisions.

I wondered: why did my parent give their blessings to our union but did not help us as a married couple?

Strangely, Mother had decided to save her family fortune to hand it over to her son instead of sharing it between Brother and me. She had conveniently used Richard's heritage as a reason not to share the family wealth; she did not wish to support a foreign invader!

I could not have predicted her plan before I married Richard, and I felt that I was not treated fairly by my family. The realization of their betrayal had been devastating.

Unfortunately, Mother's decision affirmed the theory tabled by my in-laws; the notion of me being a gold-digger. Her plan to instigate a rift between me and Richard's family was successful and would eventually crush my happiness in my marriage.

All in all, I realized that Mother had planned to make me feel as if I was standing on quicksand in my marriage; I had to walk on shaky grounds, always expecting to disappear into oblivion.

Milly's provision of an unacceptable breakfast was the last straw. I needed to take action to get fed to nourish the baby. I slowly got out of bed and looked for Richard's father. I found him in the veranda, reading the daily newspaper.

"Could you help me contact my brother?" I asked.

"What seems to be the problem? Could I be of any help?" he inquired.

"I need to eat before feeding the baby," I responded.

He immediately walked in to find his wife, wondering why my breakfast had been delayed. Out of respect to his wife, he did not examine the evidence of her misdeed. Instead, he asked her to feed me. Although she eventually provided me with some suitable food, I felt she had clearly exhibited her opinion of me.

That was the beginning of a torturous path Richard's family took to ensure that I would suffer because of Mother's neglect.

Then, something unfathomable and sorrowful started to infold. The point-of-no-return was about to arrive in my life.

From the start, I felt that our lives while in Sri Lanka could never be happy. No one came forward to help us. Both families tried to wreak our marriage.

Ultimately, Mother's decision to withhold the family fortune would force Richard to search for other avenues to support his new family.

Yet, what Richard planned to do would lose my trust in him for the rest of our married life. I would start to understand the predicament I had been placed in, yet it was too late.

Naturally, Richard's family would support his pursuits whole-heartedly. How could I blame them? Yet, in those efforts, they all have forgotten about the future of our little family.

The after-effects of Mother's irrational and cruel decisions would be revealed through Richard's efforts to find ways to support his new family; the outcome was unbearable.

Mother had made the wrong decision, and she would soon feel the negative effects of her own making.

The tragic outcome of Mother's cruel decision: I lost every conceivable important facet of my life, and most of all, the privilege to bring up my son as a family with Richard.

I wondered why the universe did not step in to save us from this impending tragedy. Perhaps bad Karma gathered from my past lives and those of our son had surfaced?

The downfall would be inevitable.

CHAPTER 16

Sophie's Choice

This was how I was forced to drown.

After giving birth to our son, Mother's plan to control my life took a new direction, which had unanticipated disastrous effects on all our lives.

Since I had married Richard, I sensed several willful hands coaxing me to the deepest end of a body of dark, murky water. I felt that my moves were being monitored to see how I would survive. Mother was the strongest force; a few others systematically followed her.

I had to design a new plan to come out of the deepest ditch she had created for me. I recognize now that I must have had a strong belief in myself; neither Mother nor those who followed her knew the power that surged through me to survive.

For a long while, I saw the world before me as a cattle trail with heavy dust; unclear and bleak. How did I come up for air? Indeed, with all of my strength, my unwavering will, and my built-in resilience.

I had to climb mountains and pass through fires that burnt my spirit. I had struggled through illnesses, had lost my way several times, and had to travel in darkness, only guided by my instincts. I would endure many hardships for more than ten years before I would finally experience the elusive light.

Then, I would feel like Danté re-entering civilization as the *Count of Monte Cristo*.

The year I had witnessed the miracle of childbirth, Sri Lanka was a peaceful country. It had natural beauty, an endless summer, and all that I had considered good.

The land was rich, enamelled with tea plantations and dotted with magnificent temples. It was a country of simplicity, a paradise many Europeans desired, and many locals had enjoyed for centuries. There were no cycles of seasons to detect any changes in human behaviours. Except for a few sporadic incidents of unrest among the youth, all inhabitants lived in harmony.

Therefore, leaving this wonderful country had never once crossed my mind.

In November, however, only one year and four months of marriage, unusual events lined up that would force me to leave the bosom of my motherland. The direction of my future was beyond my comprehension and control.

In a matter of days, I lost the two things I had valued the most: all the achievements I had gained up until that time and the person who needed me the most—my infant son.

On the 26th of November 19.., I sat on a cold bench in an unfamiliar building—an airport—surrounded by many strangers. On that cold November day, I had landed in a country that I had only seen on a map—Canada. The day I arrived, I would learn, was their first major snowstorm of the year.

Looking across a sea of people, I could see many pale faces and others with different shapes, sizes, and skin colours. Some did not notice me, some viewed me with surprised eyes, some were openly insolent, and some were mildly interested. I was petrified. I needed to find my bearings.

I took a vacant seat close to where I entered the lounge.

Richard disappeared into the crowd after asking me to sit for a while. I found it hard to keep my eyes open because I had not slept for more than twenty-four hours. My mind was foggy, and so were my eyes. I was exhausted beyond my capacity, but I needed to keep my eyes opened to get myself acquainted with my new surroundings.

I started to notice various activities around me. Some travellers were rushing out while clutching their travel bags. Some were wearing woollen hats and long, heavy coats and moved with their heads held high. There were choruses of screaming babies. A man with a loud voice directed the crowd to a swinging door. No one had smiles on their faces; they all looked exhausted and cranky.

What I saw around me that night was unfamiliar and different from what I had known my whole life, signalling me that my current situation would be not only the beginning of a new era, but also the beginning of a new life in a new country. Who would have thought that I, who was born in a village and grew up sheltered in a school hostel, would end up in a foreign country?

I had no choice, as the decision had been made for me by others.

We only had a few hundred dollars to begin our new life, which would hardly be a surprise. because we only had enough income that barely covered our monthly expenses. Now we had become even poorer after converting our Sri Lankan rupees to Canadian dollars. The only glimmer of hope we had was the stars in Richard's eyes; how could we build a new life in a foreign country with that?

At this unexpected beginning, I only had a few items packed, including the clothes on my back. Did I have any money of my own? Not even a single penny to my name. However, I did not care about being poor, because I thought that one day I might be able to have an income through hard work and determination.

Over the last few days though, what I had lost could not be replaced: The relationship I was planning with my infant son. In contrast to Richard, I had a heart filled with sorrow and despair and eyes filled with tears.

While seated on the cold airport seat, I reminisced about the events that had unfolded turning my life upside down.

During the third trimester of my pregnancy, my focus was on preparing myself for confinement, but Richard and his family had a different focus. Without my knowledge, they had designed a plan to encourage me to leave my post at the university and accompany him to Canada to support his post-graduate program at Dalhousie University in Nova Scotia.

That University had offered Richard a Killam Doctoral Scholarship, which was unprecedented for an international student. From the time the offer letter had arrived, without my knowledge, discussions had been held among Richard's family members. Without any discussions with me—his current family—he had accepted the offer.

A month before my departure from Sri Lanka, Richard had coaxed me to sign a document to attest that I was willfully resigning from my post at Ruhuna University. A pen was handed to me, and Richard said that I did not have a choice.

The Dean of the Faculty, to whom the letter was addressed, spoke for several minutes, effortlessly trying to make me change my mind. He might have felt my agony to leave a post that I had earned with great efforts. He was deeply concerned about how Richard had used his authority towards me, putting me in this difficult position.

My hand shook with fear and helplessness, and my signature was hardly recognizable, because it became clear that I would be unemployed for a very long time.

No one had given a thought to how I would feel about finding myself in a foreign country without having any firm offer to go into post-graduate studies or find employment while Richard would carry on with his studies.

It was quite probable that Richard's family expected me to be a housewife, just like all women in his family had become after their respective marriages. They most likely would not have appreciated my effort to be an independent and employed woman, and never a housewife.

Now, even after all these years, I still feel that Richard should have thought through his forceful decision to remove me from my post. The events that unfolded since then would enlighten him to make him regret this bold move.

What was most incomprehensible and alarming was how Richard and his family had decided that we leave our baby in Sri Lanka, while I would accompany Richard to Canada. No one had considered the distress that would be inflicted on our baby, during a time when he needed his mother's milk and her love.

With Richard's thoughtless decision, all those who lived around us expected me to abandon my son. He was only four months old.

I had become a mother who, in Sri Lankan society, had the primary responsibility of taking care of the baby. But if I was expected to be the responsible mother, why would the baby's father decide to separate the child from the mother?

Finally, I realized that I had no power to change any of the plans others had made.

Richard's decision on how we could bring our son to Canada once we had settled in that new country was unacceptable. There were too many uncertainties in his plans. I could not see what he had in mind for our future as a family with our son.

After I was informed that my place was beside my husband and not with my infant son, my hesitation to leave my country based on other's suggestions was very clear to Father and me. Yet, the opposition from Richard's family concerning my reluctance to accompany him was even clearer.

"Don't you want to see a wonderful world that you have never seen before?" my father-in-law inquired.

"I would accompany my husband no matter what," Ramona, Richard's eldest sister, added.

"I would take my baby if I could while I accompany my husband, but you don't know whether you will have a place to live with an infant," Bridget, Richard's second sister, rationalized.

But Milly, his Mother took the cake.

"Do you know that there are beautiful women in that part of the world, and one might become attracted to Richard? You would have a problem bringing him back," she stressed.

She had a nail of hard strength and lacked compromise; she was rightness in the face of all opposing wrongness. Most of all, she loved her family even more than the God to whom she prayed with every breath.

I was in my twenties and naïve enough to believe her words; eventually, Milly got her way.

As a new wife, I believed that Milly had good intentions to protect our union, and I had to make every effort to prevent any interference from another woman. How wrong I was to believe that her purpose was honourable. With her words, she robbed the happiness of both my son and me.

Surprisingly, Richard's brother Ben had no opinion. I considered him my only friend, yet he had no verbal support to rescue our family either; silence did not mean that he did not support his only brother.

All in all, I had to face the reality: Richard had a strong support system behind him to carry out his future endeavour.

There had been an alternative path that I was directed at. In October of 19.., soon after Richard had accepted a scholarship in Canada, he requested me to find someone to help out with the baby—if I would like to stay in Sri Lanka until his return after his post-graduate studies.

Naturally, the first person I thought of was Mother.

I hoped she would encourage me to stay in Sri Lanka and would help me raise my child to prevent separation from my baby, but based on my past experiences, I was reluctant to ask for her help. Yet, I was desperate, so I begged her to consider. She refused to help me by stating that she needed to continue her job as a school teacher to receive her maximum pension.

It was clear to Father and I that she already had the number of year's necessary for her eligibility, but neither of us had the courage to change her mind. Mother had exhibited her selfish behaviour one more time, but this time she would regret her decision.

I had no one else to ask for help. Then, Richard suggested that *his* mother would take that responsibility; he had already discussed the possibility with her, and Milly had agreed to his proposition.

But, there was a catch.

Milly informed me that she would take care of our child only if I would accompany Richard to Canada. Not only was I reluctant to hand over my baby to her—because I hardly knew her—but I was furious about how she expected me to follow in her footsteps in becoming a housewife to her son, but not a mother to my baby.

Her proposal was unreasonable as she would have never left her children in the care of any other human; she took care of them all until they reached adulthood.

Yet, did I have a choice? No.

It was obvious that others had taken over the power to make decisions for my life and my child. It was clear that Richard, Milly and Mother had forced me into a difficult situation.

Much like *Sophie's Choice*, I thought, *Stay back, with no support to take care of my child and lose my husband, or accompany him and lose my son.*

Even then, I could not make that decision for our son, as Richard intervened; he had determined that his mother would take good care of our baby and I would be there to take care of his needs.

Unfortunately, he would realize that his confidence in this plan was unfounded.

Some years later, a lengthy discussion on this subject surfaced. Richard revealed that he decided to leave our son with his mother because of the many uncertainties surrounding the living arrangements in a new country, while taking care of an infant.

I agreed that his concerns were valid; however, making that decision without any discussion with me was inexplicable. Even after all those years, he could not clearly answer my questions on why I was separated from my son.

It might have dawned on him that he had inadvertently created more losses for himself: a wife who would fall into depression, and a son who would learn of his father's scheme to abandon him at the time he needed his parents the most. The unfortunate end result of his decision was a family that did not receive the happiness that all parties deserved.

With that heartbreaking decision, I lost all that was precious to me and my reasons to live.

Time had been ticking away. I had been waiting patiently in the airport lounge for Richard to return from wherever he had gone—out through the door with the Exit sign—and continued to reminisce about the day of our departure.

Three days before, I had left Sri Lanka.

I remembered how Richard's family had been very proud of his ability to secure a scholarship to attend a Canadian university. They had been spreading the news among friends and family about his future and constantly spoke of how he would return to Sri Lanka with a doctorate in chemistry.

There was no pomp and pageantry specifically meant for me, because my life was about to slide downhill into oblivion. Personally, there was nothing I could celebrate, but there were plenty of reasons why I could cry. I needed to keep my hopes up and expect the unexpected that the future would bring.

It was an emotionally charged and difficult day.

On the day of our departure, Milly prepared a lunch especially to celebrate Richard's achievement. She served cooked fish, steamed vegetables, fried rice, curried potatoes, and poppadom; all that was favoured by Richard. The aroma of the food filled the home, and the family sat together and enjoyed the meal. I was glad my parents joined the lunch party, but there was no chit-chat among the participants.

The silence was tense and uncomfortable.

With the uncertainty of my future, I had lost my appetite altogether. I could not taste anything. However, I realized that the familiar smell of a Sri Lankan meal was a proper ending to life in my country. At that moment, I was grateful for the presence of my parents and that we could share a meal for the last time.

A few minutes before departure to the airport, Richard's two sisters sang hymns while playing the piano and the rest of the family stood around in the living room with solemn thoughts to bless his new journey. Richard was in harmony with all that was around him, but he had forgotten the precious part of his life that he was about to leave behind—his infant son.

I stood close to the small bassinet where my baby slept peacefully. He had no inkling of the difficulties he would have to encounter and endure in the upcoming years. As a young mother, I was in deep sorrow. Tears rolled down my face like an uncontrollable leak of a damaged reservoir.

I had the most difficult time accepting Richard's decision to leave our baby behind, especially since I had no knowledge of when we would reunite our family. It would be a torturous journey that I had to take, which I would never wish upon anyone.

I picked up my baby from the bassinet and hugged him for the last time. He woke up from my closeness and looked at me. I could not believe that I had to leave him behind. I kept him close for as long as I could while numerous activates swirled around me.

The smell of Ponds baby powder, which I had dabbed on him after his regular morning bath, filled my nostrils. The touch of his skin on mine alerted me that this would be the last time I would feel him; if and when I could feel him again against me was beyond my control. I promised him that no matter what, he would always be my son and that I will return to unite him with his family.

Oblivious to what was happening, he smiled, and I cried uncontrollably. The aroma of his soft skin would travel with me halfway across the globe to keep me close to him.

Father was in deep sorrow; he did not speak much that day. He looked at me with sympathy and stood close to me until the moment of departure. His presence soothed my painful nerves, and what he said at the last minute stayed with me for a very long time.

"The only way out of deprivation is education. Do not worry. No one could stop your progress in life; you will one day become well educated and will hold a position better than anyone in your family; the stars that shone on you at birth would not betray you."

I held on to his encouraging words, like a human grasping onto a withering grass bush while drowning in a mud pool. I was determined to act on his wisdom at the moment opportunity would arrive.

As the hired taxi travelled through the streets of Colombo, heading to the airport, I felt like I was one of those women who lived at the end of the Second World War during Fascist Italy: they had no rights, no voice, no equality, and no say in their own lives, and many had small children.

I contemplated the lives of those women and realized that if I were to survive, much like them, I would need to find courage, imagination, and selflessness to fight to make myself truly extraordinary. I was inspired, and that thought had briefly consoled me.

It was the afternoon of the 23rd of November. The sun was beating down on all that was wonderful in Colombo. Men and women were going about their ways of life; the traffic was horrendous as usual, but the car dashed through the crowded streets to ensure our departure on time.

I sobbed softly. Tears stained my face and drips of mothers milk-soaked my shirt.

I felt that my heart was being pulled away from my own flesh and blood—the pull was too painful. My grief became deeper with the increasing distance between my son and me.

It was clear that my situation was hopeless.

The chill in the air at the airport brought me back to reality. Time had passed, and I had been sitting on this seat for nearly thirty minutes. I wondered what was keeping Richard away.

Suddenly, the burning desire to hold my baby and feed him overwhelmed me. Alone on a cold bench, I endured the painful memories of leaving my son. I forced my tears to retire to its source.

It was unbearable.

I shivered as the airport lounge was very cold—it was a chill I had never experienced before. I had a pink overcoat on, which was handed down to me by one of Richard's relatives, "The best winter coat you could find in Europe," she said. I thanked her profusely as I had no idea what a winter coat was or how suitable a European coat would be to keep me warm while in Canada.

I realized that the coat I had on was not the best for a Canadian winter, but I was grateful that I at least had a coat. How was I supposed to know what a Canadian winter would be like? When we were getting ready to leave the country, time was of the essence, and every activity and decision was rushed. Any charitable donations from friends and relatives who had travelled to foreign countries were most welcome.

Underneath the coat, I only had a shirt suitable for a hot day in Colombo; that was where I had been there three days ago. I wrapped my arms around myself to warm me, but I had very little success as my hands were cold.

I noticed that many people in the airport were wearing gloves. I could not recall any discussions on how to purchase gloves before departure, because such items were not commonly available in Sri Lanka, except those seen in funeral homes worn by the pall-bearers. I decided to keep my body warm by keeping my hands in my coat pockets.

As I waited, I noticed that the airport had been gradually emptying. Time had elapsed, and I had been seated in the lounge for more than forty minutes. The lights had dimmed, and there was no one I could speak to. I was alone. I wondered whether this might have been the sign of things to come.

I looked at my watch to find the time.

Tap. Tap. Tap. I tried to wake up the dead watch. It read a time, but the hands had been frozen in place. Could it be the dreadful cold that had frozen the watch hands? I blew on it for a few minutes to warm it and lifted it to my ear, hoping to hear its tick, but there was no ticking sound. The watch had stopped at 2:00 p.m., sometime after we had flown out of the International Airport in Colombo. Seemingly, time had stood still from the moment I left my country. *How strange*, I thought.

Later, I tried to find the reason for the watch to die; it was a manual wristwatch, so the reason could not be a dead battery. Apparently, the reason was that my body's magnetic field had aligned with that of the earth, because I was very close to the North Pole, which resulted in freezing the watch hands!

I felt that my time on this earth had come to a standstill.

I presumed that the universe had sent me a message to prepare myself for a bleak future.

A few years later, I had replaced the old watch, but the new one also did not function on my wrist. I never had the luxury of wearing a regular wristwatch for the rest of my life in Canada.

With every minute that had passed, I felt anxiety as I could not fathom where Richard was, and there was no one I could ask for help. I had no choice but to wait until his return.

Before we left Sri Lanka, he had been informed that someone would meet with us at the airport in Nova Scotia to take us to a residence. Richard's intension was to locate the friends who would provide us with a ride. I waited and waited. Eventually, I no longer had the energy to sit, and I decided to lie on the bench as I could no longer hold my head in place.

I might have dozed off.

...I felt the warm sea breeze, but the sea was sound asleep, like a labourer after a hard day of work. Only the splash of long oars from working fishing boats moving along the blue waters was audible. The clouds moved slowly across the blue sky, merging with and skirting each other. There was nothing sinister in the slow movement on the soulful mass of the clouds

...A woman wearing a colourful cloth walked, carrying a large basket of fruits on her head while heading towards the local market. Uniformed school children walked in groups while chatting and laughing along the shoreline. Three cows were lingering along the road, looking for food. The familiar sound of the seagulls could be heard, and they floated in tandem. The bell hung on the rooftop of the local church and rang rhythmically, informing me of the time of day—it was 8:00 a.m. I was seated on a rock very close to the beach, and our home in Matara, facing the Indian Ocean stood still and empty. A teardrop emerged and ran down on my face . . .

An unfamiliar voice close to my ear woke me, and I was not certain of my whereabouts. A gloved hand touched my shoulder, and two blue eyes peeked into mine. Had I arrived on a different planet? I had never seen blue eyes before.

I sat and faced the stranger. Thankfully, he smiled. I must be in a land of friendly people. I smiled back.

"What are you doing here? All the passengers have left the building. Do you not have anyone picking you up from the airport?" he asked.

Airport! That was where I was supposed to sit and wait until Richard return from wherever he went to meet our escort. I tried to find an answer to the stranger while I came to my senses.

My explanation for being on the bench bewildered the man.

"No one can return after going through that door unless they buy an airline ticket for another flight," he said while pointing to the door where everyone, including Richard, had left more than an hour ago.

After receiving Richard's description, he left me. I stared after him and hoped that he would return. A few minutes later, Richard returned, escorted by the same man. Finally, we were able to exit.

Later I would learn that Richard did not know the rules of this airport. He had to explain to the security officer at the door why he had left me in the lounge. Apparently, convincing the guard to let him return to the arrivals lounge had been a tedious task, most likely because of Richard's Sri Lankan accent.

Because of the uncertainty of finding our escorts—people he had never met—he had thought that leaving me at the lounge was the best option, because I was exhausted and distressed after such a long flight.

I exited the airport with Richard; for the first time, I faced a dark and bitter cold world. The air had blended in with the blackness of the world, creating a thick unpleasant mass. The darkness had engulfed any possible views of the surroundings, and a gloomy and patriated repellent exterior of an unknown land stood before me.

It was surreal.

The fierce frost had come with negative degrees of temperature. I felt like I had landed on the North Pole. A witch-whirlwind howled and was sweeping the paths, making wavy white swirls on the ground, blinding any opened eyes, powdering winter coats and their warm collars, men's mustaches and animal hair. I had never seen such an ominous scene in my whole life.

For the first time, I had experienced the dreadful Canadian winter.

I stepped onto a slippery path in my poorly insulated pumps and closed my eyes to protect them from the flying wet snow. Where had I come? I could not imagine living on this land; I could not imagine how I could survive, let alone thrive.

I was frightened and confused.

I was asked to get into a car that looked like an iced cake, notably covered by a thick layer of snow and ice. Someone opened the door for me, and I slid in, with Richard sitting beside me. I looked at him, hoping to understand his feelings about this unusual place and was stunned to find that what was repellent to me had been opposite for him in unbroken silence; the stars in his eyes were still bright and burning.

I was happy for his optimism.

I sat in the warm car. The two Sri Lankan-Canadians who came to fetch us were polite and friendly, making the existing situation a bit comforting. Yet, my mind kept travelling back to my son. When would I be able to see him and cuddle him in my arms again? When would I be able to feel the warmth of my motherland again?

I covered my face with my cold palms and sobbed.

The car moved ever so slowly on the slippery road. The dashing white, wet snow continuously covered the car's windshield, making driving difficult with the poor visibility of the tar-paved road lit by the headlights. I could hear communications between our new friends and Richard in the background, melding with the swish of the windshield wipers; I had no interest in the details of the discussions.

My mind was numbed by the uncertainly of our future and of any possibilities of getting back on my feet to reunite with my son. The dreadful winter and its wrath had frozen all my senses.

For the next four months, I did not see a single green leaf on any tree, and I could not visualize the true nature of this solidified land.

I slept all day and cried all night while my body continued to convert my blood into milk, which stained my clothes and killed my spirit to live. My infant son would grow up deprived of his mother's love at the most important time; the first two years of his life.

Ironically, after I had left Sri Lanka, Mother also had lost much too. Father had great difficulty handling my departure. After saying goodbye to us at the airport, he refused to visit Richard's parents or return to his own home. Richard's sister Ramona had to step in to accommodate my parents for a while until Father was ready to return to their home.

Apparently, Father had expected Mother to step up so I could raise my son in Sri Lanka, with the love of his grandparents and other extended family members until Richard's return. But Mother could not be selfless and because of that, she had lost her husband's affection forever. Father had stopped taking his regular meals and had become a skeleton of a man. He started to withdraw from his daily tasks and began to neglect their residence beyond repair.

He eventually had become deeply depressed.

Mother had realized her mistake only after one year following our departure. She might have expected Father to forget and forgive her despicable behaviour. To compensate for her mistakes, she had regularly visited our son at Richard's parent's home and had offered to stitch his little clothes.

Eventually, when Father's depression did not improve, she offered to take the baby to their home during the school holidays to help Father be close to his grandson. Yet, Father could not forget that Mother had neglected to help me and their first grandchild.

I wrote to Father as much as I could, but he never revealed the status of his relationship with Mother. Two years later, I would learn that my parents had lost their affection for each other beyond repair. I believe Mother lost the most important aspect of her life: Father's affection. Still, what I had lost was distinctly much more.

Later in Canada, I read many spiritual books to learn about Christianity. In [5]*Becoming a Better You* by Joel Osteen, he wrote, "Out of our greatest rejection comes our greatest direction." I considered the predicament I had been placed in showed me the greatest direction for the rest of my life.

I was about to be tested and tried. I had to learn what I was up against and how I should persevere. I had to believe that the obstacles I was about to face were opportunities to grow. I took that idea seriously to move forward.

I also had remembered Father's words as I was getting ready to leave Sri Lanka, and with that, I had assimilated hope in my heart. From the early days of my rejection by Mother, I had built ample resilience.

Now, I had to use all my emotions to build courage. I waited for the right moment to step forward, and I was determined not to stop until I found my way back into life.

After many years later, I found a way.

---

5 **Joel Osteen**. *Becoming a Better You: 7 Keys to Improving Your Life Every Day* (Tennessee: Howard Books, 2009. PP15)

PART II

$\mathscr{I}$NTRODUCTION

Several years had gone by.

There was a blank sheet of paper sitting before me; it was suggesting me to tell the story about my ten-year-long struggle on how I got back on my feet, and my efforts taken to bring up our son.

I wish to admit that, eventually, I reached my goals in my life while enduring poverty, discrimination, and running a labour-intensive home all by myself. I believe that anything is possible if one has love in their heart and determination in their soul.

I looked at the white sheet of paper again, and it remained empty. With uncertain thoughts, I wondered how I should tell the rest of my story.

I finally decided to share flashbacks of poignant moments in my past, detailing where I had been and how I had arrived with fulfillment.

$\mathcal{W}$HEN $\mathcal{O}$NE $\mathcal{D}$AY $\mathcal{B}$ECAME THE '$\mathcal{D}$AY $\mathcal{O}$NE'

I t is strange how in moments of great crisis, the mind whips back to dark times.

Nearly forty years after I had entered Canada as a wife of a graduate student, who had been a penniless pauper, and a naïve and gullible young woman, two moments of great crises arrived.

It was surreal and unpleasant.

On the 31st of December 2019, snuggled under a fleece blanket, I laid on the couch with sleepy eyes, as celebratory performances leading to the dawn of another New Year flashed on the TV screen. Richard sat at the edge of the couch and enjoyed the ball dropping at New York's Times Square. "Happy New Year," he murmured as soon as the ball touched the base, echoing the host Anderson Cooper's wishes to the world.

At that dawn of 2020, Canada was a thriving G7 economy and had a great leader to look up to. It had been a wonderful time to be a Canadian citizen. Yet, I wondered what changes would come about in the New Year.

Lo and behold! When March of 2020 arrived, Canada and the whole world dramatically changed on a dime.

On the 11th of March, the City of Ottawa, where I lived, announced the first confirmed case of COVID-19, the new Coronavirus that had supposedly originated in China. Since then, Canada had closed down all its institutions to prevent the spread of the virus. Millions lost their lively hoods, poverty was beckoning at the doors of many, and it was a time for some to envision a difficult life ahead.

I was one of those people who started to wonder how it would be if I were to be infected by the new virus and whether poverty would knock on my door again.

Poverty had been part of my life from the moment I arrived in Canada, and for a long while since then. Naturally, I did not wish to return to those dreadful days. Such unpleasant thoughts crossed my mind, not because I was poor in 2020, but because of the past difficulties I had endured.

While the virus killed thousands within a few weeks and continued to threaten people around the globe, another disaster started to loom on the horizon and brought back a different set of undesirable memories from my past: social discrimination.

Even before COVID-19 pandemic, society had been plagued with the age-old problem of systemic and societal discrimination against people of colour. I could clearly recall the effects of this plague during my struggles to establish myself in Canadian society. But, over several years, I cleared those hurdles with determination and hard work.

Unfortunately, on the 19th of May, the haunting memories of discrimination crawled back into my mind.

On that day, the killing of a black forty-year-old unarmed man named George Floyd in Minneapolis, Minnesota, resulted in a new pandemic, the violation of human rights at its worst level.

The image of the gruesome killing of this unarmed man by a uniformed white policeman—by pressing his knee on the man's neck after he had been thrown to the ground—flashed on television screens and confirmed that humanity had never evolved. The dark side of the mind had survived beneath the falsehood of lovingkindness.

The potential poverty, resulting from the COVID-19 pandemic and the danger of social discrimination that flashed on TV, brought back the suppressed memories of my past, like oil springing up to the surface after adding water on it.

I started to reflect on unforgettable and unpleasant moments: who was I, where did I come from, what difficulties did I have to overcome, and where am I heading?

Indeed, the thoughts of rejection embedded in me had stemmed from the very source of discrimination I had experienced from the day I married Richard: first from my own family, then Richard's family and later from the Canadian society.

Between the three sources of discrimination, the most difficult to accept was that enforced by my own family.

I contemplated: how could the forceful interventions on my life by those who had the power over me, be any different to the use of humans as slaves in North America—or in any other parts of the world—by those who had the audacity?

The more I thought about my past, the more I had realized that my life story had more similarities to those innocent people who had been suffocated against their will, centuries ago and also seen again in 2020.

One day, I sat at my writing desk and tabulated the items of freedom I had before marriage and those that were taken away from me since then. That had been a remarkable revelation.

Based on the unpleasant events that unfolded in 2020, powerful sentiments related to the times I had suffered through indignation emerged; those then ignited my mind to whip back.

Nearly four decades later, I still clearly recall when that one day became 'day one' of my life in a new country, and all the days, months and years that followed.

On the morning of November 30th 19.., the day after I had landed in Canada, I woke up in a basement apartment on Henry Street in Halifax, Nova Scotia. I expected my body to be wrung out and exhausted. Surprisingly, I was fully awake to face a new world.

In that basement apartment, there were no windows or a door that would open to a street so I could see life on Earth. It was daunting to realize that it was the first time I had ever woken up to a day below ground level.

The apartment had two sets of windows, yet they both did not have the capacity to see outside. The shutters of the front window had seldom been opened because two metal bars had been nailed down across its dirty frame. The one in the rear was openable, but no one had attempted to open it as a snowbank was pressed against it that had not been cleared since the first snowstorm of that year. Therefore, the room had no chance to circulate air. The dampness of the air had been infused with a musty smell, reminding me of the one-room apartment that we had lived in Matara.

The interior of this place was in the wildest disorder, with broken furniture thrown about in all directions.

There was no bedstead, it was an open space; an old bed with a dirty mattress had been thrown in the middle of the floor. There was a stove and a refrigerator right next to the bed. They both looked ancient; the refrigerator, which struggled to do its due diligence, sounded like a steamroller on a gravel road, and the stove was orange-brown with peeling edges.

The floor had been covered with an old fraying carpet that no one had cared to clean; it imparted a filthy odour. I feared to step on it without proper foot covering, but I had none.

A small rickety chair stood next to the wall with peeling brown paint; a razor sat on it, and a few curly thick tresses of grey human hair had been captured in its blade. On the floor next to the chair was a multi-coloured toy truck laid on its side. The drawers of a small brown bureau, which stood in a corner, were open and seemingly rifled through as many articles remained within them.

While seated on the bed, I wondered who had lived in this dump, but I had no strength to think about it during my own insignificant existence in this place. I decided to focus on what I needed to do to get out into the natural world.

Suddenly, at the entrance to our room, a small figure appeared from nowhere. It was a little boy about two years of age. He had black hair, more or less of the texture of wool, black skin, and dark eyes. While standing in the dark corner, he beamed at me.

I had never met anyone of African origin before. But from what I had seen in books and photos, which had been sent to me by my school day Nigerian pen-pal, I concluded that this little boy must be from that continent. To my relief, a large woman also appeared right behind the boy. I imagined that she must be the boy's mother.

"Good morning, I am Lulu, and this is Mandela," the woman spoke with an unfamiliar accent pointing to the little boy.

Mandela cuddled beside his mother, holding onto her long worn-out robe, and beamed at me again. The mother rubbed his little head with affection. He looked up at her in response with love and acknowledgment.

The sudden appearance of these two strangers in my space not only surprised me, but also bewildered my mind.

At that moment, I was distracted by the howling wind that had pushed against the door to the basement. A blast of winter had created a vortex of cold air at the entrance to the basement apartment. It ran through the dark and damp space like a frozen snake rubbing against my lukewarm body.

Yet, that wasn't what woke me to the harsh reality. No. It was the warmth in Mandela's mother's eyes set on her young son that jolted my memory of loss and despair.

I felt the wetness in my dress in response to the unexpected scene; mother's milk drained along my body. I could not breathe. I choked on my own spit with sadness, and I felt the urge to run to where I had left my infant son.

I wondered where my baby was at that moment: was he being fondled by anyone to keep him safe and happy. Was he being fed on time and tucked in his little crib, or was he crying and asking for me? A million questions passed through my mind at that one moment, seeing the shared affection between little Mandela and his mother.

The most important question that came to my mind was how was it possible that this little boy had the opportunity to tag along with his mother while my son had to stay behind? I had no answers but a laundry list of questions.

I started to feel anger towards all those who had been instrumental in taking my baby away and suggesting that I follow Richard. Most of all, I began to gather anger towards Richard for his role in separating me from my son. Yet, I decided to keep my personal feelings to myself.

I needed to respond to the woman who had graciously introduced her little family. I introduced myself, not comprehending where these people lived or how they ended up in this one-room dirty dungeon with me. The woman finally explained.

"Welcome to Canada. I am a student at Dalhousie University, and Mandela and I live here with you."

"Thanks for explaining because I did not know that we were expected to share the space," I responded with hesitation, as I was not certain how this arrangement would work out.

"We could schedule a time to share the stove to cook meals, and I have already cleared some space in the refrigerator, if you have some food to save."

Wonderful, I thought, *she knows how to cook, perhaps I could learn from her*. Yet, I realized that we did not have any food to save or to eat.

At that moment, I interrupted Lulu to ask the most important question that nagged me from the moment the pair appeared before me.

"Did Mandela's father travel with you to Canada to help you with your son while you study?"

"No, he stayed in Uganda to carry on with his job. Mandela belongs with his mother, so I brought him with me, and I have daycare facilities for him during the daytime while I go to school. It is subsidized for students. Mandela will see his father in two years." She responded in detail.

After hearing about Lulu's efforts to bring her small child with her, although she was expected to spend many hours studying and probably had to make a great effort to care for her child after school, a strange feeling came over me. I felt a deep hatred towards my mother, mother-in-law, and most of all, Richard.

Deep down in my heart, I felt that it was the beginning of my mistrust towards Richard. I felt that Richard could have made a favorable decision for our son, like Lulu and her husband did.

The winter storm that hit Halifax on the day we had landed had blanketed every conceivable surface with clean, white snow. The stillness of the surroundings had blanketed my sorrowful mind as if to console me.

While in Sri Lanka, Richard had received information from Dalhousie University that suggested Halifax and the Nova Scotia region had a lot to offer: the stunning scenery, the booming economy, the friendly people, and the incredibly rich cultural scene. That's all well and good, but there's one thing that I was not aware of—the weather.

In his early communications, the International Student Coordinator had written to Richard: *Sure, Canada gets cold in the winter, but Nova Scotia really feels the freeze. Temperatures have been known to plunge as low as -30 degrees Celsius, meaning that you'll need more than just a thick jacket to get you through the long, dark winter nights.* Yet, all of those unpleasant details had been kept from me, so I could not use them as a reason not to accompany Richard.

The coordinator also had stated that winter in Halifax could be considered a thing of beauty, with very fortunate visitors getting the chance to see the Atlantic Ocean freeze over once in a blue moon. Yet, he had stressed that we might need to learn how to do outdoor activities to make winter in Nova Scotia just a little bit more bearable.

It was easier said than done!

Before enjoying any outdoor activities, we needed to learn how to walk on ice. We did not have suitable boots or clothes to keep our bodies warm; the very first walk from our basement apartment to the Dalhousie University took much longer than ten minutes—longer than the locals take.

That day, the very first tedious walk on ice felt like climbing the slippery pole during outdoor New Year celebrations in Sri Lanka: one step taken forward with great difficulty followed by three steps slipping back to the origin.

Richard had been instructed to register for the Doctorate program on the 30th of November; it was the last available day for his enrolment. He suggested that I accompany him to the university. We dragged ourselves along Henry Street and then down Coburg Street, heading to Le Marchant Street to enter the university. We slipped and fell several times together, as Richard's decision to hold my hand during the walk was counterproductive.

By the time we entered the Arts & Administration (A&A) building of the university to meet the registrar, our outer clothing was soaking wet, and our shoes needed to be replaced. Since we did not have replacements, we had to stay wet and cold for a long while.

There were no humans in the wide-open space in front of the A&A building; it was deserted. Several bushes that had been caked with piles of snow were visible. Also, mounds of snow on either side concealed the bottom half of several evergreens that margined the pathways to various buildings. Among all that, instead of humans, it was crowded with many pigeons.

I sat on a bench in the hallway while Richard proceeded to meet the registrar. I looked around. This had been my first encounter with North American university students. I could feel the mentality of those young people who gathered in hallways. Their bold movements informed me that they had a firm mindset and believed that the entire world was their oyster.

It was fascinating how those students' thought processes were not different to those I had encountered at Ruhuna University. Their communication between their peers, the sharing of thoughts and their eagerness to get involved were comparable. At that moment, I wished for another opportunity to be a student. I would wait for that opportunity with an open mind.

Almost an hour went by, and I wondered how Richard's registration had been progressing.

By the time he returned, I was famished and parched, as I had not had breakfast because we did not have any food. After inquiring from a student, it was clear that we had to depend on a vending machine to feed ourselves; only snacks and some canned drinks were visible, and the price of each item had been printed below. I sat on the bench and waited for Richard to bring us food, but he returned empty-handed, and I could not understand the reason.

"What are we going to eat?" I inquired.

"I am not sure, because the amount of money needed to buy anything from the machine is far above the amount I have on me," he responded.

"Could you buy anything with what you have?" I insisted.

"Sure, only a pack of chewing gum."

I could not believe my ears. My heart sank, and tears started to swell.

"Let me see whether we could find a store that sells bread." Before he finished his sentence, Richard disappeared among a crowd of students.

He returned with directions to a food store, Capitol Grocery—the walk to the store would be a fair distance away on snow and in hunger. A life in poverty flashed across my mind. Seemingly, that would be unavoidable because I did not have a penny for myself. I would have to beg for it from Richard. For several years, only Richard would earn and manage the family money.

It was the beginning of the end of my faith in survival in this country; there was no one to ask for help.

We stepped out into the frozen land heading to the grocery store. As we turned the corner from Coburg Street to Henry, we met Nihal and Sheela, the two Sri Lankan friends who were our escorts from the airport; they were walking to their home on Coburg.

I had learned later that coming from the same country would make people cling together, as if they were from one family, to survive in a new country. I considered our meeting with Nihal and Sheela a source of strength for our survival.

"Where are you going?" Nihal inquired.

After listening to our story, Sheela responded quickly.

"Please come and have some lunch with us; we are on our way to the grocery store, and then to home."

The hospitality of the couple was extraordinary. The meal they provided us at that most opportune time was heavenly. We chatted and shared the meal and enjoyed the company of the two fellow Sri Lankans. Afterwards, Sheela offered a wonderful cup of Sri Lankan tea. The warmth and the aroma of the ginger-infused tea woke my withering nerves and brought back life to my wet and cold feet.

Remarkably, the aroma of fresh ginger steeped in hot tea filled the air in their cozy living room, making me think: that must be the way freedom smelled, or justice, or luxury, or perhaps vengeance. The aroma of the ginger dragged me back to my childhood, when we used drink ginger-tea after a heavy meal.

Then a sound of a box guitar brought me back to the present moment. Nihal had started to sing a familiar Sinhalese song, originally sung by W.D Amaradewa. The tune hung in the air like the nectar of a tropical flower and touched my soul deeply.

Unknowingly, I had been waiting for this moment. The tune touched me with everything I had been waiting to feel: complete power over my life, total freedom to earn money, perfect justice, and the fulfillment of my heart's desires.

While I watched the movement of the guitar strings that were strategically manipulated by Nihal's fingers, all my hopes and dreams joined in the depths of my soul, sprouting hopes to bring my son over to Canada to join his family.

In the past, music always had the power to console me and to alleviate distress.

On that day, Nihal brought back my senses to feel that music—a piece of my memorable past—which might have had the capacity to save me from difficult circumstances in the future.

The haunting melody created by the box guitar signalled that I would need music to help me escape from the harsh realities of my future. Fortunately, I had brought with me a few music cassettes; however, finding a player to listen to them was difficult, as I had no money.

Much later, I found a player, and those taped songs would keep me company when no humans would come to rescue me.

Sharing time with Nihal and Sheela on that cold wintery day, initiated a lifelong friendship. For the next two weeks, to our greatest joy, they provided us with meals and escorted us to various shops to buy essentials for the winter survival. I did not anticipate their generosity to that extent; unfortunately, I did not have a suitable gift to offer for their kindness, which made me feel embarrassed.

I decided to express my gratitude at a later day and I did.

We lived in the basement apartment for two weeks, then, one of the university professors had suggested that Richard find a suitable apartment in Saint Mary's University student housing. We were fortunate to rent one immediately after meeting the building manager.

Although the distance to Dalhousie University would be far more from there, I considered this find to be somewhat fortunate, as it was affordable based on Richard's limited income from the Killam Scholarship, and it had freshly painted walls, clean floors, and windows to bring in much-needed natural light.

I was happy to have the opportunity to live above ground.

The new apartment had one bedroom, one full bath, a living room, and a small kitchen. Yet, it was an empty space that needed to be furnished. With our limited income, we were able to buy a mattress and one chair for fifty dollars from a thrift store ran by the Salvation Army.

When they were delivered, we realized that the chair did not have its necessary support below the seat cushion, making one to fall right through!

That had been a crushing revelation, as we had spent a large amount of money—calculated based on our income—without understanding the value of the chair. How could one know the deception in people, even if they were living in an industrialized country such as Canada?

We moved into our new place on the 15th of December, with our two suitcases and the clothes on our back. Slowly, we gathered a few more items by scavenger hunts in local yard sales. The Kemese Annual Yard Sale would become our main source in finding suitable clothes and household items for unimaginably low prices.

The university graduate program started in the first week of January. After having breakfast, Richard walked out into the wintery morning, and for the first time, I was left alone in our empty apartment.

He did not return until dinner time. We had no telephone, so I could not contact him. The day dragged on as if it would never end.

During that very first day, I started to feel the emptiness, isolation, and loss, which led to stress, as I felt abandoned in a place that I knew no one and had nothing concrete to do. It would gradually drag my will to live, down in a dark pit. There was not a single person I could speak to and not a single option to look forward to.

Eventually, hopeless thoughts engulfed my whole being.

It is well known that loneliness and solitude are two different aspects of life. Living alone would need emotional resilience and self-sufficiency, but nobody relishes the prospect of isolation. I felt lonely without having any directions on how I could eliminate it.

With the passage of time, I would feel the toll of my loneliness, and it wasn't just emotional. I was in my late twenties, yet I felt tired, distracted, and unable to concentrate. I had no energy and could not make an effort to get up and do anything worthwhile; I could not find the reasons.

For most of the time, I just felt sad.

I knew that loneliness was linked to depression, anxiety, interpersonal hostility, increased vulnerability to health problems, and suicide. All those negative thoughts swirled in my mind, making me sick to my whole being.

Recently, I read in an article in the local newspaper, *Ottawa Citizen*, that in some cases, isolation had taken to gothic extremes. In Britain, a young woman named Joyce Carol Vincent died and wasn't discovered for three years. Neighbours ignored the strange smell coming from her apartment. When her body was finally found, the TV was still on. She became the subject of morbid fascination and a documentary.

Now I could only imagine what might have happened to me during that period if I did not take action to alleviate loneliness.

I was petrified and felt panic washed through me. I did not wish to die because of loneliness, so I wrote my very first letter from Canada to Father, explaining the current predicament I was placed in, although I had to borrow postage from Richard to mail it.

I would learn that after reading my letter, Father was hospitalized due to dehydration and serious pains in his stomach; unintentionally, I had transferred my distress to my beloved Father. If I had known of his vulnerable situation due to my departure, I would not have put him in that difficult position.

I realized that I had been in a desperate situation having no one to ask for help, and Father had always been my sanctuary.

Days turned to weeks and then arrived the month of February. Still, there had been no sign of a change of the dreadful winter weather or my loneliness. I had spent every day alone in the same empty space for a whole month.

Day in and day out, I sat on that broken chair, which sat in the middle of our empty living room. I looked around, and there was nothing to see and no one to talk to—physical and emotional emptiness had engulfed my world.

While my life was being wasted on a broken chair in an empty apartment, the Canadian winter dragged on mercilessly, and I felt as if the whole world stood still with me. It would be a winter I will always remember with regret.

One morning, I asked myself the question: what do I have to live for? The answer was, "Only my life." I had lost every other thing in my life: my son, job, family, and my country.

That was my darkest moment.

[6]"The Song of the Reed" by Rumi would perfectly describe my sentiments at that moment:

Listen to the reed and the tale it tells,

How it sings of separation:

Even since they cut me from the reed bed,

My wail has caused men and women to weep.

---

6 **Mathnawinby Kabir and Camille Helmiski**; *The Pocket Rumi*; (Shambhla Publications Inc., 2001)

I want the heart to open with longing, to share the pain of this love.

Whoever has been parted from its source, longs to return to the state of the union

I had no hope for the future, no faith in any person, including Richard, and worst of all, I had no one to whom I could express my true feelings of the predicament. I felt that I had been trapped in a vacuum, and its walls were slowly closing in on me.

I wanted to die.

Then one afternoon in late February, I fell asleep on that old chair and had a dream. *My son appeared before me and smiled; he had the gentlest face, and although about two months passed by since the day I left him, his face looked the same.* Perhaps it was a nudge from the universe to help me remember the need for my existence for my son.

Instantly, that image changed my mind about the future. With that change, instead of making plans to die, I started to take charge of my destiny. I had become a warrior, wanting to live again; I wanted to rebel.

Soon after, Father's response to my very first letter arrived. By that time, I had given up hope to hear back from him, but his response, filled with loving words was most encouraging.

Father's kind words and the image of my son in my dream made me turn a corner from a dreadful past to visualize a better future.

With wisdom, I adapted much like seaweed on the intertidal zone of the Earth. I bent with the tide to survive and thrive without letting the force of nature take away my natural existence.

I practiced patience, then persevered and prevailed!

CHAPTER 18
$\mathscr{T}$HE $\mathscr{R}$EUNION

Almost two years after we had landed in Canada, a letter from Mother, received on the 6th of April of 19.., changed the course of our lives. I felt a sudden weakness in my legs and literally fell to the ground after reading it.

It read, "Your son is gravely ill. If you do not find a way to take him to Canada as soon as possible, there is a great possibility that you would lose him forever." I read the letter many times, most of all, the fine print to understand what danger my son was in and what Mother was signalling.

Unfortunately, her details were sketchy.

Imminent danger to my son would be the last straw. By this time in my life, I had been through too many difficulties, and I would not withstand the stress if I were to lose him for good.

However, based on the Mother's past behaviour, it was difficult for me to believe her words. After much thought, I decided to take her message seriously. It was time to gather every penny we had and make the return journey to reunite our little family.

It took a few more months and great effort to make that journey back to Sri Lanka a reality. What was revealed during our reunion would destroy my trust in Richard's family.

Mother's journal would reveal her true sentiments related to her involvement in our lives, to bring about this outcome.

For the first two months of my life in Canada, I wallowed in despair, yet after having a dream of my infant son and receiving an encouraging letter from Father, I felt a fire within me to prevail in my new life—and I had asked Richard to either borrow some books from the local library, or buy some from a yard-sale.

By reading, I hoped to take my mind off the difficult predicament I was in. I assumed it could be the initial step for my recovery from loneliness and lack of enthusiasm for life.

I also believed that I needed to recover from my painful past to be happy in the present and look forward to a renewed future. I imagined that reading about other's life experiences would help me accept my current situation.

I was right.

With determination, I constantly visited local yard or garage sales looking for useful books. Unfortunately, the selection was limited, and I had to choose from books that others did not wish to keep. Yet, I did find some books written by women about their lives.

The most interesting find was *Moments of Being: A Collection of Autobiographical Writing* by Virginia Woolf. She described her relationship with her father, Leslie Stephen, who played a crucial role in her development as an individual and as a writer. I related to this writer; she brought tears to my eyes. Wondrous hopes emerged for a better future, because her written words reminded me that I have a loving father who wished me to live, progress in life, and love my son.

Finally, with my focus on good books, life began again. Books taught me many different ways on how I might find a place in life and in society.

While reading, I started to write little notes and kept a journal on my daily progress. I read frequently and copied interesting passages that intrigued my senses. The early stages of a personal journal came to light.

It was interesting how those valuable documents had sprouted while I sat on a broken chair in the middle of an empty living room during a dreadful period of my life. There would be hidden gems in those notes; they would eventually help me to tell the story of my life.

Life could be hard! You lose treasured and valuable employment. You cannot pay your bills, and the one you thought loved you, would take advantage of your emotions to get his way. Yet, you muster the courage to write your thoughts—dark and gloomy, like the middle of a wintery night—on a piece of paper. Those thoughts eventually lead to writing longer narratives and help you forgive all those who damned you.

Ironic how life can move you forward, hinting that the power in humans is nothing compared to the power of the universe; seemingly, the universe knows it all!

Soon after seeing my son in my dream, I also started writing letters to my in-laws Milly and Ronald, asking for any details of my son's physical and mental development. I needed to connect my life again with his in any possible method. Richard's parents responded well to my requests, and in some instances, they managed to send some photos with the help of one of Richard's friends.

Back in those days, there were no cell phones, and very few people in Sri Lanka owned cameras. Only the super wealthy had telephones, and our families did not belong in that group. The best we could do was to communicate with the family through letters; it would take three weeks for a letter to transfer between the two countries.

The very first time I saw a photo of my son was memorable.

He looked different, yet the same to me, as it had been only a few months since I had seen him last. He appeared to have grown and had chubby cheeks and curly hair like his father. He had the most lovable smile, which reached his eyes, indicating the truthfulness of his momentary joy.

In one photo, he was being carried by Milly, and his little fingers were circled around her thumb! I sat on the floor and cried for several minutes. Carrying my son should have been my job; those little fingers should have been held around my thumb.

I started to feel hatred towards anyone who had been instrumental in taking away my baby; I struggled to control my emotions.

Ronald stood next to Milly in that photo, and his eyes had been captivated by the little one's smile, making Ronald's face light up like a Christmas tree. I was grateful beyond words to see how caring they were towards my son. Perhaps I had misjudged their capacity to care for him.

I was thrilled to read that his grandparents were teaching him to read, write, and draw pictures at that young age. He also had been taught to sing little songs. I appreciated their efforts, but what I wanted the most for my son was to be healthy, so that I could bring him back into our family unit. I had trusted his grandparents to take the responsibility of his well-being seriously.

Unfortunately, my trust in them was unfounded.

Later, I realized that my instincts were right about their pretentious attention and affection seen in photos. I had no one to blame but Richard. It is remarkable how a mother always have instincts to recognize true love towards her child.

It took several more months for them to gather the next set of photos. Those exhibited a vastly different appearance of my son. In one of them, he was crying. In another, he had been picked up by someone, and their gesture had made him unhappy; he looked as if he had seen a ghost. His eyes were filled with tears and fear.

I discussed the matter with Richard, but he had no time to pay attention to speculations. How could I do anything about my child's well-being when I was separated from him by 10,000 miles? I decided to ask Milly about the fearful appearance of my son. His sad little face filled my heart with sorrow, and I wept with despair while writing the next letter.

Hoping to find details of the circumstances surrounding those photos, I wrote at length about my distress at seeing my son unhappy. I did not receive a favourable reply. I, the mother of this child, had not been granted access to his life. It was painful.

By the time I saw the next set of photos, it was obvious that my little son could stand and walk. He stood under a little flowering plant while supported by Ronald. His little face had a very pleasant smile, and I thought it resembled mine. I wished that I could carry him and hug him to feel his warmth.

I constantly wondered what I had done not to have the privilege of experiencing my firstborn child's growth.

I did not see my son's first crawl, the first time he sat, stood or walked. I did not have the opportunity to hear his first words, and no one had the courtesy to tell me what they were. Did he call out *Amma* (mother) or *Thaththa* (father) as most children would? Or did he say something very special?

The pain and misery lingered in my soul for all those missed opportunities.

I noted in one of the photos that his hair had been dishevelled and unkempt. I wondered why no one would keep his hair brushed for his comfort. Much later, I would learn the real reason for the noted neglect, which made me extremely angry and distressed.

Since the day I started writing letters inquiring after my son, I anxiously waited for a response from Sri Lanka each afternoon. That had become an important duty to fulfill for each agonizing day.

I would run down to the mailbox in the basement of the family residence building long before the mail had been delivered, and waited patiently for the mailman to sort the collection. Immediately after, I would open our mail slot, hoping to find a letter. Although we often did not receive a letter, on a rare day, I had the privilege to see the blue aerogram with stripes along its edge for international mail, and my heart would pound like a drum.

Those moments were memorable and joyful as I waited anxiously to know anything about my son.

The time dragged on; the anxiety of not having to bring up my child pressed hard on my chest, while Richard continued with his studies. There seemed to be no source of solace for my despair. Richard did not have time for me, and he did not express any regrets for placing me in this deep, dark place.

Then I thought of another way to keep my son close to my heart. I started collecting small items such as clothes, toys, and children's books from any sale to send them by air or sea.

At first, we thought of sending some items by sea. Although sea mail was cheaper, it would take much longer time to reach the destination, and facing customs at the other end was noted as a tedious process. To send by air, it would cost much more. Based on Richard's income, we had difficulty covering airmail postage for large parcels, so the compromise was the size of the parcel always had to fit our budget.

Every other month, a small parcel was mailed; we hoped that even a few items would make our son happy. Although I wanted to send items regularly, the frequency had to be controlled based on the availability of sale items.

Unfortunately, according to Mother's account, the clothes and items we mailed to our son with much difficulty and with great love had been given to Ramona's children by Milly.

Our gifts arrived from a foreign country; they were valued more in Sri Lanka than those purchased locally. In their place, hand-me-downs from Ramona's children had been used for my son. After reading one of Mother's accounts, I felt like I had been taken to prison and stripped bare without a justifiable conviction.

To this day, it is unimaginable why Ramona had behaved that way. In my opinion, she must have been an unconscionable woman to stoop to that level.

In June 19.., I realized that on the 8th of July, my son would be celebrating his first birthday without his parents. I had many sleepless nights wondering how I could make it up to him for not being there for his important milestone. I suggested to Richard that we find a way to send him a brand new suit, a few toys, and a blue candle to light for his first birthday celebration.

In the local shopping mall, I found a little blue suit with *Snoopy* appliqued on the shirt, which I thought would be suitable for his special day. We were able to mail the collected items on time; I hoped and prayed that the new suit would be used for him instead of being given to Ramona's children, although I had no control over Milly's plans.

Finally, after weeks of waiting, we received photos of my son at his first birthday party. I shed tears of joy and sadness when I saw my little boy wearing the suit we had sent. This time, Milly had respected our wishes to dress our son appropriately. He looked beautiful and smart. The suit fitted him as if it had been customized for his little body.

Seemingly, it had been a joyful moment for the family. Ramona had decorated a cake—a sleeping dog with white and brown patches—and the blue candle had been placed on the dog's head. The cake had been carefully placed at the centre of a silver tray with decorated edges.

In one of the photos, I saw my little one cutting his birthday cake. He was standing and holding a long knife with support from Milly. His poise and confidence to participate in the activities warmed my heart like a crackling fire on a cold winter day. This wonderful view uplifted my spirits, much like the happiness that would bring a mother after reading her child's first report card, who had excelled in all subjects.

I was impressed beyond words.

At that moment, I knew I was the luckiest mother in the world to have given birth to such a strong and intelligent little boy. My sentiments would prove to be true in later years.

Ramona and her six children, Ben, Ronald, and Milly, were the only participants at the birthday celebrations. I was very sad that my parents had not been part of my son's special day. Although I wanted to know the reasons for their absence, I decided to refrain from questioning their motives.

Soon after his first birthday celebrations, I decided to prepare a cassette tape to speak to him. I included some songs for his pleasure, such as "You Are My Sunshine" to help him remember my voice while falling asleep. Richard also participated in this effort, and that single cassette with his parent's voices apparently had become my son's lifeline from then onwards.

He had requested to listen to it every night at bedtime.

How could he not like our voices? We were his parents, and he belonged with us; he had the intelligence to recognize his identity within his family unit.

During that period, the cassette and the gifts were the best we could do to keep him included in our little family. We had hoped that he would appreciate our efforts when he grew up; perhaps we had expected too much.

From the time we received Mother's letter about our son's condition, I started making plans for our journey back to Sri Lanka. It took more than four months to gather sufficient funds for the trip and a few gifts for the reunion with our son. Even after those months of preparations, we still had to wait until Richard was allowed to leave the country, based on his progress in the post-graduate program.

While waiting patiently, I constantly wrote to Mother requesting her to visit our son to keep an eye on his health and provide us with any details of his well-being. Surprisingly, Mother followed my instructions and wrote as much as she could.

At that point, I did not know her true reasons for getting involved in our lives as she had not given much concern for my life as a child or my family after my marriage.

Later, I would find out her mysterious reasons to step into our lives.

In August of 19.., soon after Richard was granted permission to take leave from his research work, we travelled back to bring our son to Canada with us.

We took a very long journey—more than twenty-four hours—which included two layovers: one in London, England, and another in the Middle East. Yet, it was the most important journey of my life. I was determined to travel even if we would become paupers again.

In preparation for our son's arrival, with much effort, we furnished the only bedroom in our apartment to accommodate him. We were able to find a small wooden cot, a little writing desk, a bookshelf, and a toy box from the apartment sales of students who were leaving the family residence at Saint Mary's University.

Fortunately, the cot was furnished with a comfortable mattress. From a local Zellers store, we bought a little pillow, bed linen, and a cotton blanket. We did not have enough money to buy him a comforter, but eventually we would, as winter was still a few months away. Brand new toiletries were purchased, and a rubber shield cap for his head baths was borrowed from a friend.

Finally, we were ready to receive our little one.

During preparations for our travel, I discovered that we did not have enough leftover money, not because we have used all our savings to travel to Sri Lanka. No. Without my knowledge, Richard had sent his first saved five hundred dollars to his brother Ben who was unemployed, unmarried, and had a remarkable attraction towards alcohol. Unfortunately, his brother's needs had superseded the needs of our little family.

I learned of Richard's secretive action to release family money to his brother only after I asked for money to purchase a few gifts for my parents.

I was furious.

That day, I decided that I would find a job, any job, and open up a bank account to save some money of my own. Yet, it took over ten years to save a bankable amount of money. My struggle to find a job was like finding a needle in a haystack during a tropical storm.

Social discrimination and the overwhelming responsibilities at home, including raising our son was a strong barrier for me to break through. I was forced to do odd jobs to collect small amounts of money at a time. I did not enjoy the work, but I needed to start somewhere to initiate my financial freedom.

My struggles in that regard perpetuated, as potential employers seemingly saw my skin colour before they saw my abilities to work hard with the skill set I had. Gradually, I lost my hope of becoming financially independent.

It took several more years to find my place in the Canadian society as an employee, who could apply the knowledge gained through education. Finally, after many years, I found a way to be financially independent.

After living in Canada for over two years, on the 17th of August, 19.., we landed in Sri Lanka; a memorable day indeed. My hopes and expectations to see my son overwhelmed my whole being.

For a long time, I had been nostalgic to see my son and the rest of my family. It is a powerful feeling when we wish to relive those memories and emotional experiences that make our life what it is today, as a means to bring back comfort and happy feelings in the past. Finally, the day had arrived for me to experience those emotions in real life.

The KLM (Royal Dutch Airline) jet was about to land at the International Airport in Colombo. It was a clear fine day for air travel, and we arrived in Sri Lanka on a warm, humid morning. I was seated at a window, which gave me an opportunity to see my country from the air for the first time.

I can tell you that what you see out of the window of a plane is raw footage. It has no narrative or soundtrack. Yet, seeing your motherland from a bird's eye view is not only emotional but memorable and fascinating.

For the first time, I had the sense of the underdeveloped nature of our small Island: the majority of land was covered with coconut palm trees. Only a few buildings were visible among them, and they were barely noticeable from that distance as they were not skyscrapers.

I could clearly identify the nooks and crannies of the margin of land where it met the ocean. The outline of the Island matched those detailed in maps that I had studied in school.

At a moment's notice, with the tilted movement of the plane, I witnessed the vastness of the deep, dark Indian Ocean. We started to fly down close to the ocean as if we were about to crash into that ferocious rumbling water below. It was a dramatic view. Until that moment, I had not comprehended the vastness of the ocean compared to the size of my little country.

Suddenly, a runway appeared beneath us, and we landed at Katunayake, Sri Lanka. I was home. Excitement bubbled within me to meet my son after all that time; my emotions were mixed in with feelings of the sheer joy of returning home where I firmly believed I belonged.

A few minutes later, the plane pulled up at a tiny terminal that looked like an old Canadian gas station. It seemed like we had landed right at the doorstep of the airport. I should not have been surprised at how small the airport was, as the size of the Island itself was estimated to be a little bigger than the Nova Scotia peninsula where we had arrived from.

I expected to have extreme exhaustion and unimaginable jet lag, as the time in Sri Lanka was ten or more hours ahead of Atlantic Canada. We had travelled forward in time, making morning in our destination while it was the middle of the night in Nova Scotia.

Yet, with all that excitement, I was fully awake and ready to hold my son.

I've clawed my way from the depth of unimaginable pain, suffering, and sorrow, again and again during the last two years. There had never been a day, hour, minute, or second that I stopped loving or thinking about my son. It was the unconditional and universal love of a mother to her firstborn child. I wanted to say and hear his name, to speak about my son all the time as any other mother would do.

Finally, on that day, I would have the opportunity to hold him in my arms and call him by his name for the whole world to hear.

I expected one look from him, to connect his heart with mine forever, even if we hadn't really met before as mother and child. No matter what our circumstances had been, there cannot be any greater bond than the connection between a mother and child. My love for our son should shine through. My hopes were very high.

When we disembarked at the airport, I deeply felt mixed emotions: the love, the grief, the joy, and the pain. Out of all those, I expected the meeting to be a joy that would reverberate through every pore of my skin and every bone in my body.

That was my hope. That was my ultimate expectation. Yet, the reality I faced would be vastly different.

When we entered the main lobby, it was fascinating to see several members of the family waiting to greet us: Richard's father, my parents, and Maxim, Richard's brother-in-law. I glanced through everyone, as if they were invisible and transparent, to find my son.

I had seen him as an infant over two years ago, and I now had to catch up with our lost time, but I did not know where to start.

My expectations, collected memories, bubbling emotions to meet him were all justified, but nothing could have prepared me for the moment when I first saw him.

Finally, I stood face-to-face with him.

Mother held him in her arms, and I was stunned to see how thin and frail he looked; nothing like what I saw in the last set of photos. He had long hair and a sorrowful face. He looked at me as if I were a stranger; an unknown woman who just appeared from nowhere to meet him.

My heart sank in fear and distress. Will he not remember me, let alone come to terms with his memory of his mother through the photos we sent and the voice cassette? A million other questions rushed to my mind, thousands of regrets surfaced, and hundreds of angry feelings towards Richard crowded my soul. I would never be able to accept my son being a stranger to me.

From that moment, I was determined to help him change his mind.

Motherhood had made me a more compassionate person. I can put myself in someone else's shoes. I can notice small things more—the simple, beautiful everyday moments of life. There are places in the heart that you never knew existed until you love your child. I could see things from a different perspective after I became a mother. My little son had been instrumental in all those changes in me.

Therefore, as his mother, it was up to me to bring my son emotionally closer to me.

I wanted to pick him up from Mother's arms and hug him till he could feel me, but I realized that he had never seen me in real life as his mother. Despite sharing photos with him, which he apparently had kissed each night before bed, I was a stranger to him; therefore, my touch could frighten him.

I controlled my emotions and stepped aside.

A nine-seater van, driven by Maxim, was ready to take us to Richard's family home. Mother sat next to me while holding our son on her lap. I was so close to him, but I felt like I was a million miles away from my own flesh and blood. I could see him examining me with great curiosity. I thought that would be my opportunity to find his emotional connection to me. So, I spoke the same words on the cassette tape that we had sent to him from Canada.

"*Putha* (son), this is *Amma*. I hope you are keeping well and staying happy. I love you very much."

His eyes lit up, and he kept them on my face for a countable amount of seconds. It felt like an eternity, but I held my breath to see his reaction, like a new mother who would wait for her newborn child to utter their first cry.

Then he smiled, making my eyes water. I found my little son. I was exhilarated as tears of joy rolled down my warm cheeks, soothing my skin like a slow-moving brook, sprouted from a snow-capped mountain.

I had to trust that he would recognize me and would decide to come home to me. Yet again, I refrained from touching him, giving him more time to think about the unusual events he was experiencing that day.

While we were travelling from the airport, there had been some serious preparations to welcome us, and Milly had been instrumental in all efforts. We sat together at the same table before our departure two years ago and enjoyed a tasty meal while our son sat on a high chair next to me.

We were grateful for the welcome and the reception; however, the reality of the conditions under which our son had been kept during our absence was yet to be revealed.

On that afternoon, the hot and humid air was more intolerable compared to the time I had lived in Sri Lanka. The everlasting summer-like weather made me perspire profusely, as I had now been accustomed to the cool and crisp air of Nova Scotia.

I decided to take advantage of that hot and heavy air to make my son comfortable.

I sat beside him and started to feed him the grapes I had brought from Canada and kept in the refrigerator for a while. First, he was reluctant to accept food from me. After a few attempts, he continued to open his mouth when each peeled and seeded grape approached him, like a little bird who responds to its mother's generosity. Each grape, placed in his little mouth, garnered his attention towards me, more than the one before.

Suddenly, he stopped eating and looked at me with wide eyes and smiled.

Seemingly, he knew that no one else would have the patience to feed him one grape at a time, unless it was a person who truly cared about him. He was an intelligent child.

I could only give him mother's milk for four short months, but that day, by feeding him one fruit at a time, I had opened his eyes to see me as his mother for the first time.

I was successful.

Since then, he began to respect all of my attention on him. Immediately, I emerged from my misery of separation from my son. I used all of my energy to exhibit my love for him.

The evening arrived, and I had another opportunity to get even closer to my son. I asked him whether he would like to have a cool bath because it was very hot. He was still wearing the same clothes that he wore during the trip to the airport and must have felt very uncomfortable. He looked at me with pleasure and indicated that it would be fine. Although it was only a nod, I took the opportunity as if he had fully agreed with words.

I located a new set of cotton pyjamas and a washcloth that I had purchased in Canada and had placed in my travel bag. I took his little hand, and we walked together into the bathroom. I asked whether I could remove his clothes for the wash. He smiled and helped me remove them.

Then became the moment of truth on how much care, or lack thereof, the family had given to my little son during my absence.

To my great horror, his little body was covered in red wounds. Some were opened and bloody, and some were beginning to blister. He had developed a skin disease. Later, I would find out the reasons for this illness. His caretakers had neglected to bathe him regularly to cool his body and clean it after long days of playing outside in the hot sun. To add insult to injury, no one had cared enough to take him to a doctor for medical advice.

At that moment, I realized why Mother had written a letter to me, exhibiting her concerns for my son's well-being. She might have seen the gravity of his illness.

Ironically, Mother's journal would reveal the reasons for *her tattle*. Indeed, she always had her reasons for being selfish. No one was allowed to cross her path, for she would react like an angry cobra and spit her venom at her enemy.

The entry in Mother's journal: *I have regretted not helping my daughter in her time of need so she could raise her son in Sri Lanka until the time for her to join her husband. To make it up to her, I requested that Milly allow me to take the child to Kaduwela during school holidays. It worked out well for a while until Milly had the audacity to disrupt my plans. Her excuse was that I have been too liberal in the way I brought up the child, and that has created a difficult task for her with disciplining him after returning. Also, Milly did not pay much attention to his cleanliness, which eventually made the child sick. Since she refused to let me take the child after much pleading, I took the authority to request that the child's parents take him away from Milly.*

Whatever the reasons Mother had to write to me about the illness, I was grateful that Mother warned us about my innocent child's predicament, which enabled us to take action to prevent an impending tragedy.

I would learn later that the abuse and neglect by those who took responsibility for my infant son was far worse than what was visible on his skin. It was heartbreaking. Although the tragic events were behind us, I could not remain silent. I expressed my disgust towards Richard for his unacceptable decision to depend on his parents to care for our son.

Milly expressed her reasons for the neglect. "You did not pay me to take care of your son", she blurted. Her words crushed my soul.

Richard had expected his mother to care for our son as a gesture of good will to support him in his post-graduate studies. There had been no understanding of payed services from his family; such would have been impossible, as we barely had enough money to survive in a foreign country.

Still, I could have cared for my son even with a limited income, as my love for him would have surpassed any difficulties that we had to endure. I was deprived of this right; the consequences were inevitable.

My heart fell apart into million pieces when my son Sumudu looked at my face and pointed at one of his ruptures, and said, "Wound."

His innocent brown eyes had no tears, but they expressed pain and unhappiness. The sorrow in his eyes pierced my heart like an arrow. I felt that finally, he trusted me, his mother, to express the suffering he had endured during my absence.

While holding my son next to me as gently as I could, I sat on the wet floor of the bathroom and cried.

He patiently waited for his bath.

CHAPTER 19

𝒯HE 𝒫OINT OF 𝒩O 𝒭ETURN

It had been over forty years since our little family was reunited. Year after year, I had witnessed gradual growth in several areas of our lives.

During all those years, I felt like I had been confined to my home, while the sun rose and set each day making the light and the corresponding darkness shifted within the confines of the walls, changing the view dramatically.

I could compare such movements of imaginary light to the joy and sorrow I had experienced while we grew together as a family in Canada; much like looking through a View Master that would exhibit the chronology of multiple events.

In 20.., I started to recall several of those memorable events after I was awakened by an unusual dream.

I visited the Schatz, a private beach on the west coast of Aruba, an island lying southwest of the Lesser Antilles in the Caribbean Sea. With squinted eyes, I stood on the sandy coastline and gazed at the blue water that touched the horizon in the distance. The sea greeted me with roaring waves and a warm tropical breeze.

The last time I had been on this beach was for my son Sumudu's wedding. It was a day filled with emotions; the sun was brighter, and the heat was harsh, while the wind that swirled across the land was gusty and unfriendly.

The wedding took place in February, and I could recall waking up in Hotel Riu Palace Aruba.

The couple decided to have a destination wedding, and the guests spent one week at this resort and participated in their wedding ceremony. I bathed in the blue Caribbean Sea, enjoyed wonderful tropical meals, and met the guests and the locals. It was a holiday I could have remembered with happiness. Yet, in the back of my mind, I knew that the memories of this holiday would not be as joyful as I wanted them to be.

On the afternoon of the wedding day, we were escorted to Schatz beach in a limousine; a short ride, but everyone had been in a joyful mood, filling the crowded space of the vehicle with laughter and chatter, as if we had a long-distance to travel across the Island. We arrived in good time to settle down for the ceremony. The beach had been decorated for the occasion, and it was buzzing with the guests.

The wedding party was dressed in white or shades of pale yellow. Many guests were dressed to match the summer-like weather. The merriment of the day was shared by all attendees, except me. I did not know how to feel. My soul was filled with multitude of emotions such as sorrow, distress and most of all inadequate courage to face the realities of the momentous day.

My heart felt heavy, as if a concrete block had been placed on my chest.

Surprisingly, in my dream, the beach was empty, and the sun warmed my body steadily, and calmer winds made my mind serene. Indeed, a contrasting view had resulted in different emotions.

I floated around, just like I should in a dream. I looked up to find the infinite blue sky above, and the big fluffy clouds added a touch of ecstasy. As the memories poured in, I headed over to a rock I could recall from my last visit. As before, I stood on it and took a deep breath. The salty air filled my nostrils, releasing a spell-like hypnotic trance in me.

I took a few steps along the sandy beach. The gritty sand irritated the skin between my toes during my last visit, and it still had the same annoying effect. Yet, this time I embraced the discomfort with calm thoughts because, in my dream, I did not have formal wear to manage.

I turned to face the location where the ceremonial canopy had been. The make-shift altar protected by a canopy of white silk fabric, which was decorated with beautiful white flowers, had been taken down. I had witnessed many activities under that canopy on that day.

They had engraved some feelings of loss in me.

I visualized the priest, who stood close to the canopy, preparing for the ceremony. I remembered the beautiful sounds created by the fiddler, who stood across from the altar and enchanted the crowd by playing songs like "Fools Rush In" by Elvis Presley and the "Wedding March." Now there was no music, and the surroundings were quiet and tranquil.

I looked down, and strangely, I could see the countless footprints made on the soft, silky sand by those who had witnessed the union. The shape of each foot had left a lasting imprint. Apparently, the sea did not have the power to wash those with its high tide much like the eons of time could not erase my memories of that day.

I thought of the smile on my son's face when he saw me for the first time as I walked towards the altar. The sound of his fiancé's giggle when they exchanged the rings could still be heard within my ears. The kiss my son planted on the lips of his new bride when the priest verbalized the famous words, "You may kiss the bride," had made the guests go wild with cheers.

The tear that had rolled down my cheek had felt warm, much like the loads of emotion that had erupted within me.

All that was sensed in my dream were real, but at the same time, they disappeared much like a normal dream. Still, those visions, etched in my memory, could not be dissolved. Although they should not have brought hurt and sadness because it had been a moment of happiness in my son's life, they always did.

This beach was like a sepulchre; my losses and suffering lay buried in that sand. So, my firm thought at that moment of my dream visit was: *there would be no resurrection.*

My return to this beach was not to enjoy the tropical weather or re-live the ceremonial events of that wedding day. No. It had to do with the emotions I had stored in my memory. I needed to forget the agony, pain, regret, and frustration I felt on his wedding day and to feel calm and at peace again; perhaps, I had expected the beach to do me a favour.

In reality, I woke up from my dream in Canada, which had frozen ledges and leafless trees, and found myself lying on my bed more than 3,000 miles from that warm Caribbean breeze and its surrounding greenery. I sighed, stretched my tired body, turned, and was bewildered by the darkness I saw outside the bedroom window even at 6:00 a.m.

I made a mental note: several years had passed since I had witnessed my son taking this bold step in his life. The whole process had the outward appearance of being cordial, but it had been fragile and deeply schizophrenic in its entirety.

The memories of my past experiences with my son as a child, a young adult and an adult, and those I experienced on the Schatz beach in February were worlds apart, almost like two different lifetimes of two different men. The emotions stirred up by my dream crowded my soul, urging me to find their meaning. I concurred.

I sat on my bed and re-evaluated our life in Canada during the past decades.

It had taken a very long time for me to find a path to fulfil my desires in life: educate my son to reach his full potential, somehow for me to return to my passions in life, and to be financially independent.

I could remember how I had gathered enough strength to push away the many demons that blocked my path. How I kept my mind in check and how I kept my sanity in balance over those difficult years would be my accolade.

Although, at times, I felt madness in me due to how Richard approached our family life, I had the strength to see the silver lining in those dark clouds. Perhaps that was either because of the love I felt for him as my partner in life, or it was the strength within me to make lemonade using the lemons that were thrown at me. Perhaps, it was both. Yet, none of those were my principal reason.

It was our son, who had become a part of our lives and had acted as the glue for our family.

In September 19.., when the autumn colours were radiating across the land, we were given a second chance to be a real family. It was a turning point in our life. I looked forward to being a mother to our son, who was about two and a half years old, and to build a close relationship with him with the support of Richard.

The day I arrived in Canada with our little son Sumudu in my arms, I had many hopes and dreams to build a strong and healthy family.

Although it has been written that "It takes a village to raise a child," I realized that it would be my responsibility to bring him up all by myself, while Richard was pursuing his graduate program. I did not mind that at all, but the only conflicting thought that crossed my mind was "Will I attend to his needs above and beyond what Mother had given me?"

With that thought, my determination to beat the odds became unwavering and strong.

It was remarkable how well our son had adapted to his life in a new country; he was an intelligent boy beyond our expectations. Even though we had to live in a small one-bedroom apartment, our life with Sumudu had been filled with many joyful moments.

The three of us poured all of our possessions into our limited apartment space. One never knew what one would find in the only bedroom closet by disinterring: Sumudu's toys, Richard's discarded binders of lecture notes, or a box of books that I had saved after reading each once, thinking that they might become handy again if I ever decided to write a book of my own.

All that were collected in that closet had been justified, as they were considered re-usable. Being immigrants, we believed that some of it might come in handy on a rainy day.

Among all of that, the closet also had a collection of biscuit tins containing letters sent by our family in Sri Lanka. A sentimental collection that accompanied us from one home to another, although they did not hold any value to support our future endeavours.

As we adapted to life in our tiny apartment, I had to continuously remind myself that this little home had a major purpose, more than to deal with difficulties and our frustrations. It was to give our son a fair shot at growing up in a friendly and loving environment to become a man of confidence with great love in his heart.

I enjoyed every moment of supporting Sumudu's physical and mental growth, which brought much more energy and satisfaction to my life, to look forward to spending another day with him.

Eventually, we all achieved our intended goals; yet, Sumudu's unexpected decision as an adult would baffle me.

I remember my first walk with Sumudu on the soft snow, our first outing to the Jungle Gym at a near-by park, and his first party in Canada to celebrate his third birthday. Each of those activities enabled him to relate his life with his parents' and develop close relationships.

Yet, there had been moments of distress too.

I recalled a moment of deep sadness when he was four years old. For the first time, I had to leave him in a daycare as I started to work at a chemistry laboratory, hoping to ignite a carrier in that field. Although I had explained to Sumudu during his breakfast, he would be going to a daycare for a few hours that day, the moment I entered the facility, I saw his eyes filled with sadness; perhaps he felt that he was being abandoned by his mother yet again.

The moment I turned to the door, leaving him with the caretaker, he burst into tears.

I felt the distress in his mind, and my feet refused to move. It was painful to leave my little boy with strangers; yet, I had to leave the premises. I contemplated returning and holding him in my arms and saying that I would never leave him again, but I had to proceed to help us both: for him to get accustomed to the world and for me to extend my efforts in finding my way back into the world.

Today, I believe I took the right path.

After exiting the building, I sat outside the daycare where I could still see him to ensure that he was alright without his mother. It was a moment where I had to find courage to let nature take its course. He kept looking at the door, so I waited until he stopped crying. After several minutes, he realized that I would not return and that he needed to start believing in his current surrounding. Finally, he turned to look at the children who were playing together. After the caretaker spoke with him and hugged him, he wiped his tears.

I sobbed all the way to the laboratory. It was a very sad day for both of us, but it was the beginning for us to grow as individuals.

When I returned to the daycare to pick him up, his eyes informed me that he understood the predicament I was in to care for him in a way that he could move on with his own life. He knew that I would never abandon him again.

We continued to bond well with warmth and love, and as new immigrants, the three of us grew together in our new country, Canada.

A single income from a student's stipend prevented us from providing Sumudu with all that he wished to have as a child, but he never complained, almost as if he understood the true nature of us being an immigrant family.

The only time his heart was broken was when one of his wealthy classmates ridiculed him, for wearing outdated clothes to school. My heart broke to pieces hearing the distress in his voice. Since then, I decided to purchase brand new clothes for him, forgoing any additional purchases for the home or for his parents.

Although we were poor, I was determined to provide a sibling to Sumudu, knowing that one day he would not have extended family in Canada after his parents' demise.

That plan did not materialize as I had wished.

As soon as Sumudu started his schooling at the primary level, I felt that I needed to further educate myself, if I wish to find employment in Canada. Yet, I wondered whether I could handle studying while juggling all the responsibilities that were already on my plate.

I believed that the universe had designed a plan for me to make the right decision. Two angels - a close friend and a professor in the local university- came forward and extended a helping hand to make my decision easy and my dream a reality.

After seeing the acceptance letter from the university, I had no doubts that I should follow through the program even with difficulties.

I boldly accepted the challenge, first as a part-time student to make the transition more bearable. But, after commencing the full-time participation, I could not find any spare time to care for myself.

When I wanted to expand our family, I had been under unimaginable stress. I was responsible for taking care of Sumudu, attending to household maintenance, all the while carrying out full-time research for my graduate program at the university.

Unfortunately, those responsibilities had distracted me to the point that I was oblivious to being pregnant with our second child. I lost the child during my first trimester due to the stress and the unintentional neglect. That loss made me fall into a deep depression. The fear instilled in me due to this experience prevented me from trying again for a second child.

I feared the future for our son without having a sibling, and the images I foresaw were not pleasant.

Eventually, I decided to direct my energy to provide the best education for Sumudu to enable his full potential in life. Perhaps, I had also envisioned a successful life for him in finding a supportive partner.

When Sumudu became a teenager, I knew challenging times would arrive, but we were ready.

We immersed him in sports, such as badminton and baseball. To our joy, he did very well, much like in his education. We supported his interests to the best of our abilities, although our income did not match the expenditure for a long while.

He was obedient and hardworking because he knew his place in the Canadian society. He had comprehended that, unlike a locally born person, he might need to work extra hard to reach his goals. We encouraged him to follow his dreams for success.

By that time, I was confident that I was the most fortunate mother in the whole world to have a son like Sumudu. Yet, at that time, I did not comprehend how my life had been intertwined with his; a symbiotic relationship akin to a grey wolf and striped hyena hunting together.

My closeness to Sumudu began early in his life. This was because he had strong instincts to sense my distressful moments and provided me with emotional support to keep my life afloat.

Sumudu's presence in my life during a tumultuous period bonded me to him, much like to a loving sibling or a trustworthy friend who would stand by me for life. He would become a shining lifeline, which I grabbed tightly to keep me on track to the purpose of life, more so than what the umbilical cord would have done to connect him to me.

I believed it was natural for a human to become emotionally attached to another who exhibits compassion; I should have been more realistic.

I also should have anticipated that my little boy would gradually grow up. Yet, over the next several years, I failed to observe the natural progression of the emotional gap growing between mother and son. Unknowingly, I had held onto him until nature eventually revealed that I could not belong in his life the way I had hoped; a future with Sumudu living close to his family.

Alas! I had misjudged his sentiments altogether. Just like any other man, he had been waiting to leave the nest to look for an opportunity to become an independent man.

How could I blame him for being normal?

I graduated with a Master's Degree during Sumudu's adolescence.

It was the time for me to look for employment. In that venture, I did not anticipate the numerous barriers that would fall across my path to find a suitable position in Halifax or in Dartmouth. It was daunting to see the realities of discrimination.

In the end, I had to leave home to be employed.

With a heavy heart, I left home to live in Kentville, a small agricultural town more than one-hour driving distance from our home in Dartmouth. The tragedies of this move were multifold because Sumudu was at a delicate stage in his life, Richard was still looking for steady employment, and neither of them knew how to cook a meal.

In addition, I had to live, yet again, amongst strangers one week at a time. I returned home every Friday, and most of my time during the two days at home was spent cooking for the coming week. I had no time to spend with Sumudu and be in touch with his day-to-day activities. It was difficult and had devastating consequences.

I knew a calamity was just around the corner that would haunt me.

After more than a year of commuting and struggling to keep up with my responsibilities at home and attending to work, which demanded my time and energy, an unexpected incident made me lose my hopes, yet again, to fit into the Canadian society.

On a regular grocery run at a small local store in Kentville town, my eyes were opened wide. A little Anglophone girl, about ten years of age, stepped across my path and looked directly into my eyes and said,

"Leave this country and go to wherever you came from."

I looked at her mother, who was standing next to her, to see her reaction. It was worse than the words the girl spoke. She stood without any emotions and patted her daughter's shoulder. Later, I would learn that in rural Nova Scotia, the discrimination towards immigrants was far worse than in the city.

I immediately left the premises and called home, but none of us could find a solution to the problem, except to find employment elsewhere. I had to dig deep to find strength to carry on in Kentville.

That weekend I returned home with sadness and despair. Yet, my determination kept me at my rural job, as I could not find any other place where I could fit in.

Then, a daunting event of the consequence of my absence from home happened.

One Friday, when I returned home, I could not locate Sumudu. Richard informed me that he was out with friends. Such would have been known to me in the past, making me realize that the lack of attention on Sumudu resulted in a drift in his behaviour. Sumudu did not return home until very late at night, and I had already turned in with exhaustion.

The next morning, it was very clear that my son had been exposed to alcohol for the first time. It was the turning point for our family. I was determined to find a path to keep our family together until Sumudu reached adulthood.

Finally, Richard stepped forward to find a solution for the problems we faced in Nova Scotia: explore employment opportunities in the nation's capital, Ottawa. He was successful.

Sumudu was completing his first year at Dalhousie University when Richard accepted a position in Ottawa, which required our family to move from Nova Scotia.

This move made many changes in our lives.

It provided me with my very first opportunity to find steady employment, but it also separated Sumudu from us for yet another period before he was reunited after a transfer to the University of Ottawa.

While working towards a degree in biochemistry, Sumudu sat for the Law School Admission Test (LSAT). With his results, Sumudu was able to open a fruitful avenue for his future.

With his very high percentile LSAT results, he could have attended any school, including the local law school. But to our distress, he selected the University of Toronto, which was more than a five hours drive from home.

This selection had sealed the deal for his future, professionally and personally.

In 20.., Sumudu packed his belongings and moved to Toronto to attend law school. That move changed my life forever. Our family cat Pussia (Sinhala version of Pussy), who had been very close to Sumudu, also felt the loss and would change her gentile behaviour. So, while I lost the most trustworthy person I had in my life, I had inherited an unhappy cat, who demanded attention from me for several more years to come.

With Sumudu's departure, the magnitude of the loss for me had become unbearable, making me immerse myself in work. It became my escape from reality. Yet, since the day Sumudu left home, there had been nothing that could fill the space he had left in our home and in our hearts.

Sumudu never returned home to spend any extended period of time with us since his departure. Even during his university holidays, most often, his visits were limited to a day or two. When asked why he did not wish to visit for a longer time with his family, his answer was very clear:

"I now live in Toronto."

His answer made me feel like my only son had abandoned me. I sensed that moment as a point of no return.

I wondered whether the decision to stay far from home was made based on his knowledge of earlier events, such as his father's decision to separate him from his mother at infancy, making him to live with a family who did not care for him well. I would never know the answers to these questions.

I decided to respect his decision not to speak of them, but I felt that I already knew the truth.

After graduating from law school in 200-, Sumudu secured a position as an associate in a law firm on Bay Street in Toronto (Canada's equivalent to Wall Street in the USA).

In my eyes, he had now reached a marriageable age.

Finding a suitable life partner for a person who had migrated to Canada at a very young age would always be a challenging task. That is because, while children are associating with locally born children, the parents may prefer selecting a partner from their original country to facilitate a comfortable alliance with the in-laws.

Therefore, when Sumudu selected a woman whose family originated from a culture similar to Sri Lanka, I considered this meeting as a stroke of luck.

I was excited to have a daughter in our family since I missed having one during my life. However, the new member in this family would be a daughter-in-law, not a daughter, and I needed to be prepared for a new way to associate with my son.

It was clear that Sumudu had selected a suitable partner; however, since then, Sumudu's attachments to his own family began to diminish.

I presumed that such a change in behaviour in a man after marriage is universally recognized.

After waking up from my dream visit to Schatz, I sat on my bed and acknowledged that I had visited my past memories of Sumudu for a lengthy period; then, I dozed off again.

Strangely, my dream on the Schatz beach continued while I napped, and the images that had started to cross my mind were a clear contrast to the beginning and the middle of the original dream.

I was still on the beach, looking across the Caribbean Sea. The view of the horizon had dramatically changed while I roamed, so had my perception of the surroundings. Without me noticing, the sun had almost set. The sky was more purple than red, highlighting the impending transition from day to night.

My inner voice whispered, "Change is inevitable; one has no choice but to embrace it."

Much like that day had changed from dawn to dusk I realized that my thoughts of the past had to be changed to accept the present.

I gazed out onto the horizon and sensed that all negative feelings that had been stored in my thoughts had been dissolved. They had become smudged at the periphery, like a watercolour image exposed to a spray from the vast ocean.

Peace, serenity, and contentment. The mixture of these unmatched feelings overwhelmed me. I leaned back and stared at the sky, noticing the different hues. I watched the constant ebb of the waves and breathed in deeply as I lay down.

Although my eyes had been shutting involuntarily, I did not fall asleep; I had sensed that I was fully awake.

I had been awakened from the dream to accept what it was. I hugged my pillow, and my tears stained the cover to imprint my feelings. They were not all bad; some brought hope for the upcoming days.

While trying to wake up to a cold, wintery day, I wondered: did the beach visit in my dream help me find peace after several years of suffering? I believe it did. Seemingly, it had directed me to a path to resolve the conflicted thoughts within me.

Then the telephone rang, making me jump out of bed. It was a call from Sumudu.

"Hi, Mum, how are you?" I sensed his loving feelings and his 'invisible smile' in my soul.

"I am good, how are you?" I asked with joy.

That was all I wanted—my son, asking me how I was.

At the end of Sumudu's phone call, a feeling of emptiness engulfed my heart. As usual, I started to imagine when his next call would be, and I wondered why I was visualizing an image of Picasso's deconstructed face with respect to a future phone call from him.

I craved for my little boy's image to replace it.

After reminiscing on my life with Sumudu and Richard in Canada, I wondered about Mother and the after-effects of her dreadful influence on me and how it might have affected my child's upbringing. Did I bring up Sumudu vastly different from the way Mother did?

The answer was very clear. Indeed, unlike Mother, I had exceeded my expectations in providing love and support to Sumudu. His future had been secured, and the love I had expressed had been extended to others, making him a popular man.

My momentary realization was that I had overridden the selfish behaviour of Mother and had succeeded in bringing a well-balanced and educated man to the society.

It was a victorious moment in my life.

CHAPTER 20

*T*HE *C*OLOURS OF *M*Y *L*OSS

It was the middle of September of 2020. I walked along the path facing Major's Hill Park in the heart of Ottawa to see the stunning colours of the Fall Rhapsody. As usual, summer had ended, and autumn had arrived to prepare the ecological surroundings for the incoming winter. Although the annual seasonal changes had followed the same pattern as any other year in Canada, when the cold winds started to blow across the land in 2020, Ottawa faced a new critical point in the COVID-19 pandemic.

The second wave of the new Coronavirus had arrived.

I looked around me to see how different the appearance was of those who came out to see the colourful foliage this year compared to the last; the powerful virus had changed human behaviour forever. I could not recognize anyone as they all had covered faces. I was glad that I could still admire and enjoy the colourful landscape.

Face masks had become a norm, and I did not even feel it on my face.

I took my time to admire the stunning contrast between the clear blue sky and the wonderful colours of the maple and other trees. I wondered whether any other land on this earth has this magical colour change during this time of the year.

Suddenly, I came across a large tree covered with orange-brown leaves. That tree stood out among others that donned varying

298

colours of yellow to deep red. Its unique colour combination created a powerful rush in my mind; I remembered why. That colour mixture took my mind back to the date that I had lost the most valued human in my life—Father.

The orange-brown colour combination of the leaves matched the colour of the unusual flowers that decorated the satin interior of the casket that housed his body. A tear rolled down my cheeks, and the cold air froze it, making an impression on my face.

More than ten years had passed since his death, but the memory of those exotic flowers was fresh and vivid in my mind. Then, the orange-brown colour reminded me of Mother's death too; the saree which draped her body, lying in the casket, had the same colour combination in its design. At that moment, I realized that this particular tree signified the two great losses in my life. *How strange,* I thought.

With that revelation, my mind started to peel the layers of the past, re-surfacing the memories of my parents.

While my relationship with Mother had been a harrowing experience, Father had been my beacon and the best friend. His engagement in my life was much like the efforts of a horse pulling a cart up the steep hill of life, while it had been filled to the brim with baggage that Mother had burdened it with.

Father helped me see the sunrise over that steep, dark hill. His vision had been the foundation for my life, much like a mansion that had been built on an unshakable ground.

If I would be inclined to describe Father and his influence on my life, I might have to write another book. My memories are vivid and incredibly interesting. However, if I were to sketch him as I knew, not only for me but for the whole world at large, I would describe him as a man full of love, who was a legend for making others laugh because he had the ability to initiate numerous joyous incidents.

Sometimes people around him would laugh deeply at his humorous expressions, while holding on to their stomachs as tears of joy rolled down their cheeks. He had a great capacity of bringing happiness to those who came across him.

To my great pleasure, I still laugh out loud when I recall some of those hilarious moments I had experienced with him. He had a great sense of humour.

But, if I were to appreciate him as being Father to his little girl, I have many details that I would like to share. His qualities, which I admired, were countless, but those that still energize me were his honesty, unworldliness, and perfect sincerity in expressing his love to his family.

He had a godlike yet childlike character when standing among the immediate and the extended family. Remarkably, he had the capacity and courage to be silent during the most disturbing and aggressive outbursts of Mother. He would come out on the other side with a solution to a hypothetical chaos Mother would have instigated.

He was a wonderful father to both Brother and me, although Brother, even to this day, believes that Father had a deeper connection to me. I would not dispute his sentiments, as I felt that too.

But the most wonderful memories I have are related to many activities Father and I did together, and one of those stands out.

During my school or university holidays, on afternoons after a sumptuous meal at lunch, we regularly took long walks down to Kaduwela town. He considered those walks as opportunities to fill me with his wisdom to develop a successful life. His instructions on how I should follow my heart and when not to follow it were my guiding principles.

He had been my mentor and my lifeline. Although I sincerely wished to follow his directions in all my decisions, I know that I did not, and I had realized the error and its regrettable outcome.

Although I had lived away from my family home for the majority of my life, I constantly felt his presence. I always had the pleasure to see his eyes upon me when we met, as somehow, when his eyes were fixed on me, they made me feel that we two were in a league together. There was something we had in common. I remember his pleasure when I came into his workroom to speak briefly about anything of interest to me; he always made time for me. Indeed, I was often on his side, and he was on mine.

We were a team until we parted in life.

When he was about seventy-five years old, I had the pleasure of spending time with him in Canada. By that time, I had been married and was living in Canada for nearly thirteen years. I expected to spend time with him until his death; however, that would be dramatically cut short by Mother's aggression and unpleasant display of disrespect towards Father and my family.

One particular incident would alter the lives of all.

For over eleven years, we lived in Halifax in students' housing. Finally, in August of our twelfth year, we bought our first home in Dartmouth.

Halifax and Dartmouth were considered twin cities, separated by Macdonald Bridge. As the home prices in Halifax were too high for our budget, we crossed over to Dartmouth. The home we bought was in the old section of the Colby Village.

In 19.., our son had graduated from his primary years at St. Francis Catholic School in Halifax. It was the right time to look for a suitable first home closer to a junior high school. We were fortunate to find one next to Astral Drive Junior High.

Our home in Dartmouth fitted well within our budget and the plans we had for our future.

There was a separate room for our son, who was approaching his teenage years, and a large French window in the upstairs living room to keep a cushioned bench next to it for our family cat Pussia to look out and be mesmerized by the movements on the road. Most of all, the home had a basement as a separate unit, which we thought would be suitable for our parents for their privacy and comfort, if one day they would come to live with us.

In 19.., during a visit to Sri Lanka, I asked Father whether he would like to come to Canada either for a visit or to live with us. I remember how Mother's eyes lit up hearing my invitation—Mother exhibited greater excitement about the idea than Father. Yet, based on my relationship I had with her in the past, I was uncertain how she would adjust to the new environment and how willing she would be to live with her daughter.

After asking several questions, gradually, Father warmed up to the idea. Just before we left Sri Lanka, he assured me that he would make arrangements for their travel to Canada.

I informed him that we would do our best to accommodate them. I also assured him that if he were willing, I would be delighted to take care of him for the rest of his life. His assuring smile provided me with the greatest comfort.

In March of that year, the snow started to melt away after a long winter, welcoming the early spring. It was the perfect time to travel to Canada.

I still remember how my parents, in their seventies, flew halfway across the globe to come to our home. We welcomed them with great love. They entered Canada as new immigrants, and I felt it was my duty to care for them the best way I could during the sunset years of their lives.

I firmly believed that would be my only chance to return the favour for Father's generosity for the care he gave me when I was young.

I wished to care for Mother too, since she was supportive of several important aspects of my life, although, in the back of my mind some uncertain thoughts started to nag me from the moment Mother entered our home, like a pin-prick on an open wound.

My instincts were correct; my plans to care for either of them did not materialize, as Mother would decide to change the expected outcome.

Mother had been a thrill seeker in life, so I was certain she would have looked at my invitation as an opportunity to experience a new adventure. Eventually, I realized that Mother's plan to travel to Canada with Father was part of her devious plan to make my life miserable, by imposing her powers on Father and his life.

My troubles with Mother during that period began when I first suggested that she help me prepare meals, as the family was now extended. She immediately refused. Day-in and day-out, I laboured to prepare meals for my family. I did not have enough time to look for jobs or attend to my son, who was a teenager that needed parental guidance in his life. A few months dragged on, and Mother did not budge, although my struggles were very clear to her.

One day, Mother complained that she was not satisfied with her accommodations. She felt slighted as she and Father had their quarters below ours.

After all the efforts we had made to accommodate them, she wanted more than what we could offer. From my younger days, I knew she believed herself to be superior to everyone and had demanded privileges to meet her comforts. I firmly believed that the accommodations she demanded from us were ridiculous, as my family of three needed more room than my parents.

But I wondered, was that the real reason for Mother's outbursts?

She continued her escapades of unreasonable demands and rude remarks that made us feel uncomfortable. Father did not speak a single word to intervene. A few weeks into her bad behaviour, she realized that I would not give in to her demands.

Then one evening, Mother started to scream, informing us that she would immediately leave unless we would comply. She might have been out of her mind; how was it possible that she did not realize her sudden plans to travel in the middle of a night would not work without having an airline ticket?

Obviously, she was being difficult and disrespectful to us.

Around 8:00 p.m. that night, Mother flared up like a combustible liquid that encountered a flame. I decided to stay calm and quiet. By that time, we had experienced the first snowfall for the arriving winter and the ground was partially covered in snow. While screaming, she opened the front door and walked out into the darkness to mimic her departure at that late hour in the cold.

I looked at Father, wondering what his reaction to Mother's behaviour would be, and to my surprise, he did not follow her or persuade her to stay inside. Instead, he walked into his room. So, we also walked away from the scene to attend to our tasks at hand. I started serving dinner and everyone, including Father, gathered around the kitchen table.

After more than thirty minutes, I heard the front door opening and Mother walked in. I was glad that she had realized her mistake and that no one in the family would tolerate her disrespectful behaviour. She exhibited her true character of being the perfect drama queen.

Sadly, she did not have the courage to join us at the kitchen table; she had decided to forgo dinner that evening. No one spoke of it the next day.

However, Richard and I had to decide for her.

I expressed my concerns to Father about Mother's intolerable outbursts. I informed him that she should leave as planned if she were unhappy. I was very clear that we were unable to provide any more comforts than what we already had. I did not urge Father to stay behind, as he had to decide where he wished to live.

Unfortunately, Father did not wish to let Mother leave alone. He expressed his concerns for her travel plans, and with tearful eyes, he informed me how sorry he was to leave me and my generous offer to care for him.

Mother knew that I did not have the opportunity to live in Sri Lanka to take care of Father. Richard and I had become citizens of Canada, which automatically disqualified us as being citizens of Sri Lanka. She also knew that if I were to take care of them, Father would give me my share of their properties and any other belongings.

Did she plan to disinherit me completely and support my brother instead, or did she feel that she might not receive the care that *she* expected during her final years while being with my family?

The decision was made, and their bags were packed. It was time to say goodbye. Even before the heavy snow could cover the land for the winter of 19.., Father left us with Mother to return to Sri Lanka.

I was devastated.

For more than three years after their departure, I had no contact with Father because Mother had refused to communicate with us. In fact, she had placed the blame at our door for their departure from Canada!

I could not fathom Mother's thought process. I continued to wonder about it until one day I remembered an incident that occurred on their very first night at our home.

While bringing them a flask of hot water for tea the next morning—a suggestion by Father—I overheard their hushed pillow-talk.

"Are you comfortable and warm?" Father asked with a concerned voice.

"Yes, I am, but I am not comfortable going to sleep, because who knows what could happen to us if we would fall asleep?" Mother responded.

"Why do you say that? What could happen? We are in our daughter's home." Father inquired.

"How could we know whether she will squeeze our necks while we are in sleep and get rid of the bodies?" Mother said in a deep tone, as if she truly believed in her thoughts.

I froze at the door after hearing her words, which solidified her mistrust in me.

I did not know whether I should react to that disturbing conversation or not. I thought for a moment and decided to give her the benefit of the doubt. I felt she must have been extremely tired, which resulted in having such incoherent thoughts, and that she did not feel comfortable sleeping in a strange environment. After all, they had travelled for more than twenty-four hours and did not have much sleep during that period.

Naturally, Father did not respond to her remarks; he might have had the same notion for her words as I did. I slowly entered their room, left the flask and other items to facilitate making morning tea, and stepped out without saying a word, making them believe that I did not hear their conversation.

Although her words shook me to the core, and I tossed and turned that night, Mother's normal behaviour at sunrise led me to believe that she had spoken in haste because of exhaustion. After their departure, however, I believed she meant every word and that her outbursts during her stay with us might have been because of her mistrust in me.

No matter how she treated me when I was young, I respected her as my mother and loved her the best way I could. How could she believe that I could kill my parents?

As they say, it takes one to see one. Perhaps she did not trust her own mother, which led to perpetuating her thoughts towards me. Another mystery that would never be solved!

Although Father's departure was devastating, I was happy that Mother left my home, as we would not be happy together. Indeed, we were never happy for most of my life, so expecting that to change while we grew old would be unwise.

Still, I missed them very much and wondered how they would survive in Sri Lanka during their old age while I lived in Canada. After nearly three years of silence, I finally received a letter from Father. The long letter detailed his current living status.

In it, he had requested me to bring him back to Canada if feasible.

Unfortunately, by that time, we had moved from Nova Scotia and had bought a new home in Ottawa, which could not accommodate my parents. With that information, Father's hopes to spend his final years with his daughter dissolved.

Sadly, he expressed his distress of living with Mother; I was helpless.

I decided to stay in touch with him as much as possible. It was the only support I could give him from a distance. Although I rarely received a response, I frequently wrote to Father over the next several years, and supplemented his income for his comfort and good health. However, according to his accounts, he did not receive proper care during his last years.

The most sorrowful memory in this regard still haunts me. Although I had provided enough funding to treat his cataract in both eyes, Father died a blind man, as I could not be there to find the most suitable treatment to help him regain his sight.

My heart felt great pain and despair when I saw him for the last time, roaming around the home while holding onto furniture, and not being able to see any of his family members.

During my last visit to see Father, the conversation we had in August of 20.., still lingers in my mind, like the last flower at the end of summer that refuses to part with its branch.

"I cannot see you, my dear, but I know that you are still my beautiful daughter," he said on the first day of my visit.

"Can you see anything at all?" I asked.

"I can only see you as a shadow in motions, but I am glad that I could see that you are here with me now." He responded with teary eyes.

My tears could not wash away the pain that touched deep within my soul; I was desperate to find a way to help him, but it was too late. I would have helped him if he had stayed in Canada.

With her careful manipulations, Mother made me lose the opportunity to take care of Father. I would continue to suffer, thinking of that lost chance, and would continue to feel miserable

On the 2nd of January, 20.., at the ripe age of ninety-one, Father died in Sri Lanka. I was 10,000 miles away from his bed, just like I had been at Mother's passing.

That morning, Father had fallen inside his bathroom. He was taken to the hospital as he could not stand up. His hip was fractured, and Brother had decided that Father should have surgery to fix the fracture. Just before his surgery, I spoke to Father. Although I sensed his end was near, I kept my voice steady with great difficulty.

"I have sent enough money to cover the operation and your recovery. I will speak to you once you return from surgery," I said calmly.

"Bless you, my dear daughter, for your financial help" Those were his last words to me.

I never had the opportunity to speak to him again.

After the surgery, he was admitted to the ICU and died there, as his heart could not withstand the effects of major surgery at that age.

I ravelled halfway across the globe to attend Father's funeral. It was the most difficult few days that I could recall.

The plane landed at Katunayake at around 10:00 a.m., and I took a taxi from the airport. The exhaustion, combined with the jetlag, made me forget to hire an air-conditioned car, and I felt like I was about to die in that heat. By the time I reached Brother's home, I felt dizzy because I had trapped myself inside a car filled with hot and humid air.

I needed to see Father, as this would be my last chance, and it would be the most unusual visit so far in my life. Yet, I had the most difficult time to get off from the taxi.

I sat in the heated, rented taxi for a long while. Above, I could see the white strands of flowing white cloth on a string that were hung across the lane; the standard way locals signal to the community that someone special, who lived in the premises, had passed on. A gust of wind suddenly lifted the string to make the strands sway rapidly in the midair, as if Father welcomed me at the gate.

My tears wetted my face.

I continued to sit in the car as I did not have the courage to face reality to visit Father that way. The memory of seeing him alive for the last time paralyzed me in my seat.

I reminisced.

Since 20.., I travelled to Sri Lanka annually, sometimes twice a year, to visit my parents as they were passing through their senior years.

After they left Canada, they had decided to sell their properties in Kaduwela and move in with Brother and his family in suburban Colombo. This was feasible because they gifted a major portion of their income from their property sales to Brother in exchange for him taking care of them until they died.

Using that money, Brother built a massive home and our parents shared the lower level with his family in the two-story home. Indeed, that arrangement worked out perfectly for Mother, as she had the opportunity to spend time with her son. However, that joy ended abruptly soon after Father's death. Unfortunately, Mother's tactless behaviour would enrage her daughter-in-law, and Mother was sent to a nursing home for nearly five years until her death.

I had visited Father in August of 20.., but I had not anticipated it to be my last chance to see him alive. After each annual visit, leaving my family behind was always stressful, as I did not know when my next visit would be. After spending three weeks with my family, I was getting ready to go to the airport to return to Canada. I packed my bags and left them close to the front door for easy loading into a taxi.

I could now visualize how Father sat next to the row of travel bags that I had placed at the door. Although he was legally blind, he served his duty by holding the tallest bag with his right hand.

Seemingly, he had intended to guard my property.

I said goodbye to my family members, and the last person I needed to speak to was Father. As a loving daughter about to leave her father, I bent down at his feet, touched them with care, and worshiped him with kindness. I then stood up to hug him to say goodbye. I wrapped his neck with both my arms and kept my face on his shoulder.

He was silent, and so was I.

I wanted to leave soon after, but I could not. I had the strangest feeling that I might never see him alive again.

While holding each other, we burst into tears. Strangely, we both sensed that it would be the last time we would hug each other. Father and I were a team all our lives and we sensed our thoughts without having to speak. We were both right. That day, Father sent me off for the last time to find my own way, like the million other times he did in the past.

While reminiscing, I realized that now I had no choice but to visit Father to send him off on his last journey—to find his own way. I had to travel alone from then on to find my way.

It was painful.

Suddenly, Brother appeared in his gateway. He stepped out to the road to see why I was not coming in as he had heard a car arriving at his gate. He opened the car door for me, and he knew why I had hesitated to go in; he had always been attentive and thoughtful.

We walked together to visit Father. I did not recognize any of the visitors in the crowd of people gathered around the living room. I could not see Mother either. I walked across with Brother to the corner of his living room where Father's body rested.

His remains were kept in a decorative casket, surrounded by flowers and tall brass lamps lit at his head and feet.

One year before, during my last visit to Sri Lanka, I suggested to Father that it would be my duty to make his funeral arrangements, as I felt that I might not get another opportunity in the future. With his blessings, I selected the decorative casket, flowers, and other suitable ornamental arrangements and pre-paid for the services at the funeral home in Borella. He was extremely grateful for my gesture. Brother was also grateful, as he did not have to bear the expenses at an unexpected moment.

I was happy to see that Father's remains had been preserved the way I had suggested.

I wanted to see Father's face at close, just to make sure that he was no longer with us. His face was peaceful. Suddenly I realized that I was alone. I touched his arm; it was icy cold. I stood very close to his face and promised that I would never forget him. I spent several more minutes with his remains to wish him *Nibbana*, the peaceful end of a life according to Buddhism.

I turned around to leave his body, and I noted that the flames of the two lamps at his foot started to flicker rapidly; I wondered whether Father acknowledged my presence. I smiled with appreciation since we could communicate with each other, even though he was no longer present to greet me in person.

Then, an unusual aroma surrounded me. It felt like I had entered a garden filled with aromatic Jasmine flowers. I sensed its meaning; I felt its purpose.

I firmly believed that Father greeted me to say that he was happy to see me again. It might have been his undying love for me that created a wonderful aroma representing his spirit. That aroma followed me around for the next few days until Father's body was taken out of the home. I will never forget that enchanting aroma, just like the enchanting association I had with Father throughout my life.

For three days, I tried to spend as much time as possible with Father's remains, and the rest of the time, I stayed close to Mother. At night, while his body rested at home, I prayed for his spirit, and I cried when I was alone.

I kept wondering when I could see a tear in Mother's eyes, but I did not see any; then I cried some more to show Father that I was sorry for Mother's lack of emotions. I was certain that Father would have understood it all, just like he did for nearly sixty years when living with Mother.

The day of the funeral arrived in haste. I wished that it never did; I wanted to keep Father close to me for as long as I could.

The time then arrived to say goodbye. All those who had crowded the living room earlier were now seated on mats to listen to Buddhist chanting and a eulogy delivered by a close relative.

Six men carried Father's casket and started to walk out the front door. As the pallbearers stood outside the door with his casket on their shoulders, a sudden gush of wind swirled around the tall tree above the casket, which had served as a canopy. I understood that Father's spirit might have left with its body where it was housed during his time on Earth. I prayed for him to be at peace. That was all I could do.

Mother stood beside me like a granite statue with no emotions.

Brother urged me to follow the vehicle that carried Father's body as Mother refused to follow it to the cemetery. I accepted his suggestion with grace and dignity; after all, I would have followed Father to the ends of the earth if I was asked to.

At the cemetery, just before his body was taken into the crematorium, Brother decided to open the casket for the last time for those who could not visit Father's body at home. After one look at Father's face, my body fell to the ground. For some unknown reason, after coming to, I could only remember the unusual orange-brown coloured flowers that decorated the satin interior of his casket. I vaguely remember Richard lighting the funeral pyre enclosed inside the crematorium.

I walked back with Brother while in a daze.

I returned home with exhaustion and sat beside the side table in the living room. When I turned my head to place my purse on the table, I noticed a small bunch of orange-brown flowers had been placed right next to where I decided to keep my purse. I felt delighted by the mysterious gift, as though it bore a message from Father who was transferring his gratitude towards me for the last time, just like he used to, whenever I had done anything small or big. I held the bunch with love and kept it until it withered away.

The colours of those tropical flowers had remained within my memory for years to come.

During the weeks following his death, I saw my surroundings as a skeleton bush on a summer's night. I waited for new leaves to arrive on the sorrowful bush, much like the way I anticipated new green leaves to appear on trees at the end of each dreadful Canadian winter.

In the days following the funeral, Mother stayed in her room, and I sat on her bed to find a reason to speak with her. I could not find any.

Richard decided to spend time with his family who lived in Colombo, as visiting them was not possible until the funeral services had ended. Brother was extremely busy bringing normalcy back to his home and to his family.

Seemingly, Father's death had left us all ill-adjusted, growing painfully into relations that his death had distorted. Since then, I felt as if Father left me in a world where the people in it did not understand me the way he did.

The anchor I had felt before had been lifted, as if it had left with Father; I felt rudderless.

On that day, I realized that Father had taken the cloaks of protection that I used to put on with him. I felt vulnerable, like a deer in open grassland with the potential to become anyone's easy target.

It was such a fundamental maneuver that, even today, after more than ten years since his death, nothing could be decided, and nothing could be concluded without the referral to his point of origin.

At the same time, even though Father's passing had left an inextinguishable flame of rage in me—mainly because I felt that he abandoned his little girl—it reminded me of a love that I often find happiness in thinking about.

Although Mother was instrumental in taking away my opportunity to care for Father during his final years of life, I am grateful that she had no power to stop me from being happy, and of thinking about Father with great love.

Three months after his passing, in Father's memory, I offered alms to Buddhist monks residing in Ottawa. The next morning, Father visited me in a vivid dream. He sat on my bed while surrounded by a bright white glow, just like his mother had done when she had appeared at the university dorm just after her death. At that moment, the same delightful aroma I experienced at Father's funeral touched my senses with joy.

He continued to visit me in my dreams since then, just like Grandmother had done.

Mother outlived Father by over seven years. She continued to demand from those who came in close contact with her to fulfill her never-ending desires. I wondered whether she felt her husband's absence, because she never spoke of him even to the point of her death in 2016.

She had not written a single word about Father's death in her journal either.

Suddenly, I realized that I had been standing in front of the orange-brown tree for quite some time until a passer-by brought me back to reality.

"You seem to be mesmerized by the orange-brown tree. I like the deep red one over there," she said, pointing to a large red maple that attracted hundreds to its vicinity.

"I prefer this one because its colours took me back to a wonderful land I used to know," I said with a smile. She smiled back with empathy.

CHAPTER 21

𝒯HE 𝒟REAM THAT 𝒜WOKE 𝒩E

The day that Mother passed away at the age of ninety-three, I went to bed early with exhaustion, frustration, and devastation; it was a day that I needed to crawl into bed and sleep until I could sleep no more. But, Mother and her memories kept my mind flustered and sorrowful; I had anticipated a restless night.

Yet, I certainly did not anticipate a visit from her.

Based on my life-long conflicted associations with Mother, I believed that she would forget me in her afterlife, let alone have thoughts of visiting me.

I was wrong; she appeared in a visitation dream.

In the end, it was very clear that she had visited me not to express love—as in most such dreams—but to ask for forgiveness. That visitation dream profoundly affected my life; it awoke me to face an undesirable reality.

I was fast asleep, but an unusual mental signal brought me into semi-consciousness. The familiar, mild fragrance of Cuticura soap mixed in with Ponds powder touched my senses. I peeled my eyes open to see if it was Mother. *I must be dreaming*, I thought. Her presence cannot be real, as she had passed away the day before. How could she be in my bedroom?

I tried hard to discern what I saw; a small figure surrounded by a thick mist started to approach me. I watched the figure move ever so slowly—more like floating—along a well-paved road. Gradually, the associated fragrance became stronger while the clarity of the image sharpened.

Eventually, the image of Mother manifested.

She started to move faster towards me like she used to walk in haste during her prime years. Her silk saree moved with the wind, and I observed that her right hand held the fall of the saree to keep it in place, just like she used to. That was when her signature fragrance encased my whole body.

It was euphoric.

My eyes widened, and my heart thumped with vigour. Mother smiled. I was surprised beyond my wildest imagination. I cried with joy and in awe; then fear crept in. What were her intentions to visit me?

Suddenly, she bowed down on the tarmac that she walked on. Her hands were stretched towards me, and her face was tucked in between her arms; a posture of a woman in worship. I stared at the view in amazement. The surroundings where she knelt were very bright, much like dawn of a sunny day in Sri Lanka.

She held her posture for what felt like a long time. I waited for her to stand up and explain her unexpected behaviour. Slowly she stood and looked into my eyes. Her eyes were red, and tears rolled down her cheeks.

She mouthed a few words, "I am sorry for treating you differently from your brother. I love you both the same."

Suddenly, I found myself seated on the bed. I had awoken in a sweat; my nightclothes were drenched. Once I regained my senses, I recalled a discussion I had with Mother a week before her death during the lengthy, usual, weekly speaking event on Sunday mornings.

I candidly expressed how I felt about her disrespect and indifference towards me, her only daughter, while she had embraced Brother as if he was her only child.

I still could not fathom how fearless I felt during that conversation, which I never thought would be our last. It was a long and heartfelt phone discussion, speaking of things I never dared to bring up face-to-face. The visitation dream confirmed that she had taken my distress to heart.

That was remarkable.

Had she finally realized after our discussion how hurtful her reluctance to express her love had been to me, *or* had she decided to ask for my forgiveness on the day of her death, so she could feel better in her next life?

Perhaps she could not help herself. But, the real reasons for her behaviour towards me would be reveled in her journal. Yet, how would I believe her words without credible evidence? I could not make up my mind because, with Mother, her self-centred decisions were always to make her situation better.

I closed my eyes and hugged my pillow to find comfort.

I might have dozed off in exhaustion and confusion created by the dream. To my surprise, the dream continued: Mother held my right hand, and we walked side-by-side towards an unknown destination. I could see the sun shining and the horizon crisp and clear. We were both smiling and looking at each other frequently. The meaning of it was not clear; perhaps Mother felt happy after begging for my forgiveness, and with that resolution, she might have envisioned her next incarnation.

Mother asked for my forgiveness in her visitation dream on the day of her passing, but it took me nearly three years to feel the need to forgive her.

I finally would accept that forgiving her would bring the closure I had been searching for.

Three long years after seeing that visitation dream, I decided to read the last sections of Mother's journal that I had left unread.

It was a Sunday morning. I was alone in my home. It was the first winter storm of the season. The howling winds brought distress to my mind, making me feel isolated in a deserted land.

I sat by the window and read the last few pages of Mother's journal; a dramatic and unexpected conclusion flashed across the handwritten notes, and her words had an unusual power that would haunt me henceforth.

She detailed her most devastating life experience, which was daunting and harrowing to read. My soul bled for her, and in the end, I cried uncontrollably, hoping she would feel my sorrow from beyond.

It was the day that my parents left home to attend the annual overnight 'pirith' (the chanting of Buddhist verses on the night before the Vesak day) at the local temple. That day I lost control of my life.

I bathed my youngest brother just before bedtime. He was a toddler, and my mother assigned me to be his caretaker because she was too busy attending to the rest of her duties as a mother and a wife. I tucked him into bed after reading him a story. His room was far down a corridor from mine. No one except my eldest brother was at home, getting ready for his final exams in his accountancy program. His room was near the front of the home, while mine was closer to the back entrance.

After the little boy fell asleep, I returned to my room; the full moon was visible through my window. I took off my day clothes and folded them neatly, placing them on the clothes horse in the corner of my room. Many different thoughts were whirling around in my mind; among those, the strongest was Mother's instructions to keep the bedroom door ajar in case my younger brother would call for any assistance during the night. After a long day taking care of an active toddler, I thought of how pleasant it would be to stretch out in bed and fall asleep and forget about the tedious day.

Sleep had almost come to me. The room was dark, and the house was silent. Then, creaking stealthily, the bedroom door fully opened; someone entered and treaded gingerly.

"Who is there?" I cried.

"Don't be frightened, sis," my eldest brother whispered.

"And don't turn on the light, or I will hit you with all my might," he bellowed.

He flung himself on my bed and covered my mouth with his right palm while taking me up in his left.

Since the horrific encounter that night, he threatened me each time he visited me, and he got his way at every opportunity he had until his premature death at the age of twenty-one.

Yes, our parents had been strict towards their own children like a Ugandan dictator who had frightened his own people. Yet, they never knew that their beloved eldest son was also their only daughter's abuser.

I could not read any further as my heart was filled with anger and surprise. I was devastated that Mother had faced such tremulous events during her younger days. I sobbed while clutching the old journal that held her secrets with silent dignity.

Mother's experience scribed in the journal led me to search for information on childhood sexual abuse and its impact on a person during their life.

Irrespective of how childhood sexual abuse is defined, it has been well–documented that it has a significant negative and pervasive psychological impact on its victims. The majority of sexual abuse happens in childhood, with incest being the most common form. Apparently, sexual contact between an older child and a younger child also can be abusive if there is a significant disparity in age, development, or size, rendering the younger child incapable of giving informed consent.

I wished that Mother would have discussed her troubled past with me when I reached adulthood. Perhaps then, I could have made peace with her disposition to exercise better interactions with her. Now, I will never get that opportunity to console her. Why she decided to endure the mental anguish and psychological trauma on her own is beyond my comprehension.

According to records, survivors who have difficulty in externalizing the abuse think negatively about themselves. After years of negative self-thoughts, such survivors have feelings of worthlessness and avoid others because they believe they have nothing to offer. With this understanding, my mind started to fill with numerous questions with no answers.

Did Mother's traumatic experience transform her personality? Did those awful episodes of abuse make her an introvert?

Based on what I had seen in the past, one thing was very clear: Mother had difficulty having normal social interactions with others.

I left her journal in its special place as I could not read it any further. I decided to go back in time to investigate my memory of our lives in Kaduwela. I needed to find answers to my million questions.

What significant moments or events would reveal how Mother had handled her life after having horrific experiences of childhood sexual harassment? Could her emotional turbulence during her adult life be related to this personal tragedy?

I started to re-evaluate many past incidents related to Mother and me, to gather clues to rationalize her behaviour. Unfortunately, none of those were happy encounters, but with my current knowledge, I was determined to find answers to the questions that had been troubling my mind.

First, I recalled a discussion I had with my paternal Grandmother.

When Father worked as a principal in a distant school, and Mother had to take care of our family, I spent my holidays at home with Mother. It was one of those days, like many others before, when Mother used to spend time in the evenings alone with Piyal while Father was away from home.

Every time Piyal was in our home, Mother had asked me to leave the premises, suggesting that I spend time with Grandmother. I did not have the courage to question Mother, although it contradicted her past suggestions where she had forbidden my close association with Grandmother. But I delightfully agreed, although I was curious about why she had changed her mind.

I sat next to Grandmother on her bed and listened to the stories about her dead relatives and, most of all, the historical stories about the village, the British rule of the Island, and how the colonial government had affected her business. I enjoyed the time I spent with her until one day she decided to change her tone and her stories.

I could recall the words that Grandmother whispered in my ear, "She is not a good woman; she had a troubled past with men."

"Who was she?" I questioned.

"Your mother, my darling," she responded.

I was young and had not gone through life with any adult experiences; therefore, at the time, I could not comprehend her words. No matter how difficult it had been for me to love Mother, Grandmother's expression of disgust towards Mother was not palatable to me. My young mind froze, and out of respect for Mother, I refused to probe further.

Now, after reading Mother's journal, I could understand the meaning of the disgusted tone in Grandmother's voice; she must have known about Mother's past. I wondered how.

I continued to dig further into my memory to recall the past activities of Mother and her unusual behaviour.

Suddenly, I remembered a rare and very brief conversation Mother had with me after my family had recovered from Mother's dramatic tirade—when she learned that Grandmother had presented me with a gold coin to celebrate my coming of age.

"All this fuss in this family is because I was not a virgin at marriage," Mother whispered in my ear.

I could not understand what she meant, as no one had ever told me what virgin means. I learned about those secretive expectations of a man, on the first night with his bride, from my university roommate. Later, I would find out the historical facts about the Sri Lankan culture concerning a man's expectations in finding a virgin for marriage, although he might not have been one.

Now, after reading the last chapter of Mother's journal, the circle of understanding had completed.

It became clear to me that because Mother had experienced sexual abuse as a child, the trauma of the events had changed her personality. She trusted no one, and she desired misery in others.

Unfortunately, she had released her frustrations by emotionally abusing me, not only as a child but as an adult, until her death.

Had she taken revenge on humanity through me to compensate for the trauma she has experienced? If such is the case, it was utterly unfair for me to endure her abusive episodes, which made my life difficult.

After reminiscing on the past, I concluded that I had been a victim of the reverberating and rippling effects of childhood sexual abuse experienced by Mother.

Several weeks went by, and I still did not have the courage to open Mother's journal again. Then one day, Brother called to inquire about my well-being. During our conversation, I told him that I was constantly thinking of Mother and missing her very much. We had a good cry together, and I realized that Brother did not know I had been granted the opportunity to find Mother's journal in her wooden wardrobe.

Mother had selected me to read her journal. She had decided to reveal her reasons why she could not express her love towards me. I concluded that she had wished to share her experiences with me and express her thoughts on how difficult it was to see me as a happy little girl, because she never had that privilege.

The final words of Mother's journal: *Life had been cruel to me. My childhood abuse made my wedding night the worst in my life; my husband detested me from day one. I knew that my life as a wife would be similar to the miserable journey taken by Hester Prynne, who faced a sentence that exposed her to public humiliation, where she had to wear the scarlet "A" for the rest of her life. Sadly, in my case, no one knew that the letter "A" would stand for Abused instead of adultery.*

After reading her last few sentences, I tried very hard to recall whether Father had made any disrespectful remarks or statements about Mother. All I could recall were Father's words of love and affection, expressing how their married life had been joyful despite the harrowing episode of Mother losing their third child seven days after giving birth; the brother I had never met.

My sorrow was great, knowing that Mother had endured much pain in her life even after her marriage. However, Father's expressions of love to Mother, which I witnessed throughout my childhood, told me a different tale about their married life.

I could not believe that Father had mistreated her for not being a virgin at marriage. Father's kindness and affections expressed before my eyes were more reliable to me than Mother's words. Yet, it is possible that although he did not abuse her for not being a virgin at marriage, she might have imagined that he had contempt for her.

Her childhood trauma could well have clouded her perceptions of others' behaviour.

Although I believed Mother's details about her experiences, I still needed to verify the facts by speaking to someone. However, all those who would have had the knowledge of her life had passed away, leaving me in a quandary. Much like me, Brother was also not aware of the details of our parent's married life because he left home as a teenager to live in Colombo.

In her journal, Mother's words that revealed her well-concealed secret made me inherit an unresolvable mystery, a burden I would hold for the rest of my life.

However, I decided to forgive Mother for the suffering she had inflicted on me as a result of her misfortune. I was surprised that giving the gift of forgiveness to another could be self-empowering; it works in our self-interest by relieving us from the burden of hurt.

I held her journal and recited several times: "Mother, I forgive you, and may you rest in peace."

Because, now I know who stole Mother's soul.

I believe that life does not end with the death of the physical body, and death does not end our relationships with those who had lived among us and had passed. In light of my understanding of life and life after death, I sincerely hope to meet Mother again, to have a second chance to love each other.

I closed my eyes and dwelt on the ancient words of wisdom written by the Persian poet Rumi: "Out beyond ideas of wrong-doing, and right-doing, there is a field. I will meet you there."

*&*PILOGUE

It was March of 2021. The world had been in lockdown for one full year, and everyone wished for a vaccine to prevent an infection from COVID-19. I was one of them.

I looked out the window and experienced the miserable silence imparted by the frozen land. After a very long winter, it was a pleasure to witness how the tall mounds of snow surrounding my home had started to melt ever so slowly with the rising temperature.

I opened the window for some fresh air; early spring air brought a delightful scent and coolness. It was wonderful to hear the cardinals sing like an orchestra with renewed enthusiasm. I smiled after seeing a red robin investigating the leafless tree in my front lawn, as a potential location for its next nest.

I felt as if the whole world had stood still, not just to pass through one cold winter, but also for over three years while I was writing my story. It had been a long, lonely ride.

With a warm cup of Sri Lankan tea in my hand, I comfortably sat on the couch to enjoy the morning.

I have finally set aside the printed manuscript, which has details of my life experiences with my family, more specifically with Mother. I have forgiven Mother with a genuine heart; it has relived the stress I had felt since her death.

While sipping wonderful tea and enjoying its aroma, I wondered: was it worth the efforts to find my answers, at least for some of the mind-boggling questions that had troubled me throughout my life? I believe it certainly has changed the way I feel about life, about Mother, most of all about myself.

I have been unburdened from a difficult past and seemingly have developed a more positive outlook for the future.

That feeling was invigorating.

Mother's journal has helped me redeem myself by solving some of the mysteries that had haunted me for a long time, yet, some remain unsolved.

I have been looking for ways to forgive myself and those who had dared to inflict pain. I must confess that I have been successful in that venture through writing.

It is true that through writing I have regained control over most of my feelings. My past has become more tolerable after I saw its clear connection with my present. I have decided to accept the past as part of my current reality.

Over the past several years, I have lost most of those who had played a part in my life, either as a parent, a close relative, a pet, or a friend. Their departure has made me realize how fragile our lives are.

When my paternal Grandmother died, it was the first death in my family. At her funeral, our home was filled with those who admired and respected her. On that day, she had found the reciprocation of love and attention that she had given to others while living.

When Father passed away in 2010, his body, which rested at Brother's home, was also visited by a large number of his admirers and relatives. He had been a friend and a joyful companion for many. Seemingly, at death, he received accolades for what he had given to others during his life.

Yet, Mother's departure from this earth had been vastly different. Her body was kept for viewing in a funeral home only for forty-eight hours. Only Brother and his immediate family had visited; no one else had come to bid goodbye. Much like she had the desire to spend her life in solitude, at death, she had been left alone. Perhaps it was what she wanted.

I could recall a time when she had said, "I am a lonely elephant."

Mother had lived her life only to make herself happy, disregarding the natural desire of all humans for happiness through social connections. Perhaps her painful past as a young girl would have prevented her to be happy among people. It is therefore; not having anyone hover over her corpse might have been the happiest for her.

The events surrounding the death of these family members reminded me of the cliché: *what goes around comes around.* Their death changed the way I looked at life; they led me to associate with those that are living in a more compassionate manner.

In retrospect, I am grateful for the way I have been able to beat the odds and become the strong, resilient woman I am today. Was I like a phoenix rising from the ashes? Yes.

Considering what I had to overcome, I feel triumphant that I had crossed all barriers with determination. But, I have not become a new person. I simply retrieved my authentic self from the aftermath of what I had endured.

If I could view my present-self in one single framed picture, I would see a woman who is holding her head high, in a posture of authority and dignity, while having a smile on her lips and eyes wide open, viewing a pleasant future.

By thinking of my image in that solid frame, I smile.

The spring gradually changed to summer. One morning, I looked out the window and felt frustrated by the new dandelions crop blooming in the garden in spots I had cleared the previous day. I had spent hours labouring in the hot, burning sun, digging out the roots of this pesky weed.

Suddenly, my heart softened, and tears well up; I had a flashback to my life in Nova Scotia where my five-year-old son offered me a bunch of yellow dandelion he had picked from the field. He had considered those bright yellow blooms as a source of joy for his mother.

Then a moment of epiphany arrived.

This stubborn weed that refuses to die just because someone wishes to eradicate it resembled my inner culture. Like it, rejection made me dig deeper within myself and come back up with inner strength and greater vigour, by not letting those who wished to eradicate my will to succeed.

The dandelion plant is poetically known as the rustic oracle and is perceived as a weed when in actuality, it has the strongest taproot, which burrows deep into the ground; nature's magnificent creation enabling its undeniable survival perhaps because of its medicinal value. Remarkably, the plant thrives under aggression.

I felt that I had the natural instincts to survive, comparable to that of the dandelion.

By looking back, I realized that the foundation I had been presented by my family had flaws and cracks, and had been very weak on which to build a normal life. With that, I would have anticipated emerging as a woman with a million flaws.

Yet, I have proven to myself that I had reached down my deep "taproot" for mental strength to live effectively, not only as a child but as an adult. Regardless of the past negativities, I had built a meaningful life for myself and had become a conscientious woman.

I conclude that arriving at my current reality is a miracle. Like the rustic oracle, I not only survived but thrived surmounting several attempts made by Mother to obstruct my progress as a human.

Canada is now my home. Over the last several years, I tried to persuade Brother to move to Canada.

He said, "Too old to migrate and adjust to the cold weather."

I agree with his decision, but I have no desire to return to Sri Lanka. We keep in touch regularly by giving ourselves sufficient telephone time to reminisce on our past, our current living arrangements, and what might await us in the future.

I thank the universe for providing me with a wonderful sibling with whom I can associate through thick and thin. I hope one day the COVID-19 pandemic will end so I can visit Brother, and then, together, we can visit our family gravesite at least one more time—a symbolic reunion of the family of four.

AFTER THOUGHTS

September 2021: An unexpected incident occurred during an unusual encounter with a stranger that would sprout daunting thoughts.

What if Mother's spirit has incarnated in a different country and it had made a remarkable connection with someone I know?

I started to imagine how Mother's spirit would start to communicate with me through that human. Then it really happened.

Could this be the beginning of a second attempt of Mother to control me, now from beyond? Perhaps as soon as her despicable plan to destroy me had ended with her death, she had designed a new one to manipulate and control me until I die.

I am not looking forward to comprehending how the results of that plan would affect me.

But do I have a choice on this matter?

CPSIA information can be obtained
at www.ICGtesting.com
Printed in the USA
BVHW042108120522
636836BV00002B/5